TIBETAN TRADITION
of
MENTAL DEVELOPMENT

TIBETAN TRADITION
of
MENTAL DEVELOPMENT

Oral Teachings of Tibetan Lama
Geshe Ngawang Dhargyey

LIBRARY OF TIBETAN WORKS AND ARCHIVES

ISBN: 81-85102-38-4

Published by the Library of Tibetan Works and Archives,
Dharamsala, and printed at Indraprastha Press (CBT),
4 Bahadurshah Zafar Marg, New Delhi – 110002

Contents

Foreword

In response to the growing interest and wishes of many non-Tibetans interested in the teachings of Buddha (the Dharma), courses on the Tibetan Tradition of Buddhist Practices have been established at the Library of Tibetan Works and Archives, Dharamsala. The preceptor Reverend Ngawang Dhargyey, a well-qualified teacher holding a Geshe degree from Sera Je Monastic University has studied various and numerous great Buddhist scriptures in Tibet for an extensive period of time. With the aid of translators Khamlung Tulku and Sharpa Tulku, Geshe Dhargyey has given a series of lectures at the Library to several hundred Asian and Western students. These lectures have covered such quintessential teachings as 'renunciation', 'bodhichitta' or the aspiration to attain full enlightenment, and the 'right understanding of voidness', all based on the Geshe's practice and experience.

What is presented here is a compendium of these lectures translated into English. Therefore, by virtue of this, may all sentient beings, regardless of race or creed, quickly generate bodhichitta based on the universal responsibility of helping others. With every wish and confidence for the ever-increasing strength of such bodhichitta within the minds of all beings, I offer many prayers of dedicated merit for the extensive benefit of this valuable work.

3rd of April, 1974
Tashi Rabten
Dharamsala

The Junior Tutor to
H. H. the Dalai Lama
Losang Yeshe
Trijang Rinpoche (III)

Publishers's Note

In November 1971, with the blessings of His Holiness the XIVth Dalai Lama, courses in Buddhist Dharma and Tibetan language were inaugurated at the Library of Tibetan Works and Archives, Dharamsala, India. This work, *Tibetan Tradition of Mental Development*, comprises the class notes of the first year-long course taught at the Library, which covered the basic teachings of the *'lam-rim'* ('Graded Path to Enlightenment'). The course was taught by Geshe Ngawang Dhargyey of Sera Je Monastic University, whose autobiography is included here, and the teachings were translated orally into English by Sharpa Tulku and Khamlung Tulku. The class notes taken by students during the course were subsequently edited and arranged in their present form by Juan Mills and Alan Wallace with assistance from India Stevens, Lynn Pylman, Morton Much, Lia Snyder and others.

The editors have deliberately refrained from writing in a formal or literary style in order to convey something of the flavour of the oral tradition and to ensure that the teachings themselves be accessible to the widest possible readership. The great value of the book is that it provides a complete survey of the 'Graded Path to Enlightenment', combined with practical advice from the oral tradition for its gradual implementation.

Now, ten years after its first publication, we are very happy to bring out the fourth, slightly revised edition of this popular work. We hope that, with the steadily growing interest in Buddhism in general and specifically the teachings given by Tibetan lamas at the Library and elsewhere, this book will continue to be useful to students and general readers alike.

December 1984   Gyatsho Tshering
Dharamsala   Director

Geshe Ngawang Dhargyey

Geshe Ngawang Dhargyey
A Brief Autobiography

I was born in the year 1925 in the town of Yar-kyag, located in the Tre-hor District of the eastern province of Tibet called Kham. This was a small village consisting of only fifty families and it lay not far from Dhargyey Monastery. It was a lovely place to live. Dark green forests bordered the village, and the hills rising up above it were completely blanketed by a colourful profusion of wild flowers in the summertime.

Near our home was a Sakya monastery, and it was the custom for pregnant women to go there to circumambulate it and make prostrations. While my mother was carrying me in her womb, she visited there during the winter (the eleventh Tibetan month) and made prostrations. From the spot of ground where her head touched there sprang up three small yellow flowers, and she often told me that this was a sign that if I took the vows of a monk, the result would be beneficial. She also told me that of her six children I was the lightest to carry in her womb. She gave birth to me on the thirteenth day of the fifth Tibetan month of the Fire-Tiger year, and on that day my father found a monk's upper robe and a monk's bowl filled with water. This was also taken to be an auspicious sign.

When I was seven years old, I took the pre-novice vows of a monk (*bar-ma rab-'byung*) and entered Dhargyey Monastery, which was then a community of two thousand monks. However, because an uncle of mine who was one of my teachers lived in the Sakya monastery, I spent most of my time there. I began my initial studies under the guidance of four teachers: Lozang Dhargyey, Gonphel Rinpoche, who was renowned for his mastery of all the five major fields of learning in Tibet, Tracha and Wozer. Every day I recited *Chanting the Names of Manjushri* (*'jam-dpal*

mtshan-brjod Manjushrinamasamgiti), verses of praise to
Manjushri, and even as a young boy I was not attracted to
games but rather spent my free time circumambulating the
temple and doing other simple religious practices.

As I grew older, I had an increasing desire to take the
vows of a fully ordained monk and to go to central Tibet
to continue my studies. So when I was sixteen, I set out on
the long journey to Lhasa, accompanied by my uncle and
a younger brother. For about three months we travelled on
foot and on horseback over very rough tracks. But although
it was a very difficult and strenuous journey, I did not
weary of it, for I was strongly urged on by my great desire
to learn. On the twentieth day of the twelfth Tibetan
month, we finally reached the great Kagyu Monastery
called Drikung Densathil. Five days later we arrived in
Lhasa, which is known in Tibet as the 'The Pure Land'. We
immediately went to the main temple to see the famous
statue of Buddha and to pray for the success of my studies.

After a seven-day rest in Lhasa, we went to the nearby
Sera Monastery, which is renowned as 'The Ocean of
Learned Masters of Scriptures and Insight.' On the last day
of the twelfth month, I was admitted into Sera Je College
with the blessings of the Abbot, Ngawang Gyatso. During
the following few days, I made an extensive pilgrimage to
all the temples in Sera, which were so numerous that it
actually took seven days to complete. At each one I made
offerings and said prayers for the success of my studies
and the fulfilment of my wish to benefit all sentient beings.

Realizing the great importance of having a good teacher, I sought one who was well-versed in both the sutras
and tantras. And, thus, I met my first spiritual master in
Sera, Sherab Wangchuk, whose kindness to me was greater
than that of all the innumerable Buddhas. Altogether I
studied under four successive teachers at Sera. The second
teacher was Chonzey Ngawang Dorje, a great master of the
sutras and tantras. I later studied under Geshe Ugyan

Tsetan, another learned master who was filled with compassion and who was highly respected for his strict moral discipline. Finally, I received religious instruction from Dhondup Topgyal, who is the present abbot of Sera Je College. Making devotions to my masters with pure motivation and action, I comprehensively studied the Five Treatises, which cover all the main points of teaching contained in the sutras.

At Sera Monastery the system of learning commenced with a three-year study of philosophical debate and logic beginning on a very simple level and working up gradually to more and more sophisticated ways of reasoning. Then the general tenets of the Buddhadharma with stress on the method aspect of the teachings were studied for five years, using Maitreya's *Ornament for Clear Realization* (*mngon-rtogs rgyan, Abhisamayalamkara*) as the root text. Following this, Madhyamika philosophy was studied for four years, using Chandrakirti's root text, *Entering the Middle Way* (*dbu-ma 'jug-pa, Madhyamakavatara*). Then Gunaprabha's *Root Text on Ethics* (*mdo rtsa ba, Vinayasutra*) was used as the root text for two years of studies on moral discipline ('*dul-ba, Vinaya*), followed by two more years of study of metaphysics (*mngon-par rtogs-pa, Abhidharma*), using Vasubandhu's *Treasury of Higher Knowledge* (*mdzod rtsa-ba, Abhidharmakosha*). One then spent a year in the *bka'-ram* class in which both moral discipline and metaphysics were studied, and from this class the top students were allowed to enter the highest class called *lha-ram*. It was the custom to study moral discipline and metaphysics in this class for eight years except for the one month each year which was devoted to the study of Dharmakirti's text *Commentary on Dignaga's Treatise on Valid Cognition* (*tshad-ma rnam-'grel, Pramanavarttikakarika*). There are three levels of Geshes or monks who pass the final examinations after completing all these monastic studies. Those monks graduating from the *lha-ram* class in any of the three great monastic universities near Lhasa took their final examinations during the annual Prayer Festival in Lhasa. Examinations were given orally by top *lha-ram-pa* Geshes of previous years questioning the graduating monks in the presence of thousands of onlookers. The *lha-ram* monks especially are required to have the ability to interpret the great texts that they have studied. Monks having a medium calibre of intellect and understanding take their final examinations upon the completion of the *bka'-ram* class. These are given during a smaller festival which is attended by fewer people than for the *lha-ram* examinations and these monks earn the title of *tshogs-ram-pa* Geshe. Finally, those monks in the *bka'-ram* class who are of lesser intelligence take their final examinations in their own monastery. They are primarily required to recite the texts they have memorized, and they earn the degree of *gling-gseb* Geshe.

The primary methods of learning employed by the monks were: memorizing fundamental texts, attending discourses on them, practising logical debate among the students and reciting memorized texts at night.

Throughout my studies, I memorized many of the Sera Je texts, such as the *Seventy Stanzas* (*don bdun-bcu, Trisaranagamanasaptati*), Tenets (*grub-mtha', Siddhanta*) Jetzun Chokyi Gyaltsen's general (*spyi-don*) and critical (*mtha'-dpyod*) commentary to the first chapter of the *Ornament for Clear Realization* and his general commentary to *Entering the Middle Way*. I also memorized the fundamental texts such as the *Stages and Paths* (*sa-lam*), the *Ornament for Clear Realization, Entering the Middle Way*, the *Treasury of Higher Knowledge*, the *Sutra on Moral Discipline*, the first two chapters of the *Commentary on Dignaga's Treatise on Valid Cognition*, all ten chapters of Shantideva's *Guide to the Bodhisattva's Way of Life* (*spyod-'jug, Bodhicaryavatara*), Je Tsong Khapa's *Essence of Good Explanation of the Interpretive and Definitive Meanings* (*drang-nges legs-bshad snying-po*), Pandit Atisha's *Lamp for the Path to Enlightenment* (*byang-*

chub lam-sgron, Bodhipathapradipa) and other texts. I not only
memorized them but also tried to discover their meaning
by receiving extensive teachings on them.

By the age of nineteen, I was teaching to disciples of
my own while pursuing my own studies. Then when I was
twenty-one, I realized the great meaning and importance of
keeping pure moral discipline and therefore took the vows
of a novice monk during the prayer festival held in the first
month of that year. Three months later, on the day marking
Buddha's enlightenment, I also received the vows of a fully
ordained monk from the Venerable Phurchog Jamgon
Dorjechang Jetsun Thubten Jampa Tsultrim Tenzin. He was
recognized in Tibet as a human manifestation of Maitreya
Buddha and was honoured as the crown jewel of all spiritual masters in Tibet.

Feeling the thirst for more than a literal understanding
of the scriptures, I soon realized the great importance of the
Graded Path to Enlightenment (*lam-rim*), which shows how
to understand the order of all the teachings in terms of
one's personal practice. I thus received an explanation of Je
Tsong Khapa's *Great Exposition on the Graded Path* (*lam-rim
chen-mo*) from Kyabje Trijang Rinpoche, the Junior Tutor to
His Holiness the Dalai Lama. He is further a manifestation
of all the Buddhas of the three times and is emanation of
the three-fold kindnesses (the kindnesses of (1) giving initiations, (2) giving explanations of tantric texts, and (3) passing on oral traditions). In all I have had the opportunity to
attend four series of his Graded Path discourses. Other
teachings and initiations I have received from him are: an
extensive explanation of Guru Puja (*bla-ma mchod-pa*) and
Mahamudra (*phyag-chen*), four series of discourses on Vajra-
yoginitantra (*rdo-rje rnal-'byor-ma'i rgyud*) including both the
developing and completing stages, many initiations of the
three meditational deities (*yi-dam*)–Guhyasamaja (*gsang-
'dus*), Heruka Chakrasamvara (*bde-mchog*) and Yamantaka
('*jigs-byed, Vajrabhairava*)–initiations of *kun-rig*, which is one

of the yogatantras, a set of one hundred initiations called *rin-'byung rgya-rtsa*, including initiations from all classes of tantra, initiations of Avalokitshvara (*spyan-ras-gzigs*), permissions (*rjes-snang*) of the Sixteen Arhats to practise certain sadhanas and recite mantras of certain deities, permissions of the Eight Medicine Buddhas, initiations of Vajrabhairava Ekavira (*'jigs-byed dpa'-bo gcig-pa*), thirteen initiations of Mahakala (*nag-po chen-po*) all initiations of Manjushri (*'jam-dpal-dbyangs*), initiations of the Thirteen Golden Doctrines of Sakya (*sa-skya gser-chos bcu-gsum, Sitachatra*), which in ancient times were carefully guarded within the confines of Sakya monasteries, discourses on the *Six Works of Naropa* (*na-ro chos-drug*), *Fifty Verses of Guru Devotion* (*bla-ma lnga-bcu-pa, Gurupanchashika*), the *Seven-Point Training of the Mind* (*blo-sbyong don-bdun-ma*), *Wheel of Sharp Weapons* (*mthson-cha 'khor-lo*), so called because it cuts off all impure thoughts, especially those arising from self-cherishing, the *Twenty Verses of Commitment* (*sdom-pa nyi-shu-pa*), the *Six-Session Guruyoga* (*thun-drug bla-ma'i rnal-'byor*), sixteen initiations of the Kadam tradition, an oral transmission of *rgyal-chen bstod-'grel* and many other discourses and initiations.

From Lama Lhatzun Dorjechang of Sera-Mey College I have received: an oral explanation of the *Hundred Deities of the Land of Joy* (*dga'-ldan lha-brgya-ma*), the *Three Principal Paths* (*lam-gtzo rnam-gsum*), a Kalachakra (*dus-'khor*) initiation, an initiation of the Solitary Hero Vajrabhairava (*'jigs-byed dpa'-bo gcig-pa*) and one of Vajrayogini, a long-life initiation of Tara (*sgrol-dkar*), thirteen Mahakala initiations, an initiation of Manjushri Dharmachakra (*'jam-dbyang chos-skor*), initiations of the Thirteen Golden Doctrines of Sakya, and many others.

From Lama Dragri Dorjechang I have received: explanations of the *Blissful Way of the Graduated Path* (*lam-rim bde-lam*) and the developing and completing stages of the Solitary Hero Vajrabhairava, an initiation of Vajrayogini, an explanation and oral transmission of the *Eight Thousand Stanza Perfection of Wisdom Sutra* (*brgyad-stong-pa, Astasaha-srika Prajnaparamita*), explanations of Je Tsong Khapa's commentaries to the *Entering the Middle Way*, called *Great Commentary to the 'Supplement' [to the 'Middle Way']* (*'jug-pa'i tik-chen*) and *Summarized Meaning of the 'Middle Way'* (*bdu-ma'i spyi-don*), and his *Golden Rosary of Good Explanation* (*legs-bshad gser-phreng*), Nagarjuna's *Six Collections of Reasoning* (*rigs-tshogs drug*), the Five Texts of Maitreya (*byams-chos sde-lnga*), an initiation of Chittamani Tara, explanations of Je Tsong Khapa's *Praise of Dependent Arising* (*rten-'brel bstod-pa*), explanations of the root text *Wheel of Sharp Weapons* and its commentary, an explanation of the *Hundred Teachings on Generating the Mind of Enlightenment* (*sems-bskyed bka'-brgya-ma*) and many other initiations and explanations.

From His Holiness the present Dalai Lama I have received: an explanation of Je Tsong Khapa's *Great Exposition on the Graded Path* and his *Great Exposition on the Path of Secret Mantra* (*sngags-rim chen-mo*), the *Great Exposition on the Guide to the Bodhisattva's Way of Life* (*spyod-'jug chen-mo*), Guru Puja along with Mahamudra and a Guhyasamaja text by Je Tsong Khapa called *The Yoga of Pure Stages* (*rnal-'byor dag-rim*), an initiation of Guhyasamaja, explanations of the *Four-fold Commentary to Guhyasamaja* (*'grel-ba bzhi-sbrags*), the *Condensed Graded Path* (*lam-rim bsdus-don*), the *Guide to the Swift Path* (*myur-lam dmar-'khrid*), the *Seven Stanzas on Mind-training* (*blo-sbyong don-bdun-ma*) and the *Eight Verses of Mind-training* (*blo-sbyong tsig-brgyad-ma*), an oral transmission and explanation of the *Chanting the Names of Manjushri*, initiations of Avalokiteshvara on many occasions, the Kala-chakra initiation on three occasions, explanations of the *Six Collections of Reasoning of the Middle Way* and the teachings given to Je Tsong Khapa by Manjushri as they are recorded in the *Guide to the View Having the Four Mindfulnesses* (*lta-'khrid dran-pa bzhi-ldan*), an initiation of *rigs-gsum gcig-sgrub*, a long-life initiation of *rje tshe-'dzin-ma*, an initiation of

Mahakala, an explanation of Je Tsong Khapa's *Three Principal Paths* and of the *Foundation of Excellence* (*yon-tan gzhi-'gyur-ma*) and many other explanations and initiations.

And finally, from the Senior Tutor to His Holiness, Kyabje Yongzin Ling Rinpoche, I have received: explanations of *Six-session Guru Yoga*, *Chanting the Names of Manjushri* and a Vajrayogini text, *Guide to Individual Liberation* (*sos-thar-gyi 'khrid*), the *Great Exposition on the Graded Path*, numerous explanations of Vajrabhairava, initiations of Guhyasamaja and Avalokiteshvara, an explanation of a complete text on Vajrabhairava, an oral transmission of the commentary to a Guhyasamaja text which belongs to the Upper Tantric College tradition, a long-life initiation of Amitayus (*tse-dpag-med*) and many others.

These are just some of the initiations and explanations of texts that I have received while pursuing my studies and teaching to my disciples. Throughout the years of my monastic training, I spent the nights in reciting the texts that I had memorized. My living conditions in terms of food, clothes and lodging were, like those of many other monks, of a very low standard. I think it is little known among Western students that there were a great many simple monks dwelling in monasteries throughout Tibet who lived in much the same manner as did Milarepa. Such hardships were far from being rare.

Between semesters of normal lessons and debate there were a number of breaks each year. During many of these, I went into retreat to meditate on Vajrabhairava and other meditational deities for whom I had received initiations.

When I was thirty-two years old, I was appointed to be the tutor of two incarnate lamas, Lhagon Rinpoche and Thubten Rinpoche. Two years later in 1959, the Chinese suppression caused a great obstacle for the continuation of the Dharma and made it impossible to live in peace in the pursuit of inner happiness. Thus, I escaped with a number of other people over a mountain pass near Sera, and we headed towards southern Tibet through the Phenpo region. But because there were many Chinese soldiers in the area, we found that we had to turn back to the north.

We travelled on until one day we reached the town of Baka in northern Tibet. There our party was surrounded by Chinese troops. A battle then ensued, and a great number of the men in our party were killed while trying to protect the two young Rinpoches and others who were unable to protect themselves. Due partially to my practice of the Dharma but primarily to the kindness of my gurus, even at such a grave moment of life and death, my only intention was to die with a pure moral discipline and motivation. Accepting the fruits of my own karma I meditated on compassion for the Chinese. I truly felt no anger against those who were trying to kill us; and while the fighting was going on, I found a few moments to speak to the two Rinpoches about karma and compassion.

In the confusion of the battle, the Rinpoches and I managed to escape. We travelled on, still insisting on wearing our robes, even though this made us very conspicuous; and we continued our daily spiritual practices and monthly rituals. While trying to escape the Chinese, we had gone so far to the north that it took us many months before we finally reached the border of Nepal. We had left Sera during the third Tibetan month and arrived in Nepal in the tenth month and met His Holiness and his two tutors in Bodh Gaya. We attended an Avalokiteshvara initiation given by His Holiness, then proceeded to Kalimpong, making a brief pilgrimage on the way.

In Kalimpong, in addition to following my daily meditational practices, I taught the Graded Path and Je Tsong Khapa's *Essence of Good Explanation of the Interpretive and Definitive Meanings* to the two Rinpoches. I also gave several discourses on the Graded Path and Tara to large groups of laypeople. After living there for four years, I again visited Bodh Gaya. There I sought the advice of the two Tutors and subsequently moved to Dalhousie.

I had been in Dalhousie for two years when I was chosen as one of fifty-five scholars to attend a six-month Abbots' Seminar in Mussoorie. Following this, we went to Bodh Gaya and Varanasi for a tour of the Indian universities. Then we all returned to our respective places.

Back in Dalhousie I again gave instruction to a number of incarnate lamas and monks, including Khachog Rinpoche, Jado Rinpoche and Duldul Rinpoche. I gave them intensive teachings on the *Great Exposition on the Guide to the Bodhisattva's Way of Life* and Kyabje Trijang Rinpoche's *lam-rim* notes, logical reasoning, *Ornament for Clear Realization, Entering the Middle Way* and explanations of the three kinds of vows.

A few years later, Sharpa Rinpoche and Khamlung Rinpoche came to Dalhousie and received religious instruction from me. I gave them an explanation of the *Hundred Deities of the Land of Joy,* a complete teaching on the *Ornament for Clear Realization* together with Gyaltsab Je's commentary *Ornament of the Essential Explanation (rnam-bshad snying-po-rgyan)* and brief explanations of *Entering the Middle Way* along with Je Tsong Khapa's *Great Commentary to the 'Supplement',* and the *Treasury of Higher Knowledge* along with the commentary by the first Dalai Lama. I also gave them an explanation of teachings on moral discipline, on tenets and on the stages and paths (*sa-lam*), and brief explanations of the *Essence of Good Explanation of the Interpretive and Definitive Meanings* and the *Praise of Dependent Arising.*

I then began to teach them Dharmakirti's *Commentary on Dignaga's Treatise on Valid Cognition* but before completing the first chapter, we all came to Dharamsala to attend the discourses by His Holiness on the *Four-fold Commentary to Guhyasamaja* ('*grel-ba bzhi-sbrags*). I was planning then to return to Dalhousie and go into retreat for Guhyasamaja meditation. Following this, I hoped to go on pilgrimage to Nepal. However, during our stay in Dharamsala, we had a private audience with His Holiness at which time he asked me to teach and the Rinpoches to translate Dharma courses for Western students at the newly constructed Tibetan Library in Dharamsala.

Well over a year has elapsed since we began here. Although we cannot claim to be learned pandits, we are following the wishes of our lama with the hope that our efforts are of benefit to those who come here to learn. We further hope that they will in turn benefit others, bringing great peace and joy into the world.

Tibetan Tradition
of Mental Development

by

Geshe Ngawang Dhargyey

1
The Twelve Principal Deeds
of the Buddha

As you receive these teachings, you should have the motivation to use them as the means of attaining full enlightenment in order to be of benefit to all living beings. If you lack this motivation, try to develop it.

In the course of his spiritual growth, Buddha first developed bodhichitta, the wish to attain enlightenment for the welfare of all sentient beings. Then for innumerable lifetimes during three limitless world ages, he followed the way of a Bodhisattva—a life of giving. By thus eliminating all his obstacles to the attainment of enlightenment and by perfecting all positive qualities, such as wisdom, compassion, patience and so forth, he attained the full enlightenment of Buddhahood.

Previous to his life as the Indian Prince Shakyamuni, Buddha lived and taught Dharma in the Tushita Buddhafield. While he was abiding there, all the Buddhas of the ten directions urged him that the time had come for the deeds of a supreme nirmanakaya (the physical manifestation of a Buddha) to be enacted in this world of Jambudvipa, the Southern Continent. Buddha then placed his jewelled crown on the head of Maitreya, appointing him successor as the host of Tushita.

Before entering this world, Buddha made five observations concerning the time, place, caste, lineage and mother to whom he would be born. Buddha saw that it was a time of great strife in Jambudvipa and, thus, a fit occasion for a Buddha to manifest himself and act there. Buddhas manifest themselves as teachers solely for the sake of those who are able to be led spiritually. Among the two main kinds of beings who are able to practise Dharma—men and devas (divine beings)—the former are unable to go to the deva realms but the devas can descend to our realm in order to listen to Dharma. Thus, the acts of a supreme nirmanakaya are always performed among humans. Other realms, or continents, in which human beings live are so bountifully filled with pleasures that the faculties of the beings living there are dull. This dullness makes it very difficult for them to develop strong renunciation. Because of the people of Jambudvipa have extremely sharp faculties, enabling them to develop renunciation with ease, and because many of them are suitable vessels for Dharma, Shakyamuni saw that the deeds of a Buddha should be shown there.

At that time in India, there were four major castes: the caste of royalty, the Brahmin caste, the merchant caste, and the caste of the common people. Whenever Buddhas manifest themselves in their supreme nirmanakaya form, they always take birth in one of the two higher castes, depending on which is the more highly honoured at the time. At that time the royal caste was more highly revered. Shakyamuni saw that he should take birth in the royal Shakya clan, since the Shakya king was a great ruler who was devotedly served by his many subjects. Furthermore, both the king and queen were of lineages that had been pure for the previous seven generations. Finally, he saw that it was fitting for him to be born from the womb of Queen Mayadevi, who in a previous life had prayed to be the mother of a Buddha.

Following this, Queen Mayadevi dreamt that a six-tusked white elephant entered her womb through her right side at midnight. Upon her inquiring about this to the Brahmin sooth-sayers, they prophesied that she had conceived a son who would become a great Universal Emperor if he followed the life of a householder. But if he instead were to follow the life of a wandering monk, he would become a Perfected One, a Buddha.

One day, as the time of the child's birth was approaching, the queen took a stroll in the garden grove in

Lumbini. Reaching up with her right arm, she grasped a branch of a royal priksha tree, and as she looked to the sky, the son emerged from her right side. The sky was suddenly filled with a magnificent array of offerings by the devas. Brahmins approached the child with offerings of exquisite muslin, but he arose and exclaimed, "Release me!" Then, taking seven steps to the east, he declared, "I shall attain the greatest of all Dharmas." Taking seven steps to the south he said, "I shall become the object of veneration of devas and men." With seven steps to the west he uttered the words, "I am supreme in the world. This is my final birth—I shall cast off birth, old age, sickness, and death." And finally taking seven steps to the north, he said, "I shall be the Unsurpassable One among all sentient beings." Then, as he gazed down, he declared, "I shall subdue the gathering of maras. I shall let fall the rain of Dharma, which will extinguish the fire of suffering of all sentient beings in the hells." And, looking to the sky, he said, "All sentient beings will look aloft."

Seven days after his birth, the queen, who was a human emanation of Avalokiteshvara, the collected form of the compassion of all the Buddhas, passed away and her body was carried to the deva realms.

As the boy grew up, his father gave him the finest of tutors, but the prince was well-versed in all fields of learning, such as language, mathematics, logic and medicine, without even having to be taught.

When the prince grew into adolescence, the king advised him that it was time for him to take a wife and that a suitable consort should be sought. Five hundred or more daughters were offered by their parents, and the King ordered his son to choose from among them. Although the prince was perfectly aware of all the faults of desire, he also knew that the Bodhisattvas of the past had been able to provide for their wives and children without letting this hinder their spiritual practice. With this in mind, he wrote a description of the kind of woman he would accept as his wife and presented this to his father.

The king's ministers then scoured the countryside in search of a young woman possessing the necessary qualities. Finally, they came upon the princess Gopi Yashodhara, and seeing that she fitted the prince's description, invited her and many other maidens to the palace. Upon their arrival, the prince gave each of them a gift, but by the time Gopi came forward, there were no more gifts left. He then took a precious ring from his own hand and presented it to her. And the king saw that he favoured her over the rest.

A messenger was then sent to Gopi's father with the request that he give his daughter in marriage to the prince. But he replied that he would only give her to the suitor who was most skilled in athletics. This news disheartened the king, for he knew that his son was not practised in such skills. However, when the prince heard of the proposal, he readily agreed to compete with all contestants. After seven days, five hundred youths from all over the king's realm assembled and competed with one another at swordsmanship, archery, wrestling, swimming, foot-racing, and other trials of strength and dexterity. In each of these competitions the prince easily defeated all his rivals. Upon their conclusion he was given Gopi for his bride and she became his foremost queen.

And so they lived as man and wife for several years. Then one day by the power of all the Buddhas of the ten directions, the Bodhisattva prince heard a voice speaking through the notes of music played by his queens. The voice called him:

The three realms of the world are aflame with the
    suffering of old age and death.
Protectorless, living creatures remain unaware that
    this blazing fire of death arises from cyclic ex-
    istence,

And they live like bees circling about inside a vase.
The three realms are transient like the clouds of
    autumn.
The birth and death of sentient beings is like gazing
    upon a dance.
Like a flash of lightning is the passing of the life of
    sentient beings,
Running swiftly like a splashing stream down a
    steep mountain.

Hearing these words, the prince's thought turned to
enlightenment. That night the king dreamt that the prince
had taken to the wandering life, so he ordered guards to
observe him and more pleasures to be offered to him.

Not long thereafter, the prince felt the urge to explore
the world beyond the palace walls. Ordering his charioteer
to make ready his carriage, he left the palace through the
eastern gate. They had not gone far before he saw the
suffering of old age, which previously had been hidden
from him. Inquiring about this to his driver, he was told
that this misery was the fate of all those who advance in
years. And they returned to the palace.

The next time the prince ventured outside the palace,
he left by the southern gate, and saw a man ravaged by a
terrible disease. He set out the third time through the
western gate and observed a corpse for the first time. When
his driver told him that this was the deserted body of a
formerly living person, who was now forever separated
from his loved ones, the prince determined to find a means
of liberation from these miseries.

Once again the prince left the palace, this time by the
northern gate, and he saw a bhikkshu (monk) walking
along peacefully, his mind subdued. Asking his driver who
this man was, he was told that he was one who had
abandoned worldly desires, subdued his mind and, in
order to attain peace, had become a monk. Seeking that this

path was of benefit both to oneself and others, the prince resolved that he would do likewise.

When the king learned of this, he ordered that the walls and gates of the palace be heavily guarded and that the wives of the prince increase their efforts to amuse him. But the prince, far from finding them seductive, felt as if he were in a cemetery while he gazed upon their sleeping bodies. With the aid of the devas, he made his secret nocturnal escape.

His escape accomplished, the prince saw that his clothes were not fitting for the new life he had chosen. As he was thinking thus, a hunter appeared and offered him his saffron-coloured garments.

The Bodhisattva then sought out a great spiritual teacher and quickly mastered his teachings. He then went to another guru who had many disciples and quickly attained his level of insight. But still the Bodhisattva was not satisfied, for he had not attained freedom from the misery of the cycle of birth and death. For some time he practised religious austerities with a group of ascetics, but, thinking it better to live in solitude, he departed. Five of his disciples followed him, and for six years they practised meditation, severe ascetic practices, kept silence, and survived on just one sesamum seed, one jujube seed, and one grain of rice each day. But after these six years of practice, the Bodhisattva saw that this alone was not a means for attaining liberation, and he told his disciples that he would once again eat coarse food. They immediately lost faith in him and departed for Varanasi.

Shortly thereafter a girl mixed rice and fresh grain with cream, cooked it and offered it in a golden vessel to the Bodhisattva. He accepted it, and after eating it, his body was greatly revived. A village youth then brought him a bundle of kusha grass to use for his mat. Taking this, he walked to the bodhi tree in Bodh Gaya, circumambulated it three times, then laid down the stalks of the fresh green grass with their tips meeting in the centre.

He then sat upon them facing the east and vowed, "Even if my body dries up and my skin, bones and flesh fall away, I shall not move from this seat until I have reached enlightenment." And he entered deep meditation.

Countless maras came and assaulted him with rains of weapons, but he paid no heed. Then the weapons instead turned to flowers, lovely palaces, and other offerings. But thus subduing all the maras with the power of his meditation on compassion, he attained the omniscient state of full enlightenment. His body in full meditation posture rose into the sky to a height of seven palm trees. And countless Buddhas, Bodhisattvas, and devas rejoiced, casting flowers and richly adorning the bodhi tree with jewels.

For seven weeks Buddha examined the state of sentient beings. During the first week devas came and made offerings to him. During the second, he travelled to the countless realms of the universe. In the third week he spoke the words, "Here I have come to the end of suffering," as he sat gazing fixedly on the bodhi tree. During the fourth he travelled as far as the oceans of the east and west, and during the fifth he went to the domain of the nagas. During the sixth week he sat at the foot of a nyagrodha tree and ripened many spirit beings. During the seventh week he went to a grove of datura trees and was offered food by two merchants.

Then he remained in the forest and pondered the sublime, eternal Dharma, transcending all words, which had dawned upon his mind like a clear light. Thinking that no one else would be able to comprehend this Dharma, he decided to remain silently in the forest. But when many Bodhisattvas and other divine beings came and requested him to turn the Wheel of Dharma, he assented and went to Varanasi.

In Varanasi Buddha taught the four noble truths to the five disciples who had left him, as well as to many other followers. Thus commenced his First Turning of the Wheel of Dharma. In other places he taught vinaya, or moral discipline, and the practice of close mindfulness—teachings which are also included in the First Turning of the Wheel of Dharma. And his fame spread.

When he was forty-one years of age, Buddha Shakyamuni went to the deva realms to repay the kindness of his mother by teaching her Dharma. During his fifty-seventh year, he defeated six well-known non-Buddhist teachers in a test of miraculous powers.

On Vulture's Peak he turned the Second Wheel of Dharma for countless Bodhisattvas and taught the Perfection of Wisdom. In other places he gave other teachings, such as those of the *Samdhinirmochanaraja-sutra*, which are included in the Second Turning of the Wheel of Dharma.

At Vaisali Buddha turned the Final Wheel of Dharma, explaining the teaching he had given earlier. He also taught the *Kalachakra Tantra*. In many other places in Jambudvipa he also gave numerous teachings on tantra. Thus he brought many beings to full enlightenment.

In his eighty-first year, Buddha told his followers that he was about to pass into parinirvana. Shortly before his passing away, there was a non-Buddhist, aged one hundred and twenty years, who thrice asked Ananda to allow him to meet Buddha. But each time he was refused. Knowing this, Buddha called to him, and after speaking with him at length, this non-Buddhist attained Arhatship.

Shortly thereafter, Buddha Shakyamuni lay down at the foot of a tree in Kushinagar, his head pointing to the north, and entered parinirvana. Relics from his ashes are contained in stupas throughout Asia.

2
The Four Noble Truths

Of the twelve principal deeds of the Buddha involving the
three doors of the body, speech, and mind, his verbal acts
are considered to be superior because it was through this
that he communicated the path of deliverance to others.
His first teaching concerned the four noble truths,
specifically:

    I.   The truth of suffering.
   II.   The origin of suffering.
  III.   The cessation of suffering.
  IV.   The path to the cessation of suffering.

The nature of all suffering stems from the three poisons:
hatred-anger, desire-attachment, and ignorance. There are
four qualifications of suffering, which are as follows:

A.   Impermanence (*mi-rtag*), manifested in its gross
form as death, and subtly as momentary changes of
thoughts, sounds, and so forth.
B.   Unsatisfactoriness (*sdug-bsngal*), meaning that cyclic
existence is inseparable from misery.
C.   Voidness of independent self-existence (*stong-pa*).
D.   No-self (*bdag-med*), meaning that everything depends upon cause and effect.

A. IMPERMANENCE

Of the two aspects of impermanence, the subtle momentary
changes of existence are very difficult to realize. Awareness
of death, the most important example of the coarse form of
impermanence, causes us to practise and exert ourselves in
order to realize benefits in future existences. It is this that

leads us to recognize the importance of renunciation (*nges-'byung*), or literally 'authentic becoming', in order to be freed from suffering. There are three ways of remembering death:

1. Death is certain.
2. Its time is uncertain.
3. Dharma is the only means that will help us at the time of death.

For each of these there are three sub-divisions as follows:

1. (a) There is no possible way to escape death.
   (b) Life has a definite, inflexible limit and each moment brings us closer to the end of this life.
   (c) Death comes in a moment and its time is unexpected.
2. (a) The duration of our lifespan is uncertain (Note: In the beginning of this world, the lifespan was one thousand years, but now, owing to the abundance of non-virtuous acts, such as harmful thoughts and the merciless slaughter of insects and other animals, the maximum duration has decreased to one hundred years. However, when dealing with individuals we must remember that one's lifespan is totally uncertain).
   (b) There are many causes and circumstances that lead to death but which also favour the sustenance of life. The necessities of life such as food, clothes, transport, and so forth may also be causes of death.
   (c) The weakness and fragility of one's physical body contribute to life's uncertainty. Even such a small thing as a thorn in one's foot may be the cause of death if this wound becomes infected.

3. (a) Worldly possessions like wealth, position, money—all the acquisitions directed solely at this life—are of no benefit to us at the time of death. We are born with nothing and we die with nothing.

   (b) Friends and relatives can neither prevent our death nor go with us. We are born alone, bear our suffering alone, and die alone. Therefore let us not be drawn into the web of human triviality or worldliness. The Sakya Pandit, Kunga Gyaltsen has written: "The wise follow their own reason and critical intelligence, whereas the foolish follow those who are famous."

   (c) Our own body, which we have cared most for in this life, is of no help to us at the time of death.

Contemplating these nine points thoroughly, we should come to three major decisions: first to practise the Dharma; second to practise it immediately; and third to practise it purely, not diluting it with other pursuits. After fully realizing these points, we shall resemble a traveller in a distant land, never worrying that we may need many things during our travels, since we never know when we shall be moving to new quarters. Thus we should live with constant awareness of the uncertainty of the time of death. This will lead us to practice the Dharma purely.

The two aspects of truth (conventional and ultimate) and the four noble truths are the essence of Buddha's teaching. Realizing that without the abandonment of suffering and its causes, we are destined to remain bound to the wheel of birth and death, we must cultivate a sense of renunciation. We are like a sick person: suffering is our illness; the cause of woe is its symptoms; cessation is the recovery; and the path is taking effective medicine. Continually keeping the reality of death in mind causes a lessening of our kleshas (*nyon-mongs*) or karmic (unskilful) acts and attitudes, and turns all our acts towards the Dharma. Likewise, we lose all attachment to friends and relatives as well as desire for wealth or a high position.

In Tibet there is the aphorism: "Of all the yields of the earth, that of autumn is the best. Of all footprints, that of the elephant is the greatest. Of all incentives for Dharma practice, the greatest is awareness of death."

The purpose of this teaching is not to lead us to desperation but, through the practice of the Dharma, to the end of suffering and to freedom from death.

I. THE NOBLE TRUTH OF SUFFERING
(*SDUG-BSNGAL BDEN-PA*)

Our present minds are like the sky overcast with clouds composed of the three poisons. It is possible to clear away these clouds and realize the pure nature of our minds. The mind may also be likened to a rough child who may be trained and moulded under the guidance of wise parents.

When contemplating suffering, we may think of it in three ways: as having eight, six or three aspects.

A. THE EIGHT ASPECTS OF SUFFERING

These refer primarily to the kinds of suffering borne by humanity.

1. The suffering of birth.

An infant in the mother's womb must endure great pain from heat and cold. Then at birth the child feels the pain of being squeezed between mountains. Its mouth and throat are dry and its skin is very sensitive and delicate. The child cries at birth because it perceives suffering more clearly and, even when its loving mother takes it tenderly in her arms, the child is filled with fear. We may think we are finished with the experience of birth, but as long as the roots of samsara (*'khor-ba*) are not cut, we shall experience birth again and again. If we carefully consider this suffering, renunciation will come easily.

2. The suffering of old age.

As we gradually see the signs of old age appearing, it is very hard to bear, and when looking in a mirror, we come to despise our own form. We see our physical strength faltering, our legs becoming weak, the ability to digest food decreasing, and all the powers of our senses lessening. Out mental powers also grow weak, our memory fades, and perhaps we lose the ability to speak coherently. From the moment of birth the ageing process begins, and each day our remaining lifespan decreases. In our old age we become aware of the imminence of death, and while death is momentary, the period of old age may be prolonged and lingering.

3. The suffering of sickness.

When our body is ill, it suffers pain and weakness. This is often coupled with mental desperation, especially with a prolonged sickness. Bodily illness is caused by a disruption in the harmony of the four elements which constitute the body. Often, as with internal disorders, we must experience additional pain from medical treatment.

4. The suffering of death.

Attachment to the pleasures of this life and to relatives and friends causes desperation and great mental suffering at the time of death. In the case of a natural death, that is, one not due to accident or violence, we experience the signs of the dissolution of the body's four elements. First the power of the earth element dissolves, and the water element comes to the forefront of our consciousness. Outwardly our skin shrinks and becomes blotchy, and inwardly we feel panic and we grasp at life. A person who has practised the Dharma feels like they are in a dusty place, whereas one who has no experience of the Dharma feels as if they are being trampled by herds of animals and crushed between mountains. The earth element is no longer able to support our consciousness, and we lose the ability to move our body. During the second stage, the water element likewise dissolves, to be replaced by the power of fire. We now feel dry and thirsty and have difficulty speaking. One with no Dharma experience feels as if they have fallen into a turbulent river or a great ocean. The third stage begins with the dissolution of the fire element, and the element of air comes to the forefront of our consciousness. Outwardly the body loses its heat, but inwardly we feel as if we are being burned in a bonfire. At this point, a sure sign of our next birth can be seen. If the heat disappears from the feet up to the heart, we are assured of birth in one of the higher realms; if it disappears downwards from the head to the heart, rebirth in one of the lower realms is equally certain. Finally, the heat disappears into the region of the heart, where consciousness was centred at conception. The final outward sign is the cessation of breathing, when the power of air dissolves into consciousness. At this point, a person who has practised the Dharma has a feeling of experiencing a light breeze, whereas one without this practice feels like a feather carried by a fierce wind. At this stage, we have the three successive perceptions of white, red and black. The first perception of the colour white is due to the descending of the semen from its centre in the forehead to the heart region. It was previously held up by the power of the air element just as this power held down the blood, whose centre is in the navel. The blood, whose nature is fire, now rises to the heart region, and we perceive the colour red. It is this power of the air element which separates mind from body. The semen and blood now come together, forming a tent-like structure which encloses our consciousness (*rnam-shes*) at the heart centre. When this tent collapses, blackness is seen, and the death process is complete. If because of previous meditational experience a person is able to control their consciousness throughout this death process, they will be able to keep this tent, within which the seed of bodhichitta lies, from collapsing for a longer duration than normal. The last Panchen Lama remained in this state for one year after the cessation of his breathing. When the tent collapses, the semen may flow from the right nostril and blood from the left, or they may remain in the body. Then the decomposition of the body begins. After the tent collapses, we perceive our mind in its purest form, and this moment is the most opportune for meditation on shunyata, or voidness, but, as most of us are not able to take advantage of this opportunity, our consciousness immediately enters the intermediate state, or *bar-do* existence.

There are two types of rebirth. With the first kind we choose our next form and place of birth in order to be of the most benefit to others. This ability is held only by those with high spiritual attainments. With the second kind we are thrown into our future rebirth solely as a result of our past karma (*las*). During the *bar-do* state our consciousness takes on an intangible body and seeks a substantial one. As the *bar-do* state comes to an end, we see only the sexual organs of a man and a woman during the sexual act. Anger is aroused, causing the death of the *bar-do* body, and our consciousness enters the father's mouth or the crown of his head. It then goes from the father's sexual organ to the mother's and then into her womb. When consciousness assumes form during the union of the semen and blood, we feel as if we are being boiled in water. During the period of the formation of limbs, we feel pain as if our skin is being stretched.

The purpose of contemplating suffering is to lead us towards ending the cycle of rebirth and woe which we experience. If we have the correct attitude, we recognize that our suffering is solely the effect of our past karmic actions, and that we must undergo it in order to 'work off' the effects of our past non-virtuous actions.

5.   The suffering of being separated from that which we desire or are attached to.

We must recognize the impermanence of friends, things, and places in order to be free of our attachment to them.

6.   The suffering of meeting with undesirable events.

As long as we remain within samsara, no matter at which level of life we may be, we experience such things as sickness, accidents, and meeting whom we dislike. Our tendency, however, is to believe that others at a different social level have a better situation than ourselves.

7.   The suffering of not finding the happiness and pleasures of life which we seek.

Examples of this are provided by merchants who seek financial profit but without success, and those who strive for fame or a high position but fail.

8.   The suffering of having a body.

A samsaric body is like having a magnet that collects sufferings of many kinds. While undergoing sufferings from past karmic actions, it produces further karma which causes suffering in future lives. By realizing that wherever we exist within the six realms of samsara we must experience suffering, we shall see the need of cutting this karmic tie to the body. It is impossible for us to know the taste of the Dharma without critically examining and meditating upon it. This path is easier if we pray to one whom we trust, asking for an enlightened mind.

B. THE SIX FORMS OF SUFFERING

These are experienced by all beings, not only by humans.

1. Uncertainty.

Within samsara there is no fixed or unchanging state, but always the possibility of being cast into a lower or unhappier situation in this life or a lower realm in the next. Once Shariputra, one of Buddha's two main disciples, while begging for alms, came to the house of a woman who was holding her child, eating a fish, and kicking her dog. By his clairvoyance, he was able to see that in a past life the child had been the woman's enemy who had killed her, the fish she was eating had been her mother, and the dog had been her father. She then fed the bones of the fish to the dog. This furnishes an example of how friends change to enemies, and enemies to friends.

2. Greed.

No matter how much we possess, if we have greed, we can never have satisfaction. Abundance of possessions then implies an abundance of unslaked desires. Worldly pleasures are like drinking salt water, which temporarily soothes our thirst, but then leads to yet greater desire. There was once a merchant who bought a great jewel in a foreign land, and upon returning to his homeland, said he would give it to the poorest person in the country. He then gave it to the king, who although was very wealthy, had a great desire to possess more. This is one of the worst types of suffering, for as long as greed remains, we are separated from contentment. The truly contented person is the richest.

3. The necessity of repeatedly abandoning our body.

The heap of bones from all our past lives would be greater than the size of the earth, and this heap will increase indefinitely unless we cultivate renunciation.

4. The entering of consciousness into the union of semen and blood at conception.

Samsaric existence is without beginning. If one were able to form little balls from all the matter of the earth, this would still not equal the number of all the mothers we have had in all our forms of existence.

5. Uncertain level of future rebirth.

Even though we take a high birth in one life, if we fail to practise the Dharma, we will always fall back into the lower realms. Even such beings as the Chakra Kings, who rule the Continents in certain periods during which there is no war or famine, may fall to the lowest states.

6. Lack of friends or companionship.

We experience both suffering and death alone, and during existence in the lower realms, there is no one to whom we can call for help. In his *Friendly Letter* (*bshes-pa'i spring-yig, Suhrllekha*) to a king, Nagarjuna wrote, "O King, you must always be aware and be careful of your Dharma practices, for when you die you cannot take your riches, queens, or servants with you. You must go alone." In this letter he also wrote of contentment and correct Dharma practices.

When we fully realize these forms of suffering, renunciation of all samsaric matters will come easily. Once when Milarepa was living in a cave, a thief came at night to try to steal food. Seeing him, Milarepa asked: "Thief, what do you think you can find at night which I cannot find during the daytime?" Another time when Milarepa was changing his place of retreat from one cave to another (meditators do this in order not to become attached to any place), his only clay pot slipped from his hands and broke. He then joyfully sang a song on the lesson of impermanence thus given.

That which is collected separates into its components; birth inevitably leads to death; high position later leads to a lower position; and meeting results in parting. These are the four characteristics of samsara taught by the Lord Buddha. Only upon the attainment of nirvana do all karma, kleshas, and transience come to an end.

C. THE THREE KINDS OF SUFFERING

These refer to that suffered by all sentient beings.

1. The suffering of misery (*sdug-bsngal gyi sdug-bsngal*).

Sickness, both mental and physical pain, hunger, and thirst are the main examples of this suffering.

2. The suffering of change (*'gyur-ba'i sdug'-bsngal*).

This suffering is due to the impermanence of all things in samsara. For example, if we move from the shade to the sunshine, we enjoy the warmth at first. But then, when we become too hot, we again seek the shade. All samsaric pleasure has this aspect of impermanence, the nature of which is suffering or dissatisfaction that causes us to continually seek new sources of happiness.

3. The suffering of extensiveness (*khyab-pa 'du-byed kyi sdug-bsngal*).

This suffering is experienced not only in this life, but on all levels of samsaric existence. As soon as we take on a body, it acts like a magnet which attracts suffering. Denizens of the hells must endure the suffering of heat and cold; pretas (spirit beings) suffer from hunger and thirst; and animals suffer from ignorance and stupidity. In the higher realms, humans suffer from birth, old age, sickness, and death; anti-gods suffer from jealousy and continual disappointment; and devas suffer during the last seven days of their lives when they become aware that they are about to die. In possessing a samsaric body, we resemble a naked person carrying a bundle of thorns bound to their back by the rope of karma and kleshas.

Thus, we must develop true renunciation of this third kind of suffering, seeking total release from all forms of samsaric existence. It is important to recognize suffering in the world, especially when it is occurring. The root of all suffering is our belief in the concept of our own fixed, independent self; and realization of shunyata is like the knife that cuts the root of ignorance. Belief in true independent self-existence is like seeing a rope and mistaking it for a snake. Realization of shunyata is like recognizing the rope for what it actually is. With respect to a person, 'conventional truth' is the five skandhas, or aggregates, which we falsely grasp as having self-existence, and 'ultimate truth' is the void nature of all phenomena. It is our false concept of self-existence that causes the collection of karma. When the former is rectified, the latter disappears.

II. THE NOBLE TRUTH OF THE CAUSE
OF SUFFERING
(*KUN-'BYUNG BDEN-PA*)

There are four aspects involved in the arising of suffering, listed as follows:

A. The cause of suffering (*rgyu*).
B. The source of suffering (*kun-'byung*).
C. The circumstances of suffering (*rkyen*).
D. The violent development or growth of suffering (*rab-skye*).

The two causes of suffering are karma and kleshas. Karma means the secondary consciousness belonging to the primary stream of consciousness (*gtso-sems*), and it automatically moves the latter like a magnet attracting a piece of metal. The primary mind thus collects the black and white karma of the secondary mind.

In Tibetan, there are three synonyms for the primary mind, meaning the initial recognition of the nature of any object. They are: primary mind (*gtso-sems*), stream of consciousness (*rnam-shes*), and mind (*yid*). The secondary mind (*sems-byung*) includes all the reactions that follow the initial perception.

The mind in its entirety is of two kinds. The first is understanding free of illusion (*tshad-ma*), which has two aspects. The first aspect is direct understanding of the nature of an object (*mngon-sum tshad-ma*), and the second is indirect understanding by means of reasoning, as when contemplating shunyata or the law of cause and effect (*rjes-dpag tshad-ma*).

The second kind of mind is incorrect understanding, or mind clouded by illusion (*tshad-min-gyi blo*), and this has five aspects, listed as follows.

1. The moments following the initial moment of perception of an object (*dpyad-shes*).
2. Wrong views or understanding caused by the three poisons, especially by grasping to an independent, fixed ego. This is like the yellowish visual perception of a person with jaundice (*log-shes*).
3. Doubt or scepticism, that is, the mind which 'floats' between two alternatives (*the-tshom*).
4. Uncertain belief concerning that which is true (*yid-dpyod*).
5. Perception devoid of recognition or understanding; for example, while attentively listening to music, we may see visual objects later having no conscious memory of them (*snang-la ma-nges-pa*).

Of these five, the most harmful is wrong views.

PRIMARY MINDS

There are six primary minds, one for each of the senses:

1. Visual consciousness (*mig-gi rnam-par shes-pa*).
2. Auditory consciousness (*rna-yi rnam-par shes-pa*).
3. Olfactory consciousness (*sna-yi rnam-par shes-pa*).
4. Gustatory consciousness (*lce-yi rnam-par shes-pa*).
5. Tactile consciousness (*lus-kyi rnam-par shes-pa*).
6. Mental consciousness (*yid-kyi rnam-par shes-pa*).

It is important to understand that the root of virtue and non-virtue is the mind and that it is the power of the mind which motivates all acts. The mind is thus the most important of the six senses and the only one which does not rely on a physical organ. The primary mind, situated near the heart, understands directly, whereas the secondary mind, situated in the head, with its discriminating, differentiating power, understands through reasoning.

SECONDARY MINDS

There are fifty-one secondary minds which are divided into six categories.

A. (*kun-'gro*). That which always accompanies any perception of the primary mind, thus enabling the mind to make use of the object of perception. This category of mind has five aspects:

1. (*sems-pa*). The motivator and activator which connects the primary mind to an object of perception or action. This is the most active of the five aspects of mind in this category and is equivalent to karma.
2. (*yid-la byed-pa*). The consciousness that enables the primary mind to distinguish between particular objects or to understand things individually.
3. (*reg-pa*). The contact of mind and its object.
4. (*tsor-ba*). Mental and physical feeling of three kinds: pleasurable, painful, and indifferent.
5. (*'dus-shes*). Recognition of things and their various qualities, or understanding the relationship between the qualities of an object and its function. With this in mind we are able to label the object of perception.

The relationship between these five may be illustrated by the following examples: (1) the idea of going to a garden;

(2) choosing a particular garden; (3) arriving at the garden; (4) the feeling that arises from this contact; (5) recognizing individual forms and their characteristics in the garden.

B. (*yul-nges*). The aspect of the mind which understand things individually (as opposed to simple discrimination). This is of five kinds:

1. (*shes-rab*). The discriminating mind which is able to differentiate between virtue and vice.
2. (*'dun-pa*). Intention, which leads us to strive after the object of our desire, such as the attainment of enlightenment.
3. (*ting-nge-'dzin*). Single-pointed concentration or placing and fixing of the mind on one object.
4. (*dran-pa*). Memory, or mindfulness.
5. (*mos-pa*). Examination of the object of concentration.

C. (*dge-ba*). The mind of virtue, which is of eleven kinds:

1. (*dad-pa*). Faith, of which there are three kinds:

    (a) Faith in the Triple Gem of the Buddha, Dharma, and Sangha.
    (b) The firm wish to attain enlightenment, coupled with the faith that this is a realizable goal.
    (c) A firm conviction of the truth of the doctrine of rebirth and the law of cause and effect.

Faith is essential in attaining further knowledge and is thus called the mother of knowledge.

2. (*ngo-tsha shes-pa*). Awareness, or knowledge of that which is shameful, that is, a sense of self-shame.
3. (*khrel-yod-pa*). The external counterpart of (2), that is, keeping in mind how others view our actions. By

means of these second and third aspects of the mind of virtue, we may maintain our virtue purely.

4. (*ma-chags-pa*). Non-attachment.
5. (*zhe-sdang med-pa*) Freedom from anger.
6. (*gti-mug med-pa*). Freedom from ignorance.
7. (*brtson-'grus*). Self-motivated enthusiastic perseverance in following virtuous conduct (the opposite of laziness, which rejects doing anything worthwhile).
8. (*shin-sbyangs*). The power to control and use our mind and body in any way we like, resulting in mental ecstasy.
9. (*bag-yod*). Alertness for non-virtuous deeds, enabling us to keep vows purely.
10. (*btang-snyoms*). Equanimity, or even-mindedness.
11. (*rnam-par mi-'tshe-ba*). Not being able to endure the suffering of others.

D. (*rtsa-nyon drug*). The six primary kleshas, which result in our continued wandering in samsara.

1. (*ma-rig-pa*). Ignorance, specifically not understanding the difference between virtue and non-virtue.
2. (*'dod-chags*). Desire and attachment.
3. (*khong-khro*). Anger and hatred.
4. (*nga-rgyal*). Pride.
5. (*the-tshom nyon-mongs-can*). Doubting that which is true.
6. (*lta-ba nyon-mongs-can*). False views which arise from delusion. Five major examples of these are:

   (a) (*'jig-lta*). Grasping to the self as being permanent and self-existent.
   (b) (*mthar-lta*). The view that all phenomena inherently exist.

    (c) (*log-lta*). Belief that there is no karma, rebirth or cause and effect.

    (d) (*lta-ba mchog-'dzin*). Clinging to these above false views as being paramount and ultimate.

    (e) (*tshul-khrims-dang rtul-zhugs mchog-'dzin*). Believing that samsaric practices such as asceticism or idol-worship have ultimate meaning.

E. (*nye-nyon*) The twenty secondary kleshas. The 'throwing karma' ('*phen-byed-kyi las*) produced by these kleshas binds us to samsara and propels us into the lower states of rebirth. Therefore, we must recognize them in order to eliminate them. We should likewise be able to recognise which states of our consciousness are primary and which secondary.

1. (*khro-ba*). The growth of anger, resulting in action governed by this passion.
2. ('*khon-'dzin*). Grudge-holding.
3. (*tshig-pa*). Action which results from anger.
4. (*rnam-par 'tshe-ba*). The continual intention to harm others, such as killing an insect whenever we see one.
5. (*phrag-dog*). Jealousy, or not being able to endure seeing the wealth or virtue of others. At such times, our contentment is gone and our mind feels heavy.
6. (*g.yo*). Hiding our faults in order to obtain some object of desire.
7. (*sgyu*). Pretending that we are virtuous, wise, and so forth, in order to impress others.
8. (*ngo-tsha med-pa*). Inward shamelessness.
9. (*khrel-med*). Outward shamelessness.
10. ('*chab-pa*). Trying to hide our kleshas from others. It is best to speak of them, bring them out in the open and repent.

11. (*ser-sna*). Avarice, or continually desiring to increase our store of wealth. If this characteristic is predominant, we are born as a preta who continually seeks food but never finds it.

12. (*rgyags-pa*). Pride concerning such things as our health, wealth, or education.

13. (*ma-dad-pa*). Lack of faith, or taking no joy in performing virtuous deeds.

14. (*le-lo*). Laziness, or reluctance to follow virtuous conduct. This is the enemy of perseverance.

15. (*bag-med*). Being carefree and inattentive, not caring whether virtuous or non-virtuous karma is produced, but doing whatever comes to mind.

16. (*brjed-ngas*). Forgetfulness, that is, the unclearness and dullness which arise during meditation.

17. (*shes-bzhin min-pa*). Lack of alertness, particularly concerning the arising of delusions in our mind.

18. (*rmugs-pa*). Depression and dullness.

19. (*rgod-pa*). Mental agitation concerning an object of desire, making it impossible to concentrate on another object.

20. (*rnam-par g.yeng-ba*). Mental wandering, or the inability to control our mind.

The root klesha of the first five secondary klesha is anger, for six through eight it is ignorance, for the last two it is desire, and the rest of the secondary klesha relate to all three poisons.

F. (*gzhan-'gyur bzhi*). The remaining four secondary minds:

1. (*gnyid*). Sleep. If thoughts are virtuous just before sleep, the karma produced during sleep will likewise be virtuous.

2. (*'gyod-pa*). Regret, such as after having given someone a gift.

3. (*rtog-pa*). Coarse conceptual understanding.
4. (*dpyod-pa*). Fine conceptual understanding.

Of these fifty-one kinds of secondary consciousness, some (the root and secondary klesha) are fetters or delusions, whereas others lead to nirvana. The fetters are not permanent but may be cut out from the root. This is necessary in order to attain nirvana.

KARMA

Throwing karma of the three kinds—virtuous, non-virtuous, and unfluctuating—is the force which propels one into the different states of existence. Karma produced by virtuous action leads to rebirth in the human realm or one of the other two higher realms. Mount Meru is the centre of this world system, surrounded by four continents with two islands around each one. We humans live in the Southern Continent (*lho 'dzam-bu-gling*), named after the splashing sound of a piece of wood dropped in water.

Non-virtuous throwing karma leads to rebirth in one of the three lower realms. Unfluctuating karma results in rebirth in either the realm of form (*gzugs-khams*), of which there are seventeen levels of existence, or the formless realm (*gzugs-med-khams*), in which there are four levels of existence. We humans, live in the desire realm ('*dod-khams*).

III. THE NOBLE TRUTH OF THE CESSATION OF SUFFERING ('*GOG-BDEN*)

The first two noble truths are themselves klesha, whereas the last two are equivalent to nirvana and the path to attain it. The fruit of the cessation of suffering is peace (*zhi-ba*) and never-ending joy. To attain this cessation, we need to cut the fetters of the klesha; having done so, there is no possibility of falling back into suffering. Most people, however, do not have patience in applying the methods of escaping from this jail of samsara. Recognizing that one has no worse enemies than one's klesha, the truly brave person conquers the six root and the twenty secondary klesha, thus becoming an Arhat (*dgra-bcom-pa*), meaning 'one who overcomes enemies'. There are two kinds of obstacles. The first, kleshavarana (*nyon-sgrib*), includes the twenty-six major and minor kleshas, which must be eliminated before Arhatship, or nirvana, can be attained. The second, jneya-varana (*shes-sgrib*), is the instinct of clinging to the illusion of independent self-existence, and it is this which blocks the way to the full enlightenment of Buddhahood.

IV. THE NOBLE TRUTH OF THE PATH
TO THE CESSATION OF SUFFERING
(*LAM-BDEN*)

There are two goals towards which those on the path strive. The first, nirvana, or moksha (*thar-pa*), is the attainment of the level of Arhatship (*dgra-bcom-pa'i go-'phang*), and the second, full enlightenment (*thams cad mkhyen pa*), meaning the 'all-knowing state', is the attainment of Buddhahood (*sangs-rgyas-kyi go-'phang*).

In order to attain these goals we need the following:

A. The path (*lam*).
B. Awareness of the path (*rig-pa*) as the means of counteracting the klesha.
C. Practice of these means (*sgrub-pa*) with exertion and endurance, motivated by the wish to attain a high state of existence.
D. Knowledge of the method to eliminate the klesha so that they will never again return (*nges-'byin*).

THE SIXTEEN INCORRECT VIEWS
CONCERNING THE FOUR NOBLE TRUTHS
(*LOG ZHUGS BCU-DRUG*)

A. The four wrong views concerning suffering and the body are:

    1. Thinking of the body as being clean and pure.
    2. Thinking of the body as being a source of pleasure.
    3. Thinking that the body has a permanent aspect.
    4. Thinking that the body is composed of solid, independent matter.

These four wrong views must be refuted before shunyata may be realized.

B. The four wrong views concerning the cause of suffering.

    1. Believing that suffering has no cause or is its own cause.
    2. Thinking that suffering arises from irrelevant causes.
    3. Holding the view that suffering is due to only one cause, independent of conditions or secondary circumstances (*rkyen*).
    4. Believing that suffering and its causes are permanent.

C. The four wrong views concerning the cessation of suffering are:

    1. Doubting that there is any liberation from suffering.
    2. Stopping one's practice, satisfied with the level one has attained, before full liberation is reached.

3. Holding the highest level of meditation to be the ultimate attainment.
4. Believing that suffering will always return, no matter what one's attainment may be.

D. The four wrong views concerning the path to the cessation of suffering are:

1. Believing that there is no path which can be followed.
2. Believing that there is no way to perceive egolessness.
3. Practising methods which yield no fruit.
4. Believing that there are no effective remedies for one's suffering.

3
The Fully Endowed Human Body

If one has obtained the precious fully endowed human
body (*dal-'byor gyi mi-lus*), one has the opportunity to attain
the cessation of suffering. Thus, it is of the greatest
importance to recognize this body and its diamond-like
value. The attributes which comprise a fully endowed body
include the eight freedoms (*dal-ba brgyad*) and the ten
endowments (*'byor-ba bcu*).

I. THE EIGHT FREEDOMS

A. There are four freedoms from fetters within human
existence (*mi-yi mi-khom-pa bzhi*), that is, conditions
which prevent the practice of the Dharma. They are:

1. Firmly holding wrong views, such as nihilism, or
   disbelief in the law of cause and effect (*log-lta-can*).
2. Birth in a totally non-religious or barbaric land
   (*mtha'-khob-tu skye-ba*).
3. Birth in a land where no Buddhist Dharma is taught
   (*rgyal-ba'i bka'-med-pa*).
4. Birth as a demented or mute person (*glen-zhing lkug-pa*).

B. There are four freedoms from non-human types of birth
(*mi ma-yin-pa'i mi-khom-pa*). They are:

1. Birth in a hell region of continuous suffering (*dmyal-ba*).
2. Birth in the preta realm where continual hunger
   and desire prevent any practice of the Dharma (*yi-dvags*).

3. Birth as an animal lacking the power to discrimate between virtuous and non-virtuous actions (*dud-'gro*).
4. Birth as a long-life deva with so much pleasure that one has no motivation to practise the Dharma (*lha tshe-ring-po*).

If one has attained these eight freedoms, one should realize this opportunity to practise the Dharma, and protect one's body like a wish-fulfilling gem.

II. THE TEN ENDOWMENTS

A. There are five personal endowments (*rang-'byor lnga*). They are:

1. Birth as a human being (*mi-yid*), which gives one the potential to attain liberation.
2. Birth where the Dharma flourishes, or in a central land (*yul-dbus-su skye-ba*). This term 'central land' originally meant Bodh Gaya, but now refers to any place where the Buddhadharma is practised.
3. Birth with a body having all five senses intact (*dbang-po tshang-ba*).
4. Birth into a life free from the five heinous crimes, which are: killing one's father, killing one's mother, killing an Arhat, purposely shedding the blood of a Buddha, and causing a schism in the sangha (*las mtha'-ma log*).
5. Having respect for the 'Three Baskets of the Dharma', which include the vinaya, or moral discipline, the sutras, or discourses, and the *Abhidharma*, or the wisdom teaching of the Buddha (*gnas-la dad*).

B. There are five circumstantial endowments (*gzhan-'byor lnga*). They are:

1. The presence of a Buddha during the time in which one lives (*sangs-rgyas byon-pa*). The rarity of this occurrence through the ages is very great, like a flash of lightning on a dark night.
2. The presence of the Dharma of the Lord Buddha (*de'i dam-chos gsung-pa*).
3. The flourishing of the practice of the Dharma (*bstan-pa gnas-pa*). There are two kinds of teaching— scriptural and insight—the latter being one's own experience of the Dharma.
4. The existence of the monastic order, the fellowship of those who follow the Dharma and guide others towards the attainment of enlightenment (*de'i rjes-su 'jug-pa'i dge-'dun yod-pa*).
5. Being under the care of a compassionate person, a patron or a teacher, who looks after one in one's practice (*gzhan-gyi snying-brtse-ba*).

Having a body or, more accurately, a 'body-mind' possessing these eight freedoms and ten endowments, one is capable of shaping one's own future by following the path leading to higher states of birth and ultimately to full enlightenment. One then has the best circumstances in which to practise virtue and the means towards higher attainment, with the possibility of attaining full enlightenment in one lifetime. Only in this Southern Continent do sentient beings have this opportunity; thus, the fully endowed body should be considered even more valuable than a wish-fulfilling gem. This form is precious in every moment; for each moment may be used for the purpose of approaching enlightenment. The possibilities are boundless. One must first recognize this form, realize its great value and rarity, then use it accordingly for gaining higher attainment.

Like the appearance of a flower, these eighteen characteristics are the result of causes and conditions, the main three of which are maintaining pure moral practice, practising the six perfections, and offering prayers directed towards gaining higher goals than pleasure in this life. The practice of morality prevents one from falling into the lower realms, and generosity causes prosperity in one's next life. On the other hand, if not even one type of moral practice is kept purely, there is no chance of future human rebirth in the next life, so one must abstain from the following ten non-virtuous acts: killing, stealing, sexual misconduct, lying, causing dissension among others by means of slander, abuse, idle or senseless speech (the least of the non-virtues, but the easiest way to waste one's life), craving the possessions of others, thoughts of harming others, and holding wrong views. These ten form the basis for all further practice, including tantra. The path to enlightenment is one of different stages, to be taken a step at a time. Although it is difficult at first to practise virtue because of one's instincts, one must develop the attitude to be willing to undergo any hardships on the path, not expecting an easy way. Being endowed with a fully endowed human body is like having pushed an iron ball half-way up a mountain. If one relaxes, ignoring this opportunity, it will naturally roll down again. The future lies in one's own hands.

CONTEMPLATION ON THE FULLY ENDOWED BODY

Contemplation on the fully endowed body may best follow a three-fold outline:

A. Recognition of the eight freedoms and ten endowments

(*dal-'byor ngos-zung-ba*) which comprise the fully endowed body.

B. Contemplation of the great value of the fully endowed body (*don-che-ba bsam-pa*). This subject is subdivided into three parts:

    1. The temporal value of the fully endowed body in that it enables one to attain higher forms of rebirth (*gnas-skabs-la ltos-ste don-che-ba*).

    2. Its ultimate value is that it enables one to approach and attain the full enlightenment of Buddha (*mthar-thug-la ltos-ste don-che-ba*).

    3. The preciousness of each moment of a life with this form (*skad-gcig re-re-la don-che-ba*).

C. Contemplation on the rarity of attaining a fully endowed body (*rnyed-dka'-ba bsam-pa*). This is also divided into three parts:

    1. The rarity of the causes of obtaining this form (*rgu'i sgo-nas rnyed-dka'-ba*).

    2. The difficulty of obtaining this form as illustrated by examples (*dpe'i sgo-nas rnyed-dka'-ba*). The classic example is a vast ocean on which a golden yoke drifts about, moved by the wind and the currents. Once every hundred years a blind turtle surfaces for a moment, then again submerges. The chances of the turtle surfacing with its head inside the yoke are likened to those of obtaining a fully endowed human body. In this example the golden yoke symbolizes the Buddhadharma, and its motion refers to the fact that the Dharma moves from one land to another according to the needs of people. The turtle's blindness symbolizes the inability of creatures in the lower realms to discriminate between virtue and non-virtue. Its existence beneath the

ocean's surface represents one's existence in the lower realms and its surfacing, the attainment of a human rebirth.

Our 'permanent address' is the three lower states of rebirth, and to obtain any of the higher forms of birth is exceptional. Thus, within the vast ocean of samsaric existence, to obtain a precious fully endowed body is almost incalculably rare. Further examples of this rarity might be throwing a handful of peas against a wall (symbolizing human birth) with the chance of one of them sticking to the wall. A final example is pouring mustard seeds on the tip of a pin, with the chance of one staying on top.

3. The nature of the scarcity in terms of numbers (*grangs-kyi sgo-nas rnyed-dka'-ba*). The number of beings endowed with fully endowed bodies as compared with the number of all sentient beings is like a handful of dust compared with the dust of the world. Of the six realms, the hells contain by far the greatest number of beings, and each of the higher realms contains progressively fewer. Moreover, within the human realm, the number of those with fully endowed bodies is small in proportion to the entire human population.

Between the time periods during which the teaching of each of the one thousand Universal Teachers of a world age (Shakyamuni is the fourth) flourishes, there comes a minor dark age. The major dark age comes after the teaching of the one-thousandth Buddha who, in this particular cycle of one thousand Buddhas, will be a manifestation of Vajrapani. During each of these dark ages, the Dharma totally dies out. Before the coming of the next Universal Teacher Maitreya, the fifth Buddha of this world age, the average lifespan will first decrease to ten years, then slowly increase to eighty thousand years. During these dark ages people would not be able to benefit from the Dharma even if it did exist, for they would be far too immersed in delusion. Although there have been many since the time of Shakyamuni who have attained full enlightenment, that which distinguishes a Universal Teacher is the promise to deliver all sentient beings from the misery of samsara.

Having been endowed with a fully endowed body, one has the opportunity to attain full enlightenment in this life, or, failing this, nirvana, or at least a higher state of existence. If none of these are attained, one's fully endowed body has been wasted. The level of one's attainment depends largely upon one's mental scope and motivation. The person of highest scope (*skyes-bu chen-po*) strives after full enlightenment for the sake of all sentient beings. One of medium scope (*skyes-bu 'bring*) strives after nirvana, or freedom from suffering, the main aspect of one's practice being perfect renunciation of all samsaric existence. The person of small scope (*skyes-bu chung-ngu*), due to fear of rebirth in the lower realms, strives after a higher state of birth in the next life. The three types of practice corresponding to each type of person are graded, not contradictory, making the path to Buddhahood a more realizable one. The main subjects of contemplation for the person of small scope are impermanence, the qualities of the Three Refuges, and the law of cause and effect. The most important teaching for one of medium scope, seeking their own freedom, is the four noble truths. The distinguishing practices of the person of the greatest scope are those of the Bodhisattva path and those contained in the Tantrayana teaching. The so-called common path, namely that followed by persons of the lower two scopes, is the basis for all practice. Each of the progressively higher practices stems from and has its foundation in the practices of the persons of small scope.

The primary difference between a religious and a non-religious person is the level of attachment to this life. While most people spend their lives striving after worldly satisfaction and rewards, if one contemplates one's own future existence, a sense of renunciation of these sources of pleasure will grow. Contemplation of the suffering of all states of existence, and especially awareness of death and impermanence, bring about a great increase in one's exertion of effort in practising the Dharma. Death awareness is the great motivator and intensifier and there can be no good practice without it. Having this awareness, one sees that there is no time to postpone one's practice. One great lama at the age of sixty, when asked to write his autobiography, replied "I passed twenty years of not appreciating the Dharma, then twenty years of procrastinating, and another twenty years of apologizing for not practising Dharma. This is the autobiography of an empty life."

We always feel there is plenty of time for the practice of the Dharma, but our time is running out. We need to recognize the importance of abandoning attachment to this life and practising the Dharma purely, without mixing it with the eight worldly Dharmas.

THE EIGHT WORLDLY DHARMAS
(*'JIG-RTEN CHOS-BRGYAD*)

It is these eight which are to be renounced in the practice of the Dharma:

1. Pleasure derived from gaining something (*rnyed*).
2. Displeasure at not gaining an object of desire (*mi-rnyed*).
3. Happiness caused by worldly pleasures (*bde*).
4. Sadness caused by displeasure (*mi-bde*).
5. Pleasure at being praised (*bstod*).
6. Displeasure at being abused or degraded (*smad*).

7. Pleasure from hearing pleasing words or informa-
    tion about relatives, friends, and so forth (*snyan*).
8. Displeasure from hearing unpleasant words (*mi-
    snyan*).

If we recognize the samsaric nature of the eight worldly
Dharmas and renounce them totally, we can attain a state
of peace and equanimity. As a means of attaining this
complete renunciation, we may well follow the practice of
the ten innermost jewels of the Kadam Tradition, which are
found in the *bka'-gdams gsungs-thor-bu*, which is a collection
of sayings of this tradition.

THE TEN INNER MOST JEWELS
OF THE KADAM TRADITION

These ten inner most jewels (*bka'-gdams gsungs-thor-bu*)
include four entrustments, three vajra-like convictions, and
three changes in one's living status.

A. The four entrustments.

1. Entrusting one's mind and thoughts to one's
    Dharma practice.

This comes as a result of contemplating that now one has
attained this fully endowed body, that this precious
opportunity for gaining a higher state of existence will
certainly end, and that its duration is utterly uncertain. One
then further reflects that at the time of death, no
possessions, affection of others, praise, reputation, or
pleasure will be of even the slightest benefit. With this
frame of mind one should practise the Dharma.

2.   Entrusting one's Dharma practice to life as a beggar.

After developing the above attitude, one might worry, "If I don't give effort towards gaining happiness in this life, I might have to live in poverty and not even have the bare essentials to continue my practice." To counteract this obstacle one must develop the attitude, "For the sake of the Dharma, if I must live as a beggar, so be it. I shall still be able to survive eating only poor food and wearing rags for clothes. By doing so I shall be able to attain the fruits of Dharma practice!"

3.   Entrusting one's life as a beggar to death.

At this point, one might fear, "If I follow such a life of poverty, devoting all my time and effort to practice and never storing any material goods, I won't be able to live out the full duration of a normal lifespan. I'll die of starvation!" If such thoughts arise, develop courage by thinking, "In any of my countless past lives, have I sacrificed my life for the sake of the Dharma? Now, if I must die for the sake of my Dharma practice, so be it. The causes of death of both the rich and the poor are basically the same. The rich die after spending their lives committing non-virtue for the sake of accumulating wealth. On the other hand, there is great meaning in dying after spending a life of bearing hardship in one's Dharma practice. This I can do."

4.   Entrusting one's death to a barren cave.

One still might have such qualms as, "If I have no belongings whatever, through periods of sickness and old age, right up to the moment of my death, I won't have anyone to take care of me, or even to carry away my corpse!" If this be the case, consider, "None of us can be certain that he will live long enough to reach old age. So, if by practising the Dharma, I die like a dog in a barren cave with no one to look after me, and even if insects eat away my corpse, so be it."

B. The three vajra-like convictions.

 1. The vajra-like conviction to be stalwart towards any hindrances caused by friends or relatives.

After coming to a firm decision to practise Dharma in the above described fashion, one must remain immutable like a vajra towards all weeping and pleas by one's parents, relatives or friends—and with a mind free of misery or attachment, devote oneself purely to Dharma practice.

 2. The Vajra-like conviction to disregard the opinion of worldly people.

Then, as one is going off to a cave or some other suitable place for Dharma practice, if others are filled with anger and derision, saying, "You're just a miserable beggar," and so forth, one should think, "If they call me a blessed saint—fine. If they call me a rotten scoundrel—fine. It makes no difference to me. So many problems arise from attaching a high value to the opinions of worldly people that it is an obstacle to Dharma practice."

 3. The vajra-like conviction to firmly guard one's practice.

Throughout one's practice, it is essential to utterly abandon all meaningless worldly activities and to stringently guard one's vows. With a mind firmly set on Dharma, one should unify one's life and Dharma practice.

C. The three changes in one's living status.

1. Expulsion from the ranks of humans.

The attitudes and way of life of one who indifferently turns away from the goals and pleasures of worldly life are incongruous with those of people who are still striving for them. One is thus considered by them to be crazy and is cast from their society.

2. Finding oneself among the ranks of dogs.

Thus by following the Dharma, one receives only poor food and clothes and is scorned by society, but for the sake of the Dharma, one courageously takes on all hardships.

3. Attaining the ranks of gods.

The ultimate fruits of abiding in seclusion and renouncing all meaningless activity is the attainment of the full enlightenment of Buddhahood in this life.

4
Death Awareness

For those who are beginners in the practice of the Dharma, the contemplation of death, following the ninefold outline previously stated, is of the greatest importance, being more effective than deity meditation. If it does not bring about a change, contemplate the aspects of the death process, keeping in mind that there is no doubt that you shall experience death. Imagine the atmosphere of sadness and desperation at the time of your death, as your body loses its warmth, you have difficulty in breathing, and your skin pales. Death comes as a reality on a specific day and then it is too late to alter your course or correct your actions. After death, this body is simply a corpse, which is feared and cast aside by those still living. The complementary method to contemplating your own death is to examine an actual corpse. This is not something to be afraid of, for your present body is a potential corpse. By simply not being able to breathe for a few minutes, the body becomes such a corpse. The Buddha himself used this contemplation.

The disadvantages or negative consequences of failing to remember death (*'chi-ba ma-dran-pa'i nyes-dmigs*) are:

A. Not remembering to practise the Dharma (*chos-ma-dran-pa'i nyes-dmigs*).
B. Although the Dharma is remembered, its practice is not intensive or fruitful (*dran-kyang ma-sgrub-pa'i nyes-dmigs*).
C. Although one achieves some attainment, it is not pure for it is mixed with the eight worldly Dharmas (*sgrub-kyang rnam-dag ma-sgrub-pa'i nyes-dmigs*).
D. Lack of intensity in one's practice (*sgrub-pa-la nan-tan-dang bral-ba'i nyes-dmigs*).
E. Making oneself unworthy of human existence (*rang-nyid ma-rung-ba byas-pa'i nyes-dmigs*).

F. The certainty of having regret at the time of death
   (*'chi-khar 'gyod-bzhin-du 'chi-dgos-pa'i nyes-dmigs*).

Death awareness leads at least to the level of practice of the person of small scope, and, acting like one's own teacher, it is important at all levels of attainment. As a remedy for the kleshas, death awareness is second in effectiveness only to insight into the nature of shunyata. With this constant awareness, pure renunciation lasts until the attainment of Buddhahood. If it is not accompanied by knowledge of the Dharma, this awareness leads to desperation; but if combined with knowing the Dharma, death awareness is a great friend.

The manner in which one who practises the Dharma meets death depends upon the intensity of and motivation for their own practice. The person of great scope takes death willingly; the person of medium scope does not fear it but does not accept it willingly; and the person of small scope fears death but dies without regret.

At death, the pleasures from clinging desire are cut, for there is nothing that belongs to the self. It is as if all, including one's own body, is on loan. The contemplation of this leads to the desire to escape from the wheel of birth, death, and rebirth. Death is not like the blowing out of a candle, for consciousness goes on and one must experience the karmic effects of former actions. People who have not been virtuous are naturally attracted to the view that all ends at death. The *bar-do* state, the state between death and rebirth, lasts up to forty-nine days, after which one is thrown helplessly into the next existence. The Buddha has said that virtuous actions lead to birth in the higher realms.

At death, the pleasures from clinging desires are cut, and non-virtue leads to birth in the lower realms. Whichever of the two kinds of karma dominates at the time of death determines one's next life.

Only if one's own practice helps to eliminate personal

defilements is it effective Dharma practice. Death awareness gives strength to go through the hardships involved
in one's practice. By forgetting or ignoring death, one is unworthy of human existence, thinking only of the pleasures
of this life. Lack of death awareness affects one's way of
life and leads to regret at the time of death. Thus, one
should remember death in the morning, at noon, and at
night. The religious person and the non-religious person
die in different ways: the former dies peacefully, while the
latter dies in desperation, grasping at what must be left
behind. One's refuge at death is the accumulation of one's
own merit.

At the beginning, this accumulation is like a beggar's
possessions, whereas the collection of non-virtuous acts is
like the wealth of a king. Unless one practises strong
remedies against non-virtuous action, the power of evil is
stronger than that of virtue. In one's efforts to accumulate
merit, the motivation (*kun-slong*) for each virtuous act is of
the greatest importance. It is this motivation that determines a person's mental scope. Although the action may be
the same, for example, making an offering, its meaning or
value will differ depending on one's motivation. Whenever
performing even the smallest virtuous action, one should
try to have a perfect motivation (*sbyor*), a proper performance of the action (*dngos*), and dedicate the merit to all
sentient beings (*bsngo*). This dedication is specifically for
the sake of one's own attainment of enlightenment for the
benefit of all living beings, for the flourishing of the
Dharma, and for the care and guidance of a guru until
one's full attainment. It is very seldom that all of these are
present, whereas in the performance of a non-virtuous
deed, such as abusing someone, it is easy to initially have
a strong motivation, then an effective choice of words, and
finally the feeling of satisfaction in hurting the other
person. On the other hand, when a person meditation
begins with the intention of liberating all sentient beings,

his mind may wander and the final dedication of merit may never take place.

Whenever a non-virtuous act, specifically any of the ten non-virtuous acts, is committed, it is essential to apply the four opponent powers (*gnyen-po stob-bzhi*), for it is only by this means that one can eliminate its karmic effects. These four powers entail:

A. Strong remorse for the act, generated by contemplating its effects (*rnam-pa sun-'byin-pa'i stobs*).
B. The firm intention not to commit such an act again (*nyes-pa-las slar-ldog-pa'i stobs*).
C. Taking refuge in the Triple Gem, if the non-virtuous act has been directed towards them; and contemplation of bodhichitta or of universal love toward all living beings (*rten-gyi stobs*), if the act has been against other sentient beings.
D. A persistent effort to carry out the high intention of abandoning non-virtue and following virtue (*gnyen-po kun-spyod-kyi stobs*).

One should think of non-virtuous acts as being similar to taking poison, and apply these remedies to even the smallest non-virtuous act—even a little poison is harmful. One should not deceive oneself, for it is almost certain that one will commit a particular non-virtuous act again; instead of determining to refrain from it forever, one should have the intention not to do so in the near future.

By applying these remedies, one is purified and need not experience the karmic effects of previously committed non-virtuous deeds. Without this application, rebirth in the lower realms is certain. It is important to meditate upon the three lower states of rebirth, both for the purpose of gaining a greater determination to follow virtue and abandon vice and to increase compassion for those who exist in these realms.

5

The Three Lower Realms of Existence

According to the Buddhist conceptions, there are six realms of existence, divided into three lower realms and three higher realms. The three lower realms of existence consist of the following:

    I. The hells (*dmyal-ba*).
   II. The preta realm (*yi-dvags*).
  III. The animal realm (*dud-'gro*).

I. THE HELLS (*DMYAL-BA*)

The following description of the eighteen states of hell is based on a work by Nagarjuna (*smon-lam them-skas-pa*), in which he condensed teachings on this subject from the sutras. The hells described are of three types:

    A. The hot hells (*tsha-dmyal*).
    B. The cold hells (*grang-dmyal*).
    C. The occasional hells (*nyer-'tshe-ba'i dmyal-ba*).

One may have one's own opinion about the existence of hells, but without any realization of this suffering there would be little growth of renunciation and one's practice would not be intensive.

A. THE HOT HELLS

They are located countless miles beneath the Stupa in Bodh Gaya and are the lowest state of existence in samsara. They include the following regions:

1. The first hot hell, called 'Revive' is the one closest to Bodh Gaya. Here beings have the clairvoyant ability to remember the non-virtuous deeds of previous lives. As soon as such an act is remembered, weapons appear and they fight with and kill one another. In one day these beings die three hundred times, each time to be reborn again in the same hell. There is no limit to the great suffering that they endure. Humans who spend much of their lives killing, like soldiers and butchers, are reborn in this realm.
2. Beings in the second hot hell, called 'Black Line', have large bodies and delicate skins. By means of the projection of their karma, lines are drawn on their skin with hot pokers, then their flesh is cut along these lines. Harming other living beings is the cause of rebirth here.
3. In the third hot hell, called 'Mass Destruction', all the guards of hell gather all the inhabitants and destroy them all at once. The sufferings that must be experienced here are beyond imagination. People that kill en masse take rebirth here.
4. In the fourth hot hell, called 'Crying Out For Help' beings enter a large metal house seeking refuge. The doors are then locked and the house turns red hot. Monks who break their vow of abstaining from drinking alcohol are reborn here.
5. The suffering in the fifth hot hell is similar to the fourth, but here the intensity is doubled.
6. In the depiction of the wheel of existence (*srid-pa'i 'khor-lo*) a large iron pot is shown, in which beings are boiled over a hot flame. This illustration refers to the sixth hell, in which one experiences all kinds of suffering due to heat—thus its name, 'Hot'. Causing dissension among others leads to rebirth here.

7.　The seventh hot hell has the same type of suffering as the previous one, but greater intensity.

8.　There is no greater suffering than in the eighth hot hell, 'Ceaseless', in which the inhabitants become indistinguishable from a raging fire. Committing one of the five heinous crimes is the cause for birth here.

Surrounding each of these eight regions are four circles of auxiliary hells (*nye-'khor-ba dmyal-ba*). As a being's karma which caused his rebirth in hell is used up, one moves progressively outward through these four circular regions, dying and taking rebirth each time one moves from one to the next. The innermost circle resembles hot ash; the second circle is like quicksand in which one is bitten by insects; the third appears beautiful at a distance, but as one moves closer, all things turn to weapons; and the fourth is an ocean of a burning liquid, like acid. One must remain in each of these circles for a long time before moving on to the next.

B.　THE COLD HELLS

To the north of Bodh Gaya are the cold hells, the same distance away as the hot hells below Bodh Gaya. In these regions, in Sanskrit called 'pleasureless', there is no source of light, and all is covered with ice. A freezing wind blows constantly, and the denizens of these hells, whose bodies are huge, have no protection from the cold and suffer great torment. The regions of the cold hells include the following:

1.　In the first cold hell the beings have huge goose-pimples.

2.　In the second cold hell the goose-pimples break out into sores.

3. The third cold hell is so cold that bodily movement is not possible and the beings can only shiver and sneeze, hence its name, 'A-choo'.
4. In the fourth cold hell even speech is not possible, so one can only groan.
5. In the fifth cold hell one's jaws are frozen shut.
6. Due to the intense cold in the sixth cold hell, one's body cracks like the petals of a blue lotus.
7. In the seventh cold hell cracks form in one's body like the lines of a lotus.
8. In the eighth cold hell, the most severe, the cracks grow larger and one's body falls apart. Blood and internal organs flow out and are eaten by insects, and even though this matter has left the body, one still experiences suffering from it. Holding wrong views, such as disbelief in the law of cause and effect, is a cause for rebirth here. Another cause is inflicting the pain of coldness on others.

C. THE OCCASIONAL HELLS

The location of the third type of hell region varies according to one's karma. The inhabitants may live in harmony during the day, but suffer through fighting with one another at night. Or a married couple might live happily during the day, but at night the wife turns into a serpent and bites her husband. The cause of taking birth here is observing morality during the day but not at night.

There is a two-fold purpose for contemplating the hell regions: to develop renunciation and to cause one to search within for the reason for taking birth there. This will lead to a desire to apply the four opponent powers. All that separates one from these hells is one's breath and one's accumulation of merit. Whether or not one believes that hells exist as such, it is essential to refrain from non-virtue.

The Buddha did not teach in order to convert people to his views; he simply made known that which already exists and showed the path away from suffering.

II. THE PRETA REALM (*YI-DVAGS*)

The general sufferings of the pretas include feeling hot, cold, tired, hungry, and thirsty, as well as the fear of being destroyed. Pretas exist both in the human realm and in a preta world, in which nothing grows and all is hot and dry. If at the moment of death there is attachment to food and drink, one is reborn as a preta. Pretas have a tall body, a large head and stomach, and a skinny neck and limbs. They become like a dry skeleton due to lack of water, and continually search for nourishment, without success. They have no chance to practise the Dharma.

Long ago a pandit, while on his way to Bodh Gaya, met a female preta with her five hundred children. She asked the pandit to search in Bodh Gaya for her husband, a man with no right eye, arm, or leg, who had gone there twelve years before in search of food for his starving family. The pandit found the preta husband and delivered a message that he was to return home with the food. The preta then told him that in twelve years all he had found was a wad of spit which, by the force of a man's prayer, could be taken by a preta.

Pretas also experience the following three kinds of individual suffering:

A. Seeing food at a distance which disappears upon drawing near, whereas they cannot even see a drop of water in the Ganges.

B. Finding food which, as soon as it touches the mouth, turns into acid or some else disagreeable.

C. Upon finding food, not being able to swallow it because of a preta's thin neck.

Avarice, discouraging others from being generous, stealing, and envy are all causes for birth in the preta realm.

III. THE ANIMAL REALM (*DUD-'GRO*)

The main suffering of animals is fear of being devoured by other animals. They also suffer from stupidity, heat, cold, hunger, being put to hard work by humans, and being fed upon by insects and worms.

Scorning the Dharma and calling others by animal's names, like 'pig', are causes for rebirth as an animal. We cannot directly perceive the suffering of the hells or the preta world, but our human karma is sufficiently related to that of animals for us to be able to see their suffering. Contemplating this suffering will lead to a great sense of renunciation and feeling of remorse.

By means of contemplating suffering, we may develop mercy or empathy with the suffering of others. Seeing that we can bring an end to our own suffering and help alleviate the suffering of others, we are motivated to develop renunciation.

6
Renunciation

Renunciation (*nges-'byung*) is not an outward but an inward action; it means primarily that one uses the objects of the five senses but does not depend on them or become attached to them. The opposite of this is what is called in Tibetan 'hairy renunciation', referring to the sudden outward abandoning of this life. Someone, owing to a sudden passion to renounce what he thinks to be samsara, might abandon all belongings and escape to a mountain retreat, only to return a week or two later feeling very discouraged and weak. Such 'renunciation' is generally insincere and rarely lasts for more than a short time.

Attachment is the inability to separate oneself from something or someone and is also giving all of one's energy to satisfying a desire, taking it as an ultimate goal. This is what is to be abandoned. In relations with other people, detachment means realizing the truth of impermanence and the non-ultimate character of human relationships. Having developed such detachment, one should be happy to be with others but at the same time be able to adapt to changing circumstances.

The delusion of attachment is like a drop of oil on paper, because it is very hard to remove from one's mind, whereas the other kleshas are like dust. It is a desire for permanence or non-change, making one's mind stiff and frozen.

Whenever a strong desire for an object of the senses arises, rather than simply trying to negate this desire, thereby causing more conflict within oneself, one should contemplate suffering and especially the impermanence of both one's own life and the satisfaction or pleasure that would be gained by fulfilling the desire. Attachment is much stronger than desire, for the former binds while the latter may be fleeting. With non-attachment one's outward actions are not harmful, and if one is practising tantra, it is possible to attain enlightenment even while living like a king, or living in one's home surrounded by children. Strong desire for food may be counteracted by eating it like medicine, keeping the body fit so that the practice of the Dharma may be continued. When doing even small labours, one must keep one's mind on their ultimate purpose—the liberation of all living beings—for all actions should be directed towards this ultimate goal.

7
Taking Refuge

By taking refuge (*skyabs-'gro*) in the Triple Gem—the Buddha, the Dharma, and the Sangha—and by acting in accordance with the law of cause and effect, one is able to attain a higher state of existence in one's next life. In order to seek this refuge, one needs to fear the suffering and rebirth in the lower realms and recognize that the Dharma is the only means of escape. Taking refuge is the same as looking to a higher authority, or doctor, for help. Without the experience of suffering one would never seek this help. In order to take true refuge, one must entrust oneself completely to the Triple Gem. The four qualifications of a true object of refuge are as follows:

A. Being free from all kinds of fear (for example, a person who saves another from drowning must be strong and unafraid of water).
B. Having skilful means to liberate others (if one cannot swim or know how to save another, one can be of little aid).
C. Having even-mindedness, or impartiality, towards all living beings.
D. Having the will to help others, regardless of what they may have done to oneself.

One should contemplate suffering and, when seeking a means of escape, look for a refuge having all these qualities. By doing so, one avoids blind faith and sows the seeds of pure faith to which one is able to give oneself completely.

There are three levels of taking refuge. A person of small or initial scope does so from fear of suffering in the three lower realms; in seeking freedom from suffering, one recognizes that the Triple Gem is the only means of escape.

One of medium scope fears the sufferings of all realms in samsara (including that of the deva realm) and seeks one's own liberation. A person of great scope, or a Mahayanist, takes refuge because one seeks freedom from all the sufferings of samsara, has strong faith in the Triple Gem as the guide, and feels strong compassion for all sentient beings.

It is important to contemplate these three sources of motivation each day before taking refuge. The Buddha is present in all three objects of refuge, as well as in one's guru; thus, by taking refuge in the Buddha, refuge is taken in the entire Triple Gem. There are many objects of refuge that people look to, such as money, a government, and earthly spirits, but these worldly refuges do not have the qualities of a true refuge. Earthly spirits, for example, being jealous and indifferent towards humans, are neither ultimate nor dependable and do more harm than good to those who take refuge in them. Only the Triple Gem is ultimate and possesses the means to end all suffering, and the Buddha has compassion for all living beings equally. There has never been a time when the Buddha neglected ripened beings, thus we must purify ourselves—or become ripe—in order that the way may be opened to us more fully.

The Buddha possesses the following eight rare and precious characteristics of a true refuge:

A. He has attained permanent cessation from all suffering (the third noble truth) and is thus free from birth and death.
B. All his actions come spontaneously and are free of effort.
C. This characteristic can neither be understood nor described in words, for it is the shunyata of the Buddha himself. In the same way, one cannot describe the difference in taste between brown and white sugar, yet a difference is experienced.

D. He has complete wisdom regarding both shunyata and the nature of all phenomena.
E. He has perfect compassion for all living beings.
F. He possesses unsurpassable power and thus is greatly effective in leading others to liberation. Some beings cannot be led by the teachings alone, but must be given physical evidence. In such cases, he makes use of miracles.
G. The Buddha has achieved his own ultimate aim, which consists of these first three qualities.
H. He has attained the perfect means of delivering others, or the latter three of these qualities.

Each of the three manifestations of Buddha, including Manjushri (the manifestation of his wisdom), Avalokiteshvara (the manifestation of his compassion), and Vajrapani (the manifestation of his power), is the embodiment of the entire Triple Gem. The form of each is the Buddha and Sangha, and their wisdom is the Dharma. Thus, if a person takes refuge in any of them, it is equivalent to taking refuge in the Triple Gem. The Buddha exercises his power when these manifestations embody themselves on earth as Bodhisattvas. The Tibetan word 'sang-gyae' (written *sangs-rgyas*), meaning 'Buddha', has the two-fold meaning of 'awakening from all obscurities' and 'the pervasion of all levels of knowledge'.

The refuge of the Dharma is equivalent to the last two noble truths, or the cessation of suffering and the path. Scriptures, statues, and other religious objects are simply superficial manifestations of the Dharma, or symbols of these truths. The Dharma has two aspects: it is both permanent, for the cessation of suffering is permanent, and impermanent, as is the path. The Dharma is known as the 'true refuge', for it is the wisdom by means of which one attains liberation. To illustrate this, the Buddha is often likened to a doctor, the Dharma to the medicine, and the

Sangha to nurses. One cannot fully take refuge until one becomes an Arya, but keeping pure moral discipline is the substitute until that attainment. The different forms of spiritual practice are the means by which one develops the true taking of refuge, and keeping the ten virtues (the abandonment of the ten non-virtuous acts) is the basis for attaining the cessation of suffering. Any form of wisdom that arises from the practice forms the basis for the impermanent aspect of this refuge—the path. The literal meaning of the Tibetan word 'chö' (written *chos*), meaning 'Dharma', is 'to hold' (one back from falling into low states of existence) and also 'to cut' (the bonds of samsara, or karma and klesha).

The refuge of the Sangha consists of the members of the Sangha who have become Aryas. They are the true refuge, although a group of four monks is held to be representative of the Sangha. The word 'Sangha' means 'inseparable' and the corresponding Tibetan word 'gedun' (written *dge-'dun*) means 'those who have the wish for liberation'.

There are two types of refuge: 'causal refuge', which is in someone else who has internalized the Triple Gem, and 'resultant refuge', which is in oneself after the Triple Gem has been realized within. When one first takes refuge in the three manifestations of the Buddha, they are an external refuge, but as one develops, this gradually approaches an internal refuge. The external refuge cannot help without the corresponding efforts of the disciple, but when both act together, they gradually merge into one.

8
The Qualities of the Buddha

The Buddha's body in its nirmanakaya, or physical incarnate form, has thirty-two major (*mtshan-bzang*) and eighty minor (*dpe-byas*) characteristics. The former are marks signifying the Buddha's supreme attainment as one who guides other living beings, and the latter are signs of his inner wisdom. When seeing figures of the Buddha, one tends to want to look closer and closer, yet although the form is pleasing, it is not one to which people become attached.

The Buddha's voice carries far and wide, and with one utterance he answers the questions of many. At one time, upon being questioned by a great number of disciples, he answered simply, "Humanity is impermanent," thus satisfying all the questions, stilling all doubts, his speech having different depths of meaning depending upon the individual disciple's level of attainment. His voice is soft, rhythmic, and pleasing, not fading as one moves further away, and again, it is not a voice to which one becomes attached. Once when Buddha was discoursing in Rajgir, Maudgalyayana, by means of his supernatural powers, he transported himself to the outer rim of the universe, and even at such a distance one could clearly hear the Buddha's teaching. Whenever one hears the Buddha's voice, the three poisons temporarily vanish. Depending on the needs of disciples, his voice is able to manifest itself in suitable forms.

The primary qualities of the Buddha's mind are wisdom, compassion, and the ability to experience both levels of truth simultaneously. His fully enlightened mind is the dharmakaya, which is both capable of manifesting itself in any form and has the quality of omniscience. His love is equal for all living beings and his mercy is constant. We, as samsaric beings, cherish ourselves first, and our mercy is like the ocean tides in that it is present when we perceive suffering but recedes when we see joy. His purpose is to lead those who are ripe, and his mercy is the hook that releases us from the fetters of karma and the kleshas. We all have the potential, or seed, to attain the complete qualities of the Buddha, but kleshas are the fetters which separate us from this, our true nature.

The Buddha's action ('*phrin-las*, meaning 'the act of delivering tidings') is his manifestation of himself in physical forms, radiating peace and virtue in order to encourage others on the path. When we see someone whom we admire, we naturally seek to emulate him. Therefore, the manifestation taken depends on the type of beings at a particular time and place.

The refuge of the Dharma is the cause for the attainment of these qualities. The elaborateness of the seat of a teaching lama betokens reverence for the Dharma, and any language which may be a receptacle of the Dharma should likewise be given respect. Of the actions of the Buddha's body, speech, and mind, those of his speech are considered to be supreme.

When actually taking refuge, visualize the Buddha Shakyamuni with his left hand holding an alms bowl filled with nectar and his right hand in the earth-touching gesture. The visualization may be either at eye-level or above the crown of the head. Then, while repeating "Namo Buddhaya" many times, visualize a vast abundance of radiant nectar emerging from his alms bowl, entering your body, filling and purifying you. Then, as a symbol for the Dharma, visualize a scripture at his side and, while repeating "Namo Dharmaya", visualize the nectar flowing from it and likewise filling your body. In taking refuge in the Sangha, you may either visualize the Buddha himself, or a host of Bodhisattvas, again seeing the flowing of nectar while repeating "Namo Sanghaya". The complete visualization, then, is the Buddha Shakyamuni as the central figure seated on a throne formed of a lotus, a crescent moon, and a sun, one on top of the other as is often symbolically depicted in thangkas. These three represent renunciation, bodhichitta, and the realization of shunyata respectively. At the Buddha's side is a stack of scripture and he is surrounded by an assembly of Bodhisattvas.

Then visualize to your right all male living beings as your own father and to your left all females as your mother. To the forefront, imagine friends, enemies, and those to whom you are indifferent, all of them taking refuge with you. Especially, vividly imagine your enemies, so that bodhichitta directed towards them may be developed. Recollect how helplessly immersed we are in samsara and that the Three Refuges are the only means of escape.

If you have developed some degree of understanding of shunyata, this should now be meditated upon, specifically the lack of self-existence of all beings, including your own self. The Triple Gem, likewise, does not exist as an independent entity, and is not without causes, but rather depends upon the mental labelling of disciples. While developing understanding of shunyata, you must also accept worldly phenomena on an operational level, being careful not to go to the extreme of simply negating everything. Understanding shunyata as simple negation is like holding a poisonous snake incorrectly. This is very dangerous, as it ignores the conventional truth of dynamic phenomena.

A Buddhist is one who takes refuge in the Triple Gem. Taking refuge is the foundation of all moral conduct and all growth of insight and wisdom, and is thus, essential for all spiritual practice and development. It further eliminates many of the kleshas of past lives. It is possible to eliminates all past non-virtuous karma, regardless of one's past, and become an Arhat in this life. Taking refuge not only speeds one who is accumulating in-sight and merit towards attaining liberation, but can also give temporary relief from harmful circumstances such as illness. Truly taking refuge with strong faith is neces-sary in order for the power of the Refuges to take effect. Like a cave, if one does not enter, it cannot give shelter. It is essential at least to take refuge in order to prevent oneself from falling back to the three lower realms. At the time of death, if refuge is taken purely, along with the contemplation of bodhichitta, one does not need another person to transfer one's consciousness. Therefore, it is important to acquaint oneself with this now, in order that it will be very familiar at the time of death.

In taking refuge, strong faith is essential, but, far from being an irrational leap based on belief, it must be founded on reason. Faith, the great opponent of dislike and scepticism, is in simple terms similar to 'liking' or 'attraction'. There are three progressive levels of faith: the first, clear faith (*dvangs-pa'i dad-pa*), is simple admiration but with no convincing reasons; the second is admiration combined with a desire to emulate the person in whom one has faith (*mngon-'dod-kyi dad-pa*); finally, there is faith with conviction (*yid-ches-kyi dad-pa*), when one is so convinced of the qualities of the other person as to trust oneself fully to their guidance.

Faith is known as the mother of insight and wisdom. One must be attracted to the path in order to be able to progress upon it, and without this faith, the teachings can be of no benefit. Faith does not depend on outward signs but is totally inward. Milarepa once said, "Oh you people, you have faith on your lips, but I have faith in my mind!"

Taking refuge aids one in attaining that for which one strives, acting both as a temporary aid and ultimately leading one to liberation. One Indian pandit advised: "Do not depend on others for guidance, but rather on the growth of the Three Refuges within yourself. Trust yourself wholly."

Although immeasurable merit is gained by taking refuge, this alone is not enough to attain liberation. One must further be committed to following the individual practices involved for each refuge.

Those who take refuge in the Buddha should not take ultimate refuge in ineffective worldly sources. However, temporary refuge may be taken in such things, meaning that one asks for assistance, as with a friend. Further, any image of the Buddha, whatever its quality, should be regarded with reverence as if it were the Buddha himself. This is because the truth body enters such figures. Upon attaining the highest level of the path of merit (*tshogs-lam*), one sees even a clay statue as the Buddha in his emanation body form, and on the path of insight (*mthong-lam*), one sees it as the complete enjoyment body.

Having taken refuge in the Dharma, one must avoid all harmful actions, including thoughts, which lead to suffering for others. If these corresponding obligations are not followed, one nullifies the act of taking refuge, and it will not be effective. The only true offering to the Triple Gem is one's own inner offering of following the path. One should also regard any syllable as the Dharma itself, for all languages are potential vessels of the Dharma.

When taking refuge in the Sangha, one forsakes the company of irreligious people and those with wrong views. Until one has full control of the mind, one should not frequently associate with such people, for the mind, like a piece of white paper, is too easily stained. Respect should always be offered to members of the Sangha, for lack of respect is a hindrance even to highly evolved people. One should treat all other beings with high regard and humility, a trait which leads to rebirth in a respected family. Just as avarice is the main obstacle to gaining greater material wealth, so pride is the main obstacle to obtaining wisdom.

The six general obligations in relation to taking refuge are as follows:

A. One should contemplate repeatedly the qualities of the Triple Gem.
B. While remembering the kindness of the Buddha, one should feel grateful, and whatever is eaten or drunk should first be offered to the Triple Gem.

C. One should help other living beings just as one has been helped, giving to them what was effective for oneself. It is important to try to correct the wrong views and practice of others.

D. Three times each day (morning, noon and night) one should take refuge, complete with visualization and contemplation on the Triple Gem's qualities.

E. Even at the cost of one's life, one should retain reverence for the Triple Gem. If one were to abandon the Triple Gem, the foundation of all one's spiritual practice and growth would be destroyed.

F. Whatever one does should be done with complete trust in the Triple Gem. It is wise to go for refuge in the Triple Gem, for example, whenever one embarks on a journey.

The Triple Gem is like a fertile field. If you fail to reap the fruit of spiritual growth from it, you waste a wonderful opportunity. Contemplation of the suffering of the lower realms should be done along with taking refuge. First contemplate hell, then contemplate renunciation and the Three Refuges; then meditate on the preta realm, followed by renunciation and the Three Refuges, and so forth, alternating from one to the other. Review your past actions, seeing the causes for low rebirth, and know that although you now have the means to attain liberation, you also have this non-virtuous karma working against you. No one else knows all your actions, so you must be your own judge. Be aware of the effects of non-virtuous actions and contemplate the advantages of virtue. Following this, contemplate the Triple Refuge, the only refuge that is with you always, even through the *bar-do* state.

The main teaching of the refuges is to live in accordance with the law of cause and effect, that is, following virtue and abandoning vice. When you practise this every day it will lead quickly to a change in your life.

9
The Law of Cause and Effect

Taking refuge protects one from falling into the lower states of rebirth for only a few lives, whereas following the teachings of the Triple Gem gives eternal protection from these realms. Buddha has given guidance and teachings to many beings. However, these teachings can only be of benefit if they are followed. The main teaching of the Buddha concerns the law of cause and effect (*las 'bras*) and, regardless of how much one may know about the Dharma, if one does not act in accordance with this, there can be no benefit. By means of this power of clairvoyance, Atisha's guru saw that a yogi had taken birth in a hell, whereupon he told Atisha, "Until you attain freedom from the delusion of self-grasping, follow the law of cause and effect." Until the path of preparation (*sbyor-lam*) has been attained, it is always possible to fall back into the lower realms.

Just as motivation is the start of meditation, practice in accordance with the law of cause and effect the start of religious training. For beginners, right understanding means being in accordance with the law of cause and effect; later it is the understanding of shunyata and the twelve links of interdependent origination. All joy and suffering depend upon cause and effect. Although all beings in samsara seek joy, it is difficult to find, because they do not create the causes which lead to joy. In order to understand both levels of truth, conventional and ultimate, one first needs to understand the law of cause and effect. Between shunyata and the law of cause and effect, the latter is more difficult to understand fully; for, although many Arhats have realized shunyata, only the Fully Enlightened Ones are able to determine or trace all the causes for a specific condition. Understanding of shunyata and the law of cause and effect support one another, and each is incomplete without the other.

There are three levels of contemplation on the law of cause and effect:

I.   Meditation on its general aspects.
II. Meditation on its specific aspects, that is, the ten non-virtuous acts.
III. Actually living in accordance with the law of cause and effect.

I. THE GENERAL ASPECTS OF THE LAW OF CAUSE AND EFFECT

There are four main characteristics of the law of cause and effect:

A. (*las-nges-pa*). Karmic seeds inevitably ripen in accordance with their cause, that is, virtue leads to joy, and non-virtue to sorrow.
B. (*las 'phel che-ba*). Because a karmic act has many effects, just as one grain of rice produces many grains, the store of karmic seeds is ever increasing.
C. (*las ma-byas-pa-dang mi-'phrad-pa*). If a certain cause is not produced, its result will not be experienced.
D. (*byas-pa chud mi-za-ba*). Karmic seeds never lose their potency.

A. Regarding the first characteristic, the Buddha once said, "Sentient beings do not understand the law of cause and effect, for while all seek joy and shun suffering, they do not exert themselves in following virtue and avoiding non-virtue." If one contemplates the certainty of the law of cause and effect, one will surely follow virtue. Realizing that the law of cause and effect holds true both within this life and from one's present life to the next, one should carefully guard one's acts. If an unvirtuous act is performed, one must apply the four opponent powers, for there is nothing that the Buddha can do when one's non-virtuous karma has ripened into suffering.

In Shakyamuni Buddha's time, there lived a monk who had a most beautiful voice, but an extremely ugly body. One day a king visited the Buddha and overheard the lovely voice of the monk while he was chanting his prayers. The king was so attracted by the voice that he asked if he might see the monk. The Buddha replied that the monk was better heard and not seen, but he gave the king permission. Upon seeing the monk's ugly countenance, the king asked Buddha the cause. The Buddha replied that, after the passing away of the third Buddha (Shakyamuni is the fourth), or Universal Teacher, this man had been one of the workers building a great stupa in reverence to the Buddha. During its construction he had continually complained that the stupa was too large, and this was the cause for his later ugly appearance. However, when the stupa had been completed he repented of his previous complaints and adorned the top of the Stupa with melodious bells, hence his later endowment of a beautiful voice.

On another occasion, near Rajgir, where the Buddha spent many rainy seasons, there lived a woman who laid thirty-two eggs, which grew into men. Her thirty-two sons all became ministers of the king, but there was a former minister who hated them and wished to see them killed. In order to have his wish fulfilled, he told the king that the walking-sticks of these thirty-two ministers were really weapons and that they were plotting to assassinate him. The king then ordered them all beheaded and their heads sent in a box to their mother. The box was delivered as the Buddha was teaching the mother about shunyata and he, knowing the contents of the box, told her to finish hearing this teaching before opening it. During this discourse she became an Arya (one who has fully realized shunyata). Afterwards, upon opening the box and seeing the heads of her sons, she was not greatly agitated, but calmly asked the Buddha the cause. He answered that in a past life her thirty-two sons had been thieves for whom she had acted as a housekeeper. They had all stolen a cow (which later took rebirth as the king) and slaughtered it in her house.

It is essential to understand the law of cause and effect, and study and contemplation are necessary for this understanding. The following three texts are the most important sutras on this subject; having read and understood them, one will no longer desire any form of existence in samsara.

1. *mdo-sde-las-brgya-pa*, a sutra containing many instances of the working of the law of cause and effect.
2. *mdo mdzangs-blun*, a sutra showing how to discriminate between virtuous and non-virtuous acts.
3. *mdo dran-pa nyer-gzhag*, the *Sutra on Mindfulness*.

B. The second characteristic of the law of cause and effect, the fact that one's store of karmic seeds is always increasing, can be illustrated by a peach seed which gives rise to a great tree, bearing much fruit. There are many such examples of the functioning of the law of cause and effect in nature, especially in humans' experience.

The Indian Pandit Atisha noticed that the Tibetans were careful to restrain themselves from major non-virtuous acts, but not from minor ones. He advised them to be heedful of these as well, for they also would have their effects. Whatever act one commits against another living being must later be experienced by oneself. One action, virtuous or non-virtuous, may have effects lasting for many years.

With any act of giving, one's motivation is of primary importance. When offering such a thing as a mandala (offering the whole universe, while holding only a handful of grain), full use of one's imagination is essential. Further, making offerings during a time when the Buddhadharma is not widely flourishing has greater value than doing so when it is widespread.

There was once a young bride who, with very pure motivation, gave alms to the Buddha. He then prophesied that in the future she would become a Solitary Realizer Buddha and foretold when this would happen. Her Brahmin was sceptical and asked the Buddha why he should thus lie and make such a great prophecy in return for such a minor act of giving. The Buddha then pointed to a tree and replied that, just as a great tree grows from a small seed, so it is with karma and its fruit.

Once a very poor couple wished to make offerings to Buddha, so they saved firewood, exchanged it for gold dust, and gave this as an offering. In their next lives, they were born into wealthy families, and from the well in the man's garden there flowed gold. Although they had such wealth, the man attained Arhatship in that life.

Illustrating the importance of imagination, there was once a young child who offered a handful of dust to the Buddha, wishing and imagining it were gold. Subsequently, he took birth as the great Indian King Ashoka.

Simply by living in accordance with the law of cause and effect, once can attain happiness and ultimately liberation. This teaching is very difficult to understand, for one has no concrete examples from one's own experience; therefore, one needs to develop faith in the Buddha and the Dharma. There are three general levels, or types, of understanding. The first is understanding of that which is obvious to the sense organs, that is, directly perceived. The second is understanding which relies on reasoning and logic, and to this category belong, for example, the subjects of impermanence, shunyata, and the twelve links of interdependent origination. The final type is the understanding which is attained only by those with perfect wisdom, that is, the Buddhas; full understanding of the law of cause and effect falls into this category. Having such understanding, one is able to determine the causes of any condition, no matter how many aeons ago they were produced.

There was once a monk living in a cave in front of which grew a tree. Whenever he left or re-entered his cave, the tree stood in his way. One day, out of anger, he cut it down, knowing that this act was against the Vinaya rules for monks (Buddha prohibited monks from killing plants, for while plants do not have a stream of consciousness as do all animals, this act would harm the animals that rely on plants for food and lodging). In his next life, the monk was born as a naga with a tree growing out of his head, and whenever the wind blew, he was tormented with pain. He is destined to remain in this state until the coming of Maitreya Buddha. The severity of the karmic result in this case was due to the fact that the monk deliberately broke one of his vows.

At this point we may wonder if all our actions are pre-determined by the law of cause and effect. The essential teaching here is that all joy and suffering, mental and physical, are the results of causes. By means of memory and alertness throughout the day, we may avoid non-virtuous acts which result in suffering. Just as in a country ruled by a powerful dictator there is still some degree of freedom, so we have an element of freedom from karma. Our human form is an effect of karma, but this form allows freedom to follow virtuous or non-virtuous conduct. Each individual is now creating his own karma.

The Buddha's compassion for all living beings is a special type of karma, which is effective owing to his great virtue. This compassion comes into action, for instance, when a lama prays for someone who is affected or in need. Such a prayer, however, can only be effective if there exists both a special karmic relation between the lama and the other person, and the latter has an adequate accumulation of virtue. When the sun rises over a mountain, the lotus opens but rocks do not. Likewise we may only receive the blessing of the Buddha if we have acquired enough past merit, that is, if we are ripe to receive the blessing. The Buddha cannot directly transfer his wisdom to us; he can only guide us to the way which will cause this wisdom to arise from within ourselves. And it is this—his taking birth as Gautama Buddha and turning the Wheel of Dharma for the benefit of all living beings—which is the primary act of his great compassion. Only by means of exerting ourselves to understand and follow the Dharma can we take advantage of this blessing.

There are two kinds of karma, samsaric and non-samsaric. Only those who have fully realized shunyata possess the latter type, thus having the ability to choose their next birth. We ordinary beings, on the other hand, have been thrown into this present form due to the karmic actions of our previous lives. Even beings with non-samsaric karma still have some degree of delusion, and this is the source of their karma. In carrying out a non-samsaric act, some small degree of effort is required due to jneyavarana (obscurations to knowledge), or instinctive kleshas. The Buddhas, who are free from all kinds of kleshas, produce only what is called simply 'action', and this requires no effort.

Many of our actions, such as sweeping a room or cooking food, produce neutral karma. Even such acts as giving food to a beggar without any motivation to do a virtuous action, or doing meditation without any good motivation, produce neither virtuous nor non-virtuous karma. After realizing the importance of collecting virtuous karma, we should perform all actions with the motivation of helping all living beings, thus changing neutral to virtuous karma. Further, when we are about to enter a situation in which we will probably be tempted to act non-virtuously, we should prepare ourselves beforehand for any such temptation or problem. When alone, we must be especially aware of our thoughts; when with people, we should watch our speech. The Buddha taught that when a monk enters a village to collect alms, he should keep his head bowed, not letting his gaze wander, and should involve himself only in contemplation. Doing so leads to an end of both non-virtuous and neutral karma.

C. The third characteristic of karma is that if we do not produce a certain kind of karma, we shall not experience its results. The contemplation of the law of cause and effect is subtle and not something that reason can entirely understand, so it is helpful to contemplate examples from the past. A sutra dealing specifically with this aspect of karma is the *dge-slong pha-yi rnam-byed*.

A king once commanded all his subjects to throw dust at monks whenever they came to beg alms and not to give them food. All his subjects, except two ministers who objected to his command and did not comply with it, did as they were told. Some time later a dust storm buried the king's city, killing all the inhabitants except for the two ministers, who were able to escape.

Even in extremely dangerous situations, such as a car accident, if we have not collected the appropriate karma, we will not be harmed. Examples of this are car accidents in which most of the passengers are killed, while others are, seemingly miraculously, left unscathed.

A final illustration of this third characteristic of law of cause and effect is the account of a burning palace, within which were one hundred women Aryas and a maid. By means of their miraculous powers, the Aryas all rose into the sky above the palace and sought the cause of this situation. They discovered that, in a previous life, all of them, together with the maid, had come upon a hut, which, unknown to them, contained an Arhat. All but the maid, who objected, had burned down the hut, killing the Arhat. Having learned this, the Aryas all descended to the palace and were killed. Only the maid escaped.

D. The final characteristic of the law of cause and effect is the inevitable ripening of stored karmic seeds. There are many examples in the sutras concerning events which were caused by a karmic seed planted aeons before. One of these is the account of Maudgalyayana, one of Shakyamuni's two main disciples, receiving a terrible beating because in a previous life, countless ages before, he had abused his mother.

Through contemplating especially these latter two aspects of karma, we should come to the firm decision to apply the four opponent powers whenever kleshas arise, and never to let anger overcome our virtue. Of all the kleshas, anger is the most harmful, for it overcomes all virtue and leads to other kleshas. Like a dire disease, it temporarily takes over the mind, and we lose all control. Thus, the practice of patience is especially important for beginners in following the Dharma. These four characteristics of karma should be made the suject of close contemplation, for without this, learning about them would be like quickly reading through piles of books: we would have little initiative to live in accordance with the law of cause and effect.

Whenever studying or contemplating any aspect of the Dharma, our motivation should be bodhichitta, or the determination to attain enlightenment in order to lead all living being from their sorrows. Such motivation aids the growth of understanding, love and compassion for all beings. It is essential that there be correct motivation on the part of both the teacher and the disciple, the former teaching with no expectation or hope of receiving anything in return, not even gratitude.

There are three interfering states of mind to be abandoned by the disciple: the first is having a mind like an upside-down pot, that is, not listening to the teacher's explanations of the Dharma; the second is listening to a discourse with a mind like a dirty pot, that is, defiled by preconceptions, prejudices, or wrong motivations (the nectar of the Dharma, though pure and nourishing, is poisoned by our own defilements); the third is listening to the teacher with a mind like a leaking pot, immediately forgetting all that is heard. These three states of mind must be abandoned when receiving any teaching.

When listening to a discourse specifically on the Dharma, it is important to cultivate the following six attitudes.

1. Thinking of ourselves as sick people in need of help. This should not be difficult, for we truly experience terrible pains, such as those of anger and unfulfilled desire, due to the 'sickness' of our kleshas.
2. Thinking of the Dharma as the medicine.
3. Thinking of our teacher as the doctor.
4. Regarding all Buddhas as Supreme Beings and thus as reliable sources of knowledge.
5. Wishing for the flourishing of the Dharma.
6. Having the intention to overcome our own personal delusions by means of applying the Dharma.

Further, before receiving any teaching on the Dharma, it is most important to feel humility towards our guru and the vast teaching of the Mahayana.

II. THE TEN NON-VIRTUOUS ACTS
(*MI-DGE-BA BCU*)

After one has become convinced of the validity of the four

aspects of karma and desires to act in accordance with that conviction, one is ready to receive teaching on the ten non-virtuous acts. These ten are the foundation of all spiritual development and insight and are essential at all stages on the path. Nagarjuna, in his *Friendly Letter*, likened these basic practices of morality to the earth, the foundation of all spiritual growth. Abiding by them is like cultivating and fertilizing the rough, barren field of the mind, making it fit to produce a rich harvest.

Understanding and acting in accordance with the law of cause and effect is the means of attaining inner peace and acceptance of those conditions in life which one cannot change. It enables one to relax and be calm in the face of suffering and takes one beyond such notions as "but I don't deserve this" or "why me?" For example, if two people went to prison, one understanding the law of cause and effect and the other not, the latter might feel sorrow, fear, and a sense of injustice, whereas the former would remain calm, realizing that this was a result of one of his own past actions. He might even feel glad that this karma had ripened and that he thus need not experience its effect in the future. Both pleasure and pain cause followers of the Dharma to increase their efforts to abide by the law of cause and effect.

When dealing with the specific aspects of karma, (as opposed to the four general aspects), there are three subjects for contemplation: non-virtuous or black karma, virtuous or white karma, and the weight of both types of karma. The ten non-virtuous or unhealthy acts (for such acts disturb one's peace of mind both in this life and the next) result in the strongest unvirtuous karma. They include three acts of the body, four of speech, and three of the mind. They are killing, stealing and sexual misconduct; lying, harshly abusive speech, slander, and idle gossip; greed, harmful thoughts, and holding wrong views. Only by refraining from these deeds may one take rebirth as a human. In his *Guide to the Bodhisattva's Way of Life* Shantideva wrote, "As a moth, while seeking happiness, flies into the flames of a candle, so do humans, while wishing for joy, ignore virtuous conduct and indulge in the ten non-virtuous acts."

In carrying out any one of these acts, there must be: the object (*gzhi*), the motivation (*bsam-pa*), the action (*sbyor-ba*), and the completion of the act (*mthar-thug*). For example, in killing an insect there would be the insect as the object, the motivation to kill it, the act of killing, and the death of the insect as the completion of the act. If any of these four is lacking, the act is not complete, and the karma is less heavy.

A. THE THREE NON-VIRTUOUS ACTS OF THE BODY

1. Killing (*srog-gcod*)

In the act of killing, the object must be external if the act is to be complete, and the motivation may be due to any of the three poisons. There are many ways to kill—using weapons, reciting mantras, or pushing buttons—but all result in the same karma. If the recognition of the object is incorrect, then the karma is altered accordingly.

In war, the general who gives the command to kill receives the heaviest karma, for he bears the karma for all the people that are killed. Further, if eight people were to kill one sheep, their karma would be the same as if they had each killed a sheep. It is the same if one hires another, such as a butcher, to kill. The person who hires the butcher and the butcher both receive the ensuing karma, so it is better to kill the animal oneself, rather than to cause two people to bear such karma.

The sages of Tibet taught the people to refrain from killing any living beings, and they were usually successful in their efforts. We also should encourage others not to take the life of any other being, for to do so results in the worst non-virtuous karma that can be produced. Since every living being, even an insect, cherishes its own life more than anything else, there is no excuse for taking the life of another, be it insect, fish or human being.

One naturally refrains from eating meat when one fully realizes that many living beings are needlessly killed for food. Buddha taught, however, that it is permissible to eat meat if one has neither seen nor heard that the animal was specifically killed for one's own consumption and if one has no doubt about this. However, for the Mahayanist, eating meat is undesirable, for this act is not conducive to the cultivation of bodhichitta, which leads one towards cherishing others more than oneself and treating all beings as one's own mother.

The final stage of the act of killing is the death of the other before oneself. If both the killer and the victim die simultaneously, the act is not complete.

2.   Stealing (*ma-byin-len*).

The object of stealing is any possession other than one's own. There is first the recognition of the object, then the intention to steal it, motivated by any of the three poisons, but especially by the poison of desire. The motivation may also be anger, as when one steals in order to make another poor, or it may be ignorance, as when one steals in order to make offerings to one's guru. In one of Buddha's former lives, he was one of five hundred disciples of a Brahmin teacher. The Brahmin once pretended to be sick and asked all his disciples to go out and steal food and necessities for him. All except the Buddha did as requested. When asked why he refused to steal, the Buddha replied, "Stealing is not an act taught in any religion." The other disciples had followed the theory that since all creatures are sons of

Brahma, to take any property is only taking what belongs to the Father, and therefore is not a sin.

Robbing by night, swindling with words or writing, and using false weights are all simply various methods of stealing. If someone has left money in another person's care and then forgotten about it, if the latter does not forget but keeps the money anyway, that also is stealing. The act of stealing is complete when one feels that the object is wholly in one's possession.

3. Sexual misconduct (*mi-tsangs spyod*)

The object of sexual misconduct is any woman or man other than one's own wife or husband. Sexual intercourse is improper in or around any temple, statue, religious relic, or one's guru. Improper times include religious holidays, nights of the full and new moon, and during the daytime, for this is shameless behaviour. This rule was prescribed by the Buddha in order to make clear what is and is not proper. The main reason that adultery is a non-virtuous act is that it causes disputes and violence. The Buddha said, "Because sexual desire is strong in all human beings, it is very important to make strong efforts to restrain oneself from adultery."

In the practice of tantra, a monk may have sexual intercourse with a woman, but only if he has attained the path of insight. Otherwise, this act would be a violation of his vows. If this path has been attained and the monk has a female consort, who must also be of the same spiritual level, he should be able to manifest his great psychic powers in order to convince his disciples of his attainment. Tantric practice is only for those willing to expend long sustained effort, not for those seeking an easy way.

One mahasiddha, who was a great master of the Heruka Tantra, had a king as one of his disciples. Moved by jealousy, the king wanted to put his guru to the test and humiliate him, so he asked him to prove his attainments. The guru, with his two children, came before the king who was surrounded by a large group of people, and transformed his children into a vajra and bell, the symbols of method and wisdom. He then came into union with his wife, and they both flew high into the sky. Marpa and Padmasambhava, for example, were both great enlightened beings before they took consorts. Milarepa compared his guru to a lion, whereas anyone trying to copy him, but lacking the spiritual attainment, he likened to a fox. Such mimicry would simply break the fox's back.

The act of physical union with one of the opposite sex has its climax and physical bliss in the completion of the act. Adultery is different from killing and stealing in that one can only do it oneself and even if there is a mistake in recognition, the weight of the karma is unaffected. All three poisons may be the cause of sexual misconduct: from anger, rape may ensue; from desire, the wish for very frequent intercourse; and due to ignorance, one may think that it is a path to enlightenment, which is fallacious, for sexual intercourse alone lacks the foundation which a path requires, whereas tantric practice has compassion and wisdom as its basis.

B. THE FOUR NON-VIRTUOUS ACTS OF SPEECH

1. Lying (*rdzun-du smra-ba*)

To speak falsely to others in orders to deceive them is lying. The motivation for lying may be desire, as when one claims to own something which in truth belongs to somebody else; or one might lie for a friend out of desire for his friendship. Due to anger, one might withhold important information or never speak the truth to an enemy. To state as fact something which one does not know, or to deny the law of cause and effect, is to lie due to ignorance. Lying may be by means of words, or by gestures such as a nod or a wink. The heaviest karma results from lying to one's parents, guru, or a Bodhisattva. The act is completed when the other person understands and seriously believes the lie.

2. Divisive Speech (*phra-ma*)

The object of divisive speech is to separate any two people or groups of people by means of speaking either truth or lies. It is a frequent cause of war. There are two kinds of divisive speech: open or direct speech, and indirect speech or speaking behind someone's back. Due to anger, one might speak in order to separate two friends; trying to separate one's friend from his other friends would be due to desire; and out of ignorance one might think that divisive speech is good. In order for speech to be divisive, there must be the intent to cause dissension—otherwise it is simply gossip. Speaking words which cause two enemies to fight is also divisive speech. The heaviest karma due to divisive speech arises when one causes a schism in the Sangha.

3. Abuse (*tshig-rtsub*)

The object of abuse may be either a living being, a physical object, or a condition, such as a thorn in one's foot, or the weather. The aim is usually to hurt another person's feelings, but there can be no false recognition, for abuse is solely dependent upon a frame of mind. Most abuse arises from anger, but it may be due to desire or jealousy, or to ignorance if one supposes that abuse is, in some cases, a virtue. Abusive speech may be direct or indirect, true or false. Sarcasm and telling a joke with the intention to hurt someone (like a rock wrapped in wool) are forms of abuse. Abusing one's guru results in the heaviest karma, and the act is complete when the other is hurt or their peace of mind disturbed.

4. Idle gossip (*ngag-'chal*)

The object of idle gossip may be two or more people or simply oneself. It includes any speech which is devoid of meaning or purpose; and is not beneficial to anyone. The motivation may be due to any of the three poisons, and there must be awareness of what is said. Out of anger one might abuse people or objects without intent; due to desire to earn money, one might tell stories or sing, and if a guru teaches for his own gain, this, too, is idle speech; out of ignorance one might talk to pass the time or tell stories over and over, thinking this is a worthwhile thing to do. This is the main hindrance to spiritual progress.

It is a source of demerit for a Bodhisattva to see bad qualities in another person. It is far better to contemplete the good qualities of others, which leads to rejoicing in their good deeds. To entertain anger against a person with any spiritual attainment is to despise the Dharma they practise. The Buddha often said, "One should never despise another, for we never know who might be a Bodhisattva."

The action is the expression of idle speech, and the completion occurs as soon as the words leave one's lips. The worst idle speech is speaking of worldly matters to a meditator, thus disturbing his meditation.

C. THE THREE NON-VIRTUOUS ACTS OF THE MIND

1. Craving (*brnab-sems*)

Craving is developing a wish to own an object which belongs to someone else. There must be the recognition of the desire, then the intention to obtain the object. The

motivation may be hate, as when one plunders the possessions of another, or ignorance in the thought that such
desire is not harmful. In all cases, greed is the primary
motivation. The action is the increasing of the desire until
there is the intention to fulfil it. All these stages occur in
the mind, and if the desire is blocked, frustration develops.

When one goes to the market, one must observe one's
mind, noticing what craving develops, as one views different objects. When a desire begins to develop, one must
contemplate the impermanence of the pleasure that would
be experienced if the desire were fulfilled. Then one must
contemplate shunyata, the lack of independent self-
existence of all things, recognizing that they are formed of
component parts and are devoid of a solid self-nature.

2. Ill-will (*gnod-sems*)

The object of ill-will, or harmful thoughts, may be any
living being or physical object. There must first be
recognition of the object, then the desire to inflict harm.
Anger is the predominant motivation for this action, but it
may also be due to desire, as when one sees one's friends
harmed and wishes to avenge them. It may also be due to
ignorance, for example, one might take the tantric teaching
to kill one's mother and father quite literally, when actually
it means that one should destroy delusion. Malice may also
arise from jealousy, as when one seeks to harm another,
thinking that the other's Dharma practice is superior.
Grudge-holding is another form of ill-will, but the worst
form of malice is harmful thoughts against one's father,
mother, an Arhat, Buddha, or the Sangha.

3. Wrong Views (*log-lta*)

The object of wrong views can be anything that truly exists,
such as karma, rebirth, the conventional and ultimate levels

of truth, the four noble truths, shunyata, nirvana, and the Three Refuges. The worst wrong view is disbelief in the law of cause and effect, as it is the basis of all spiritual practice and attainment. The proper recognition is that one clearly knows what one disbelieves. Holding a strong desire for an object, one may form beliefs in accordance with or in justification of this desire, thus creating a wrong view. One might also hold a wrong view simply in order to be hostile, but the primary motivation is ignorance, for as with karma, most unknowingly people continuously collect wrong views. The act and its completion are holding a wrong view and stubbornly refusing to abandon it. Lord Buddha said, "Don't be afraid of a wild elephant, for it can destroy only your body, but if you meet heretical friends and fall in with their view, this destroys the seeds of merit accumulated in the past and hinders further development."

III. LIVING IN ACCORDANCE WITH THE LAW OF CAUSE AND EFFECT

After recognizing these ten non-virtuous acts, one should develop the wish to abandon them, and to do so requires moral discipline. When rising in the morning, one should first correct one's motivation and renew the intention to avoid these actions. Throughout the day one must be mindful, and whenever one of these acts is committed, one must apply the four opponent powers. This protects one from falling into the three lower realms. Just before sleep one should review the day's actions and determine if they were virtuous or unvirtuous. It is important to look for one's own faults rather than those of others.

Once one of Atisha's disciples was reading a text on Vinaya (moral discipline) while seated on a leather cushion. He came across a rule stating that monks are not allowed to sit on leather and immediately threw his cushion away.

He read on further and found that this is permitted if the monk lives in a very cold climate; so he then retrieved his cushion. One should put one's learning into action immediately in this same way; Buddhahood is attained by removing one's delusions day by day. Buddha nature lies within everyone—one must realize this and live accordingly.

The six factors which determine the weight of karma are as follows:

1. The nature of the karma

The heaviest karma is due to killing, and the lightest is due to idle gossip. This is because among the unvirtuous actions of body and speech, killing causes the most suffering and idle gossip the least. The worst mental vice is holding wrong views, especially concerning the law of cause and effect, for this allows one to commit any act without the least feeling of remorse. Thus, it is also the worst of the ten non-virtuous acts.

2. The force of thought

The weight of karma varies according to the intensity of the mental force which guides the act. For instance, abuse which may result in light karma becomes a greater vice if it is accompanied by strong anger.

3. The action

Examples of this aspect are skinning an animal before it is dead or boiling animals alive, thus prolonging their death and inflicting much suffering.

4. The object

There is an especially heavy karmic effect due to harming

any of the objects of the five heinous crimes, that is, one's mother or father, an Arhat, a Buddha, or the Sangha. This is because our parents have shown us great kindness and the latter three have the ability to lead others from suffering.

5. Constant commitment

If one continually kills insects, gossips, or acts in other unvirtuous ways, leaving these acts unchecked, their karmic weight increases accordingly.

6. Opponent forces

When one is ill, the germs in the body will destroy life if there are no counter-agents. In the same way, the weight of karma increases continually in the absence of the opposing forces of virtuous action and application of the four opponent powers.

It is important to recognize and understand these six influences on the weight of karma and then apply this understanding to one's own actions. Having done so, if one were still to persist in committing grave unvirtuous acts, it would be like jumping off a cliff with full awareness.

For each of the ten non-virtuous acts there are three kinds of effect:

  (a) The immediate and main effect.
  (b) An effect which is consistent with its cause.
  (d) An environmental effect.

1. Killing

  (a) The main effect (also called the 'ripening effect') of killing is rebirth in one of the three lower states, depending on the karmic weight of the action.

(b) Then, after the person has returned from the low rebirth and again taken birth as a human being, he will have the tendency to kill and is likely to have only a short life or one with much illness. Such people often die in their childhood, or if they live to an old age they continually suffer due to illness. Further, some children delight in killing, whereas others do not, and this is due to the habits they have formed in previous lives.

(c) The third effect is that in the next human life, if the person falls ill, medicine is not effective and food gives little nourishment. In earlier times, food was much more nourishing, but now, due to mass unvirtuous karma, the level of nourishment is decreasing.

The higher teachings of the Dharma all rest on these basic principles concerning cause and effect, and the Tibetan word for 'to practise' is 'nyam-len' (written *nyams-len*), meaning 'to destroy vice and accept virtue'. Now since one has the ability to shape one's next rebirths, it should be done with care. Shantideva wrote, "Everyone is careful not to fall off cliffs only a few feet high, yet the abyss of the lower realms is vast in depth." So one should restrain oneself from following action that leads to these lower realms and also guide one's friends away from unvirtuous action.

2. Stealing

(a) The main effect of stealing, if committed to a great degree, is rebirth in hell; if to a medium degree, rebirth as a preta; and if to a small degree, rebirth as an animal.

(b) Moreover, when one is again reborn as a human, no matter what one does, there is no escape from poverty. Events like this are called 'bad luck', but this is a superficial way of thinking. Other people, while making very little effort, receive as much as they desire, and this, too, is a result of previous karma. The natural inclination to steal or not to steal is also a result of previous habits.

(c) If a person with such unvirtuous karma has crops or a home, they might be destroyed or lost. The difference in crops in adjacent fields, or in the same field at different times under different owners, may be due to the karma of the owners.

One should analyze these characteristics, co-ordinate them in one's mind, find examples from one's own experiences and then come to a firm decision to abandon vice. This will lead to rapid spiritual progress without interruptions.

3. Sexual misconduct

(a) The main effect of sexual misconduct is rebirth in one of the three lower realms, depending on the weight of the karma.

(b) After having taken human rebirth again, there may be unfaithfulness and disharmony between husband and wife.

(c) The third effect is that one will live in dirty, unendurable places, even though a pleasant environment may be available.

The Buddha did not say that celibacy is a necessity for the attainment of Buddhahood, but rather that there are different vows for different sorts of individuals.

4. Lying

(a) The main effect of lying is rebirth in one of the three lower states.

(b) Again as a human, regardless of what such a person says, no one belives one or takes one seriously. One also retains the tendency to lie.

(c) Further, one is continually deceived and cheated by others, and one's own endeavours are unsuccessful. The Buddha's words are powerful and respected by others because for aeons he lived as a Bodhisattva and spoke only the truth. A Kadampa lama wrote that one should grasp the potential lie by the neck before it leaves one's lips, for the fruits of lying are visible even in this life.

5. Slander

(a) The main effect of slander is the same as that of the previous vices, and the worst kind, separating a group of monks or a disciple and his guru, leads to rebirth in the lowest hell.

(b) In the subsequent human life, one will have a very bad reputation and be unable to get along with others. One will instinctively speak behind people's backs and slander them.

(c) One's environment will be dirty, unpleasant, and dangerous.

When contemplating the three lower states, one must actually put oneself into them, rather than detachedly pondering them or thinking of them as being simply a fabrication of the imagination.

6. Abuse

(a) The main effect of abuse is rebirth in one of the three lower realms.

(b) In the next human life, one will be abused and disliked by everyone, but for no apparent reason, and

one will instinctively try to hurt others.
(c) Such a person will find themselves in a poor environment and will encounter many difficulties.

7. Idle gossip

(a) The main effect of idle speech is rebirth in one of the three lower realms.
(b) In the next human life, one's words will not influence others, and one will have a tendency to talk whenever there is an opportunity.
(c) If one were to have a garden or field, one would not be able to reap a harvest from it.

Idle speech is the lightest vice, but it is the easiest way to waste one's life. As one purifies one's speech, it approaches the speech of the Buddha. Thus, in Tibet, devotees would sometimes maintain silence for periods of weeks or months.

8. Craving

(a) The main result of craving is rebirth in one of the three lower realms.
(b) The consistent result is that one continually longs for more than one has and never attains satisfaction.
(c) The environmental result is that one remains in poverty, bearing constant misfortune.

All desires are due to habit, and it requires teaching and much effort to become free from desire. No one needs to be taught non-virtue.

9. Ill-will

(a) Rebirth in the three lower realms is the primary result of holding ill-will.

(b) The consistent result is that one has perpetual fear, even though it is groundless, and uncontrollable anger and constant desire to harm and destroy for no reason.

(c) Such a person endures continual sickness and unhappiness and lives in places where there is war and violence.

Whenever we see a compassionate person, we feel glad and at ease; but meeting a person who is filled with anger and hate, it is like meeting a poisonous snake.

10. Wrong views

(a) Rebirth in the lowest realms is the main result of holding wrong views.

(b) On again taking human rebirth, understanding through contemplation is very difficult, and realization of shunyata requires a long time. Dullness and stupidity are also a result, and one naturally continues holding the wrong views held for so long.

(c) If one goes to a spring, the water stops flowing, or if to a mine, one finds no treasure.

Of the four main schools of thought in ancient India, three accepted the law of cause and effect, while the other believed only in events which can be directly experienced and rejected all abstract thought. For such subjects as rebirth, karma, and shunyata we need to use reason and abstract thought.

After contemplating these results, remorse should arise concerning one's past unvirtuous conduct, coupled with a strong determination, backed by sound reason, to abandon such action.

Formal meditation (*'jog-sgom*) must be preceded by examination meditation (*dpyad-sgom*). The former relies upon the latter, and the latter depends on knowledge gained through hearing and teaching. Without this, sure progress is impossible. Sakya Pandita wrote that one who meditates without first receiving teachings is like a man climbing a mountain with no hands. Formal meditation must be preceded by the use of the intellect—otherwise the vast teaching of the Buddha, the effort of those who wrote down his words and of others who wrote commentaries would all be in vain. The Buddha told Shariputra, "Those who like meditation but ignore the sutras were blessed by mara." Intellectual understanding increases the power of the rational mind and this increases the power of formal meditation.

The Mahayana attitude is to be willing to undergo any hardship in order to reach higher attainment. As for tantra, even studying it—not to speak of practising it—requires much effort.

Within Tibetan Buddhism, there are four traditions, but after gaining insight through following any one of them, one sees that they all rest on the same foundation—the teachings of Shakyamuni Buddha—and all strive after the same goal, enlightenment. They are different paths to suit different capacities and sorts of people. One should never slander the teachings of a path different from one's own, but should rather look for harmony. It is up to the individual to choose which religion or tradition one wants to follow, but not for one to impose that choice on others.

10
Virtuous Karma

Virtuous karma is not accumulated simply by refraining from the ten non-virtuous acts—one must develop the intention to totally abandon all unvirtuous action. In completely refraining from any of the ten non-virtues, there are again four aspects, listed as follows:

1. Recognition of an object.
2. Contemplating the result of an unvirtuous deed, leading to the intention to refrain from it.
3. The action of restraining.
4. A firm decision to refrain from the act in the future.

For example, in refraining from killing, there would first be an object other than oneself, then contemplation on the effects of killing it, followed by actual restraint, and finally the firm decision not to take life in the future. Again, in restraining oneself from stealing, there must first be an object that is not one's own, then contemplation on the negative results of stealing it, followed by the effort of restraining oneself from stealing, and ending in the firm decision not to steal in the future. For the other non-virtuous actions, the four aspects are similar.

The practice of restraining oneself from the ten non-virtues is the most practical of all the Buddha's teachings; and it is this practice which determines one's future, giving both temporary and ultimate joy.

The wisdom of hearing and contemplation is the only door to Dharma practice, and the measure of true practice is renunciation or non-attachment to samsara. The quintessence of the Dharma is the practice of method (*thabs*) and wisdom (*shes-rab*) and the practice of those two is essential for any undertaking. The Tibetan word 'chö' (written *chos*) or Dharma, means to cut the fetters of delusion, or karmic ties to samsara. Restraining oneself from the ten non-virtues is essential in developing means and wisdom. If one is able to refrain from the three mental vices, those of body and speech will be easily avoided. If one's mental activity is under control, it is good to live in a populated place, for this leads to love and compassion. Further, such an environment offers situations in which one's anger may be aroused, thus giving one the opportunity to apply the four opponent powers and to develop the virtue of patience. But without this mental control, it is better to live in seclusion. The beginner is like a rabbit, and his delusions like an elephant, so his remedies for delusion are very weak. If one lives as a town-dweller, it is important to check one's motivation before going out and to watch for the craving that arises as one walks through town.

There are three results of refraining from the ten non-virtues. The primary result of the most intense practice is rebirth in one of the form or formless realms; the result of mediocre practice is rebirth in the deva realm; and for a low degree of practice, rebirth as a human is the result. These three main results are graded in terms of happiness, not in terms of the opportunity to practise the Dharma. The wish or motivation behind virtuous actions and the dedication of merit determine whether one is born simply in a happy realm or in one with potential spiritual power. However, when practising, one must not expect to destroy all one's kleshas at once. The effective means is gradual, steady practice, like gathering drops of water in a bucket.

There are two types of karma, throwing karma (*'phen-byed-kyi-las*) and completing karma (*rdzogs-byed-kyi-las*). Good throwing karma leads to rebirth in one of the higher realms and good completing karma to a happy situation in that realm. For example, the condition of a human who continually suffers from illness is due to that person having good throwing karma and bad completing karma. If bad throwing and completing karma are combined, they lead to rebirth in the hell regions. The situation of a pet dog who is fed and treated well is the result of bad throwing karma and good completing karma. Throwing karma is the sole force which determines in which realm one takes rebirth.

The fruit of unvirtuous acts, in which there is both intention and fruition of the act, must be experienced unless the four opponent powers are applied. However, if there is an act without any intention, the person need not experience the karmic fruit of that act. For example, an executioner is ordered to carry out a death sentence; if he does so not by his own will and perhaps even while feeling compassion for the victim, he does not necessarily have to experience the complete fruit of the karma of killing.

There are three further kinds of karma:

1. Karma of which the fruit is experienced in this life (*mthong-chos-myong-'gyur-gyi-las*).
2. Karma of which the fruit is experienced in the next life (*skye-gnas-myong-'gyur-gyi-las*).
3. Karma of which the fruit is experienced in two or more lives (*lan-grang-gzhan-la-myong-'gyur-gyi-las*).

In order to attain higher states of existence and help others, the following eight qualities (*rnam-smin-yon-tan-brgyad*) are very beneficial:

1. Long life.

This enables one to attain one's own goals and help others. One needs a long life in order to take full advantage of the fully endowed human form, so it is important to take good care of one's body.

2. A pleasing physical appearance.

People are immediately attracted to one whose appearance

is pleasing, thus such a person is in a better position to offer help.

3. Birth in a race or caste which is highly regarded by society.

Others listen to such people, whereas they might ignore a low-caste person, even one who is very wise.

4. Wealth.

This can be used to help others, as people require food and clothing before they can learn and practise the Dharma.

5. Always being truthful.

This increases the effectiveness of one's speech in guiding others.

6. Power and fame.

A person with these attributes has a greater influence over others, and thus can effectively bring about changes for their benefit. For example, a king can cause monasteries or stupas to be built.

7. A healthy, able body and mind.

Such a person can follow the instructions of their guru and, by attempting and achieving goals which others would not strive for, attain enlightenment in one life.

8. Strong will power.

Having this, one will be content while following any practice and have the ability to live alone in a cave if necessary.

These eight are not necessary for the attainment of enlightenment, but they do make progress faster and one's acts more effective. Having them or not is like the difference between travelling in an automobile or a cart. If one lacks these qualities in this life, their causes should be recognized and one should practise accordingly.

The corresponding causes are as follows:

1. Restraint from killing and helping others out of their troubles, such as being a doctor or a nurse is a cause of long life.
2. Patience and such acts as repairing religious paintings, statues, temples and so forth.
3. Humility, overcoming one's pride and respecting one's elders.
4. The act of charity and making offerings.
5. Restraint from the four unvirtuous acts of speech.
6. Combining humility with the use of one's power to the fullest extent for the benefit of others. Prayers to the Triple Gem for obtaining a fully endowed body and these eight qualities in the next life are also a cause of power and fame.
7. Helping the poor and weak by doing for them what they are unable to do. Not hitting any living being, even one's pet animals, is a further cause of having a capable mind and body.
8. Rejoicing in the Triple Gem, having reverence for others, and reciting the Manjushri mantra.

In order to take full advantage of these eight qualities, one should pray that they will benefit all creatures.

This concludes the teaching on the law of cause and effect.

11
The Three Scopes

I. SMALL SCOPE

The essential practice for the person of small scope or for one who is starting out on the path includes the contemplation of the following.

A. The fully endowed body.
B. Death and general impermanence.
C. The suffering in the lower states of rebirth.
D. Taking refuge.
E. The law of cause and effect.

These contemplations complement formal meditation and form the basis for the practice of the person of medium scope. In his *Bodhicaryavatara*, Shantideva wrote that since all nonvirtuous actions result in misery, it is worthwhile to contemplate the law of cause and effect for a lifetime.

When attachment of this life has been renounced and one sets one's mind to working for future lives, the small scope has been attained. At this point one should not cease the former contemplations. Since one may regress, review is both necessary and valuable. One should, further, not be satisfied with one's present attainment, for it is still bound in samsara, and the higher states of rebirth for which one strives do not give permanent happiness. They may rather be likened to escaping from prison for a few weeks to be with a friend before returning to receive a death sentence.

II. THE MEDIUM SCOPE

The person of medium scope thus has a strong desire to escape from the wheel of suffering, that is, from all samsaric states. To do so, one must free oneself from the delusion of self-grasping. This freedom is attained by cutting the ties of karma and the kleshas, which results in Arhatship. The foundation of all attainments up to Buddhahood is the development of renunciation. This is one of the three principal paths which also include bodhichitta and an understanding of shunyata. All teachings on the Dharma are concerened with these paths, and at least a relative understanding of them is necessary before receiving any initiation. Of the three, renunciation must be developed first.

Whereas contemplation of the fully endowed body and impermanence leads to renunciation of attachment to this life, contemplation of the law of cause and effect results in the abandonment of desire for all samsaric states. When one is totally repulsed by worldly pleasures, full renunciation has been attained.

Contemplation of the four noble truths and the suffering of all samsaric states (including the eight, six, and three types of suffering) is essential for one of medium scope. Contemplating the four noble truths leads to a strong wish for liberation and to the attainment of bodhichitta, since only by knowing one's own suffering will one truly develop mercy and compassion for others. One must dwell more closely upon suffering, for this will result in deeper understanding of its cause. After doing so, one will be more personally interested in the cause of suffering and less inclined to simply accept the words of the Buddha, which although easy to do, is not fruitful. Without realizing the truth of the origin of suffering, there is no way to cut the ties of samsara. Through careful observation and contemplation, one arrives at the conclusion that one's mistaken belief in the reality of an independent self is the root of all suffering. Just as the sense of touch covers one's body, so is this delusion inseparable from all thoughts. While applying the four opponent powers deals with kleshas in their advanced stages, only the understanding of shunyata is able to cut them at the root.

Throwing karma, caused by kleshas with ignorance as their root, has cast one into this existence. On seeing that virtue alone leads to birth in higher states, one should ask; "What good is that by itself? It is still not freedom," and move on to this middle scope. This implies renunciation of the suffering of extensiveness. Even animals know the misery of suffering, and the suffering of change is easily perceived. But the human body itself is imbued with the suffering of extensiveness, and to realize this is a great insight. There is suffering in all states of samsaric existence (the implication of the Tibetan word: *ky'ab-pa*). The body acts like a magnet for suffering; it is like a toothache: if there is no tooth, there is no ache. Having a body, one collects ever more karma, yet one needs this body in order to attain liberation—like hot pepper which burns but which we need with some meals or the food is tasteless.

The person of medium scope should recognize the six root and twenty secondary kleshas and contemplate their karmic effects. One needs to contemplate how unvirtuous karma leads to the lower realms and virtuous to the higher, and how steady karma leads to the form and formless realms. Much time must be spent meditating on the four noble truths and sufferings as something experienced by oneself, not just by others. Then, after having determined the cause of suffering, one will have a pure wish to escape from it in all its forms.

The preceding is an outline of the middle scope contemplations for a person of lesser mental capacity. One of great capacity should contemplate how sentient beings come into existence, or the twelve links of interdependent origination, resulting in the realization that the wheel of samsara is like a bucket on a rope going up and down in a well.

THE TWELVE LINKS OF INTERDEPENDENT ORIGINATION

The twelve Links are divided into four categories, branches or causes (*yan-lag-bzhi*):

A. Propulsive causes (*'phen-byed-kyi yan-lag*).
B. The causes of existence (*'grub-byed-kyi yan-lag*). (*'grub* is the future tense of the verb 'to establish'.)
C. The result of the propulsive causes (*'phangs-bran*).
D. The result, existence (*grub-'bras*).

The three propulsive causes are ignorance (*ma-rig-pa*), throwing karma (*'du-byed*) and consciousness (*rnam-shes*), and the three causes of existence are craving (*sred-pa*), grasping (*len-pa*) and existence (*srid-pa*). Ignorance may be linked to a farmer, propulsive karma to the seed, and consciousness to both casting the seed to the ground and the ground itself. Craving and grasping, which are the immediate or direct causes of existence in samsara, are likened to heat, moisture and fertilization. 'Causes of existence' is a type of cause very close to the result, whereas a propulsive cause is more distant.

During the first instant there is propulsive karma, and in the second instant as the seed is being cast (thus requiring consciousness), it changes to potential power (*bagchags* or *nus-pa*, also translated as 'instinct'). This may be likened to wood in the first case and to its catching fire in the second. While existing in the formless realm, only the potential power of the five senses remains, but upon returning to the realm of form, the senses also return.

The instinct resulting from both virtuous and nonvirtuous acts has the power to manifest itself. For instance, if one studies something thoroughly in childhood, leaves it and returns to it many years later, one has the power to regain the former knowledge quickly. It is the same for spiritual power, or attainment, which passes from one lifetime to another. The instinct is placed in the stream of consciousness, its result manifesting in another rebirth, and it is due to this that some children have more learning potential than others.

Existence immediately follows these six causes. To elucidate the latter three more clearly: '*sred-pa*' is the strong attachment to one's present body, especially when death is near; '*len-pa*' is attachment to form for the future life; and '*srid-pa*' (the equivalent of samsara) is the increased power of the karmic seed—here at its strongest. This result in conception in the mother's womb.

The five results of the propulsive causes ('*phangs-'bras*: (*phangs* is the perfect tense of 'to throw') are as follows:

1. The dependent origination of birth (*skye-ba'i rten-'brel*).
2. Name and form (*ming-gzugs*).
3. Growth and development of the six entrances (*skye-mched drug*).
4. Contact (*reg-pa*).
5. Feeling (*tshor-ba*).

The result of existence (*grub-'bras*) is the dependent origination of old age and death (*rga-shi'i rten-'brel*).

Between the time of waking up this morning and now, one has collected propulsive karma of all types (leading to all types of birth), and each karma has its own cycle of twelve links. Contemplating the twelve links leads to insight into the nature of the self and strengthens one's wish to be free. It is impossible to experience all twelve links of one karma within one lifetime—two or at most three lives are required. Normally one experiences the first six links in one life and the next six in the next life (the Detailed Exposition School states, however, that only one life is needed for all twelve). Just before death, the strongest collection of karma, or that with which one is most familiar, takes effect and propels one into the next rebirth. However, if a person's karma is that which would result in human rebirth (thereby determining the nature of the first three links), but then near the time of death he collects karma which results in deva rebirth (the second three links having this characteristic), the latter karma will determine his next rebirth. If the karma of the first three links is different from that of the second three, the latter takes immediate effect, and the karma of the first three is stored and takes effect in another lifetime. Thus, in such a case three lives sre needed for the complete effect of the karma to appear. But for any birth all six causal links are needed.

Contemplating the twelve links of interdependent origination is extremely difficult, but understanding how one wanders into samsara is essential in order to escape. The Buddha said that if the twelve links are understood, one understands shunyata and that this leads to Buddhahood. In order to understand this doctrine, one needs to practise morality and cut off personal delusions. Although contemplating this doctrine requires much time and effort, one must not shrink from its difficulty, but rather use one's pride and let this be a source of energy.

After realizing that ignorance is at the root of our wanderings, one must find the path leading from it. In all six realms there is no better form than the fully endowed human body with the eight fully-ripening aspects. The human body is the most suitable for tantra, because it is born from a womb and has the six elements, including the four elements of earth, water, fire and air, channels (*rtsa*) and drops (*thig-le*).

Living in accordance with the law of cause and effect is the first door to general practice: the perfect path is the teaching on moral discipline, shamatha (calm abiding or single-pointed concentration) and prajna (wisdom). Our ignorance concerning the self is like a tree; clear, sharp wisdom (*Ihag-mthong*) is like the axe used to cut down the tree; shamatha is like the ability to strike the tree in the same place each time; and moral discipline is like a strong body which wields the axe. Combining these three, the tree of illusion is easily felled. There are many synonyms for shunyata (like the many names in different languages for 'water'), but all mean the voidness of the mind. Among them are the following:

1. *de-kho-na-nyid*, this very thing.
2. *chos-nyid*, the nature of things.
3. *chos-dbyings*, the sphere of things.
4. *phyag-rgya chen-po*, inseparable from enlightenment.
5. *rdzogs-pa chen-po*, great completion, freedom from samsara.
6. *stong-pa-nyid*, voidness of an independent self-existence.
7. *don-dam bden-pa*, ultimate truth, the way it exists and the way we understand it being the same.
8. *dbu-ma chen-no*, the great middle path, neither accepting nor rejecting.

It is impossible to imagine how much Buddha Shakyamuni taught, for all his teachings are not included in the Tibetan canon. His teachings lead to both higher birth (*mngon-mtho*) and to nirvana and enlightenment (*nges-legs*). Taking refuge and following the law of cause and effect give only temporary relief from the three lower realms, so that one advances to the medium scope; but then, seeing that this does fully benefit others, one progresses to the great scope, realizing that all sentient beings are one's mothers.

III. GREAT SCOPE

The main practice of the person of great scope is the

development of bodhichitta. In this development, one needs first to attain equanimity (*btang-snyoms*) towards all sentient beings, and for this there are two methods. One may visualize in succession a person hated, another loved, and one to whom one feels indifferent, or visualize all three at the same time, the hated one visualized on the right, the loved one on the left, and the one to whom one feels indifferent in the centre. The latter method has been found more effective by meditators in Tibet. When you turn your attention to the one you hate, let your aversion arise. Then ask yourself, "Why should there be this feeling?" The person may have treated you poorly in this life but has been very kind to you in a former one. There are no grounds for such a partial reaction towards him or her. Now recall the one whom you love and let all your attachment for him or her become manifest. Likewise, contemplate that in a former life, this person may have inflicted unbearable suffering on you, but because this is lost from memory, you only know how he or she has treated you in this life. By such contemplation, equalize your feelings towards these two people. View your reactions towards them with detachment, realizing how absurd they are. And finally, meditate on one towards whom you are indifferent and recall that in your countless previous lives, he or she has been both your friend and enemy. Thus, there is no reason to feel differently towards him or her than you do towards your enemies or friends of this life. This quality of change in relationships with others from one life to another is also very evident during one lifetime.

Equanimity towards all creatures is the basis of bodhichitta, and it is impossible for bodhichitta to be generated without it. As you practise these contemplations, apply them to your daily life, first towards your neighbours, then towards your community, and keep expanding it as you become more and more skilled. Recognize that your immediate reactions towards others are due to karmic forces from recent lives. It is a mistake to let your feeling toward others depend upon what they have done to you, for you thereby blindly react to their more recent actions, utterly ignoring the fact that both you and they are in a constant state of change.

Atisha had one hundred and fifty-seven gurus, but only one of them taught him bodhichitta. To receive this teaching, he spent thirteen months at sea sailing to the Golden Island in Indonesia. Whenever he heard the name of this guru, he felt deeply moved and filled with gratitude.

Shantideva wrote, "Even if all Bodhisattvas assembled to determine the best means to guide sentient beings, every one of them would say that bodhichitta is most important." Bodhichitta is essential for the attainment of all Bodhisattva levels and enlightenment, and there is no Bodhisattva or Buddha who has lacked it.

Equanimity must be developed first, then develop the attitude of thinking of all sentient beings as your own mother (*mar-shes*). You must not simply let your mind remain indifferent towards others, but rather develop love, then greater love, towards all living beings. Tracing your stream of consciousness back in time, you see that since there was no beginning to your previous lives, you have had countless mothers. Understanding the nature of past lives is necessary in order to see this and having done so, you also realize that all sentient beings have at one time or another been your own mother. To think of yourself as having only one mother is to be of very limited mental scope. Nagarjuna wrote, "If you were to take all the evergreen seeds in the world and then remove one representing your present mother, the number of the remaining seeds would not equal the number of mothers you have had." When thinking in this way, "I am only one, and there are countless other beings in the universe. How could they all possibly have been my mother?", imagine how many times during beginningless time you have been born as an insect, bird, human and so on, and it will more easily be seen how all living beings really have been your mother.

The mind is at first inflexible and tough, and it is hard to realize this. If this is the case, go to a lonely, secluded place and call out, "My mother! My mother!" Another method is to imagine that you have no mother—then it will be especially clear that you do have a mother. Following this, try to realize that your father has been your mother in a past life, then further broaden the scope to include all living beings. Atisha once told a disciple to hurry to a certain place, as his mother was in great trouble. The disciple went and found a pony strangling on a cord. Such an attitude towards other beings is what you wish to strive for.

Although you may think that this present body is your own, in actuality the blood came from your mother and the bones from your father. This feeling about the body is natural, and the feeling that all beings are your mothers should be equally so.

Meditate next on the kindness of mothers (*drin-dran*), remembering first your own mother, then the kindness of all mothers. Worldly love is mixed with attachment and passion, but the love that arises through remembering this kindness is free of these kleshas. If you think your mother has not been kind to you, it is because now you are an adult, but you should always remember that she carried you in her womb for nine months and cared for you as an infant. All mothers treat their infant children with tenderness and compassion.

All the teachings you have received should be used for the development of bodhichitta. A most important scripture is *rgyu-'bras man-ngag bdun*, the oral tradition of Maitreyabuddha to Asanga, which deals with the six causes and the fruit of bodhichitta.

If you have not developed the attitude of holding all beings as your mothers, remembering the kindness of mothers is not effective in developing bodhichitta. The kindness of mothers can be seen even among animals; for example, a mother bird stays with her young even if danger approaches, and she is willing to give her life for their protection.

Your mother carried you and bore you, raised you and made your present existence possible, so never hold a grudge for the few unkind things she may have done to you. Doing something fine, you may think, "I have done this", feeling very independent, but whatever has been accomplished has resulted from your mother's kindness.

As an infant you were like an earthworm, but your mother had great joy in you and lovingly cared for you. You could not speak, but your mother talked and laughed with you continually, never leaving you alone, unprotected. Your mother slept irregularly and lightly when you were young, always thinking of your welfare. When you were older, she taught you to walk, speak, eat, and so forth, and later on she was concerned with your education, growth, occupation and marriage. Nearly all mothers are like this.

A mother dog vomits up food for her pups, a mother bird constantly fetches worms for her chicks; but when the young are grown, they forget their mother. If you do likewise, you will be no different from animals. A mother's love and care arise naturally, effortlessly.

Realizing your mother's love, turn to your father and see that his love is the same, the only difference being that he is not your mother in this life.

The attainment of enlightenment is due to the kindness of others and is impossible without it. Following the Paramitayana, or path of the Bodhisattvas, requires one's own effort, but also the help of other beings. Without others, one could not practise the ten virtuous acts, attain a fully endowed body, or meditate on love and mercy.

Not only is there motherly kindness, but also the kindness of living beings towards each other. All superficial pleasures, such as the happiness of receiving praise, are due to the kindness of others. When eating just a handful of rice, consider the difficulties undergone by others to make this possible—sowing the seed, watering, fertilizing, harvesting, packing and sending the rice, and finally selling it. All the people involved thus worked for the benefit of others.

Shantideva wrote that spiritual attainment is half due to the kindness of all sentient beings and half due to the gurus and Buddhas.

In Tibet there was a famous bandit who made a practice of raiding caravans. Once while so engaged, he accidentally struck a mare with his sword, and her foal emerged from her womb. Even as she was dying, she tried to get up and lick her foal dry. Seeing this, the bandit quit robbing and followed the Dharma. One should strive to realize such love.

The next point of contemplation towards the development of bodhichitta is called 'repaying kindness' (*drin-gzo*). After realizing that all sentient beings are suffering due to the three poisons, it is shameful if one then does nothing to help them. The present situation is like seeing one's blind mother about to walk off a cliff and doing nothing to save her. Living beings do not know which actions are virtuous and which are non-virtuous, and are ignorant of the results. Every moment they walk closer to death and rebirth in the lower realms. It is our duty to help them, guiding them on the path to liberation from suffering.

To the charge that his wearing such scanty clothes was crazy, Milarepa replied that those who are wandering endlessly in samsara are the truly deluded ones. Although even his enemies pitied his extreme poverty, the Buddhas rejoiced in his wonderful attainments. Milarepa attained bodhichitta within eleven months, and when he told Marpa of his experiences, his guru was delighted and said, "You have lived up to my great expectations of you."

There are many ways of repaying kindness. Giving material assistance such as food to beggars and help to those in need is beneficial, but this is not the best means. To guide and liberate all beings from suffering is the true repayment of kindness, for although beings have experienced all types of birth and living situations, they still wander in samsara.

Thus it is necessary to first attain enlightenment ourselves and then lead others to it.

The next stage of this meditation is immaculate love for all living beings (*yid-'ong byams-pa*). If one has meditated extensively on the three preceding points, further meditation here is not necessary, for this love arises naturally. Having realized this great love, all beings (even worms and insects) are pleasing, for one knows that all have been of aid in attaining that state.

Relate the contemplations of the person of small scope to this meditation. If, having met with the opportunity of developing bodhichitta, you were to die before taking advantage of it, it would be a great misfortune. All beings, including animals, appreciate love and mercy.

One night when Nagarjuna was reciting a text, a pigeon listened to him all night long. In its next life it was born as his chief disciple and was able to recite the entire text. There are many such examples. When a person turns his mind to Dharma, it is the start of his happiness.

Love (*byams-pa*) arises through wishing that others may always have happiness, and mercy (*snying-rje*) arises from the wish to raise others from their present state of suffering. Develop love first and mercy will naturally follow, for the more one likes someone, the less one can endure their suffering. For beginners, just a moment of meditation on love is worth vastly more than hours spent on other practices. If one is filled with love, one will be loved by others. This is an example of the working of the law of cause and effect. Meditation on mercy for just a few hours lays a great foundation for further understanding and spiritual attainment.

All the Buddhas and Bodhisattvas are products of mercy. In a treatise, one sage paid homage to mercy, saying that in doing so, he was paying homage to all the Buddhas, for it is the cause of their attainment. He drew the analogy of a farmer who first needs seed, then heat and moisture to reap a bountiful harvest. Likewise mercy, first as a motivator, then as a source of perseverance, inspiration and encouragement, is needed in order to attain the full fruit of Buddhahood. It is also due to their mercy that the Buddhas go on teaching until all beings are enlightened.

The strength of one's bodhichitta corresponds to the power of one's mercy. There is a *Jataka* (previous lives of the Buddha) account of three brothers who, while walking in a forest, came upon a starving tigress about to devour her cubs. The youngest brother felt such great mercy that he lay down in front of her and offered his own flesh. He was later to become Shakyamuni Buddha, and his two brothers were incarnations of Maitreya and Manjushri.

The only suitable motivation for practising tantra is mercy for all sentient beings and the corresponding wish to attain enlightenment as soon as possible in order to guide them from their suffering. If a child were to fall into a fire, it would take a very strong person to jump into the fire herself to save him.

Rechung, the disciple of Milarepa, was for a time lax in his spiritual practice, so Milarepa took him many times to a place where animals were butchered. After that his practice was intense. This is an effective method which may be used today.

If a country has skilled and efficient representation in the United Nations, its inhabitants may be at ease and without worry. One is likewise a representative as one approaches enlightenment. Other beings depend upon such a one, for we have more karmic ties with those now living than with the Buddhas of the past. It often happens that a disciple of a guru can establish greater communication with a fellow disciple than can the guru himself. Only by finding the guru with whom one has close karmic ties can one achieve rapid progress.

Seek any circumstance which helps to develop mercy. While observing animals being butchered, reflect that goats and sheep are surviving simply to be killed later. Then expand your awareness and clearly realize that there are many people now who are not using the great opportunity of human existence. This is the one path leading to enlightenment—there is no way except with mercy. Exert all efforts towards the attainment of the person of great scope and let mercy grow until it becomes great mercy (*snying-rje chen-po*).

In order to develop bodhichitta, one needs first to develop equanimity towards all beings, otherwise the further stages of this meditation are like sowing seed in uneven ground. When meditating, concentrate primarily on one point, then at the end of the meditation, review briefly the rest of the points.

The sixth stage of this meditation is the pure wish (*lhag-bsam rnam-dag*). Whereas during the foregoing stages, concentration was placed on love and mercy along with the wish for the happiness of others, now one comes to the intention to act for their welfare. The previous stages were like bargaining for something and here is the actual buying. The meditator realizes that he must attain enlightenment and that this can only come through his own efforts. He thus takes the responsibility of the liberation of all sentient beings onto his own shoulders.

At this stage, one reviews what powers or qualifications one now has to lead others from their suffering and, recognizing that oneself is not capable, searches through all beings for another who does have that ability. Finding that no one in samsara is able to know the needs of each type of person or each individual, that only the Buddhas have this power, one realizes the necessity of attaining this state. When one has a natural, spontaneous longing to attain enlightenment for the benefit of all sentient beings, bodhichitta (*byang-chub-kyi sems rin-po-che*) has been attained, and one has become a Mahayanist. The Bhodisattva Maitreya has cultivated the wish to become a Universal Teacher, destined to enter the world during an era when the life-span is long and people are happy and most Bodhisattvas think there will be little chance for propagating the Dharma.

The most important scriptures on bodhichitta are:

1. *mdo phal-cher,;* a collection of six sutras.
2. *rin-chen phreng-ba;* one of the six main works of Nagarjuna.
3. *spyod-'jug,* the *Bodhisattvacharyavatara* by Shantideva.
4. *bslab-btus,* a supplement to the *Bodhisattva-charyavatara,* which should be studied with it.

One must have at least some development of bodhichitta before practising tantra, for without this, even the highest tantric practice is a waste of time. Tsong Khapa likened bodhichitta to the threshold of a house—if one stands on the threshold of bodhichitta, it is the same as entering the Mahayana way of life; but if bodhichitta is lacking, one stands on the outside. Far more than reading Mahayana scriptures, it is important for one to be a Mahayanist oneself. When Atisha first came to Tibet, many people requested initiations, but he replied, "Without bodhichitta, what good are they?" There are beings in the three lower realms who have practised high tantra, but without bodhichitta. No matter how profound one's meditation may be, without bodhichitta, full enlightenment remains beyond one's reach. But if the disciple has developed bodhichitta, initiations become very effective.

One should tame the mind and develop bodhichitta, a practice which can be done even during sleep. One famous guru proclaimed, "If one professes how high his practice is but lacks bodhichitta, plaster his mouth with human excrement." One who has attained bodhichitta—even though they may be an animal, which is possible under certain circumstances—is called a 'Prince of the Buddha'. This development is the highest Dharma practice, and is sometimes known as 'the diamond', for even a slight amount is precious. Developing spontaneous love and mercy is a prime means of eliminating one's kleshas and an important preliminary practice for tantra.

Asanga meditated upon Maitreya for twelve years, seeking a vision of him, but without success. He then left his cave and while walking along a road, saw a wounded dog covered with worms. Great compassion arose in him and while seeking to relieve the dog of its misery without harming the worms, he bent down to remove them with his tongue. At that moment Maitreya appeared before him.

Recognizing that the small and middle scope contemplations are mere branches, and the understanding of bodhichitta the main trunk of Dharma practice, use all contemplations to aid this understanding. Even if one has no other positive qualities, after developing only a little bodhichitta, one becomes an object of refuge and reverence. It does not come in a short time, but requires much effort, and one must be willing to undergo any hardship in order to attain it. If even a layperson has developed bodhichitta, he is worthy of the reverence of Bodhisattvas. After its attainment, all other goals are achieved naturally without great effort. Just as meat lying in the sun naturally attracts flies, so bodhichitta is naturally sensed by others. Thinking ahead about the advantages of having attained bodhichitta leads to the motivation to develop it.

The Buddha said that just as bowing to the new moon is automatically bowing to the full moon, so respecting one who has attained bodhichitta is honouring the Buddha. This is because bodhichitta is the immediate cause of full enlightenment. One must take very good care of one's cultivation of bodhichitta, which is like a young fruit tree.

In order to attain Boddhahood, one needs a full collection of physical and mental merit, and bodhichitta is a prime means for collecting these two. Merit must be increased until its fulfilment and perfection.

Bodhicitta eliminates mental and physical obstacles, and its cultivation is thus the best initial practice. Like a chemical that transforms all metal into gold, it turns the impurities of the human body into the three bodies of the Buddha. It is because people have not developed bodhichitta that they still have an impure human form. The rate of this development depends upon one's own effort.

With bodhichitta, one's collection of merit is always increasing, but without it such increase is uncertain. There are three stages of collecting merit, the first beginning during the path of collection (*tshogs-lam*), the second during the path of insight (*mthong-lam*), and the third at the eighth Bodhisattva level. Giving a handful of rice with the motivation of bodhichitta to one person has more merit than feeding millions without it. Any virtuous action done with bodhichitta motivation has the degree of merit corresponding to the number of beings one seeks to benefit. There is great merit in wishing to relieve one person from suffering; so much more for *all* beings.

When in pain, consider the suffering of all sentient beings and develop the wish to carry this burden in order to deliver them from misery. This will lead to the end of your own sufferings.

Whatever meritorious action one performs, such as meditation, bodhichitta should be the motivation. It should be cultivated with sincerity, not merely as a ceremony, for it is an important stage of the practice. Before stealing, one has a motivation to steal. Likewise one should make one's

motivation or reason, for doing any virtuous act bodhichitta. When beginning meditation, it is a mistake to think,
"I wish I could attain freedom, enlightenment, and so
forth." Guard the mind. All humans make a great mistake
in that they are very concerned about external enemies,
which can only harm them in this life, yet they cherish
their internal enemies—primarily self-grasping and self-
cherishing—which harm them for countless lives. One
should be less concerned with one's environment and more
concerned with the motivation to deliver all beings from
suffering. To attempt to develop bodhichitta for the sake of
one's own progress is still very selfish.

Shantideva wrote that the development of bodhichitta
destroys mental and physical obstacles like the world-
destroying fire at the end of the world. People are eager to
achieve great attainments with the least effort, and the best
means for this are bodhichitta and understanding shunyata.
One must not even entertain the idea that Buddhahood
may be attained without bodhichitta. Bodhichitta should
always accompany one like one's own shadow.

After developing bodhichitta, one experiences no fear
during the *bar-do* or even in the lower realms. One goes
with confidence. Performing the tantric preliminary practices with bodhichitta motivation for just one day is worth
far more than doing them for one hundred years without
bodhichitta. While working for the benefit of others, one
need devote no effort to the fulfilment of one's own wishes,
for this comes naturally. Developing bodhichitta is a prime
means for bringing others to enlightenment.

Some people recite mantras for sixty years in order to
attain powers for selfish reasons, but with no success. On
the other hand, there is no level of attainment that cannot
be reached if one's practice is joined with bodhichitta. With
it one is able to attain tantric powers with no external
physical aids.

In the last chapter of the *Perfection of Wisdom Sutra in Eight Thousand Verses*, there is the account of the Bodhisattva Sadaprarudita and his great bôdhichitta, his self-sacrificing devotions to his guru, Dharmodgata, and the powers he attained. One needs constantly to receive fresh inspiration for one's spiritual practice and this sutra may be of great help.

For six years, Milarepa stayed with Marpa, and instead of receiving teachings, endured many hardships. He later said, "To think that I was a Buddha in my past life is a great insult to tantra. Buddhahood is not something of the past but rather is always with you like your shadow—you simply do not realize it." With great effort and skilful guidance, enlightenment may be attained in this lifetime.

The attainment of bodhichitta itself may confer great powers. One of the Ganden Tripas (a succession of lamas who act as representatives for Je Tsong Khapa) turned back a flood outside Lhasa wholly by the power of his bodhichitta. With bodhichitta one is protected and able to achieve any goal with no obstacles.

There were once three meditators in Tibet, all of them seeking Buddhahood in this life. One had developed bodhichitta, and the earth spirits could give him nothing. To the second they gave a pen, and he became a great poet; and to the third they gave a bag of medicine, and he became a skilled doctor. Only the one with bodhichitta was left with an unobstructed path to enlightenment. Let all your efforts be directed here, for bodhichitta must be attained while still on the first of the five paths (*tshogs-lam*) towards enlightenment.

Only mental merit is gained through contemplation on shunyata, but bodhichitta balances this with physical merit. The possibility of attaining Buddhahood in this life depends on one's development of bodhichitta, and that is why Buddhist tantra is unique. Simply hearing about bodhichitta leaves a great impression on one's stream of conciousness, much more so if one actually develops it. Make bodhichitta the framework of your practice. Shantideva wrote, "If you stir milk, its essence, butter, appears. Likewise, if you stir all the teachings, the development of bodhichitta appears."

The source of happiness on all levels from Arhatship down is the direct and indirect teaching of the Buddhas, and this source is compassion. All the Buddhas have first been Bodhisattvas, and this will be the way of all future Buddhas.

Just before his death, Atisha said, "Those people in the future should not regret not meeting me. My essence is the practice of bodhichitta, and when one is developing this, it is the same as meeting me." Begin every morning with contemplation on equanimity and follow this with the other steps towards bodhichitta. Become well acquainted with them. These steps are the practice found to be most effective by Atisha.

Another method of attaining bodhichitta is given by Manjushri in the words of Shantideva. Its essence is the cherishing of others before oneself. At first, very few people received this oral tradition and they were required to meditate on it three times each day. One reason this teaching was kept relatively secret was that it should be taught only to those of high intelligence and broad mental scope. It is very difficult and is thus only given to those with a great desire to receive such a special teaching. There are different methods of developing bodhichitta. The previously explained six steps (*rgyu-'bras man-ngag bdun*) form the common path, and this latter method of Manjushri (*bdag-gzhan mnyam-brje*), meaning 'to treat with equanimity oneself and others', is the more exclusive and effective.

Though one's motivation may actually be selfish, one derives enjoyment from saying. "I shall do this for the benefit of all living beings." Examine what good this self-centredness has done for you and recognize the truly bad side of this trait. Because of the inborn defilement of self-cherishing all strife is born. Tension and conflict arise as soon as our self-desires are crossed, and all suffering is due to this self-cherishing. We only need to examine our own life for examples—they need not be listed here.

Shantideva wrote, "Look to the Buddhas and others who have reached high attainments, and look at self-cherishing and see where it has brought you." This self-cherishing attitude eats up one's potential powers for spiritual attainment like a worm in your intestines. Change the object of cherishing: let yourself become less important and make others more so.

Always be the loser, never the winner. The Kadampa Geshe Lang-ri t'ang-pa, who composed the *Eight Verses of Training the Mind*, once saw a line in a small book: "Whenever in an argument, lose. Whenever there is profit to be gained, let others have it." After reading this, he sought further teaching on the subject, and subsequently studied for nine years with the lama who had written the line. This lama told him, "You need this mental attitude whether it pleases you or not."

After fully realizing the negative aspects of self-cherishing and the advantages of cherishing others, practise 'tong-len' (written *gtong-len*), giving all your merit to others and taking all the sufferings of others upon yourself. First visualize a black spot in the centre of your body, representing selfishness, and when inhaling, imagine taking in all the sufferings of the world—all of them converging upon and destroying this black spot. When exhaling, send out your virtue and merit to all sentient beings for the sake of their happiness. This is a great method for increasing your own merit. When one is very competent in this practice, it is possible to transfer another's suffering to oneself, providing there is a close karmic relationship between the two beings (both the meditator and the other being must have committed a virtuous act together in some lifetime, both of them having the desire to take on the sufferings of others). Once while the yogi known as 'The Compassionate One' (*Byams-pa'i rnal 'byor*) was giving a discourse, someone nearby hit a dog with a stone. The yogi cried out in pain, and a bruise appeared on his body. The dog had been relieved of its suffering. The main object of 'tong-len' however is not to relieve another individual of his suffering immediately, but rather to attain bodhichitta. Likewise, the greatest blessing of the Buddhas is not their power to relieve individual suffering, but the giving of the Dharma.

This practice is the greatest means for collecting merit. During each meditation one comes closer to Buddhahood without even realizing it. If at first it is difficult to imagine taking all the suffering of the world upon yourself, imagine taking on just your own suffering which you will experience tomorrow. As you progress, imagine in one meditation period taking on all the sufferings of your whole life, then the suffering of a small group of people and further expand your scope. At first this seems very difficult, but after one becomes acquainted with the practice, it is easy. You can be sure that this will be a direct cause of attaining Buddhahood, and that there is no other way.

When beginning the practice of 'tong-len,' do not do it with your breathing, but rather use only your imagination. First imagine taking on all the sufferings of others, then send away your virtues and happiness. Likewise, for a person whose body is on fire you would not first offer them a piece of candy, but would put out the fire and then give them something pleasing. In the full meditation, take on the sufferings of all beings from the lowest hell to the tenth Bodhisattva level, but exclude the Buddhas and your own guru. The tenth level Bodhisattvas have no suffering, but as they still have instinctive kleshas, relieve them of those. When accepting suffering, visualize a sharp black line piercing your black spot of selfishness and utterly destroying it.

The main enemy of Bodhisattvas is self-cherishing, and it is at this that the anger of the wrathful deities is directed. When practised, this visualization will decrease self-cherishing. One Bodhisattva said, "I show my side (in attack and defence) to all kleshas, and my front (in compassion) to all sentient beings." If you perform this meditation thinking that it will not work, it will not be effective, but if you have trust in it, it will be very beneficial. Signs of success are a feeling of heaviness in the area of your heart and a feeling of fear during the meditation.

When accepting suffering, imagine the misery of the six realms coming to you and destroying your selfishness. However, this may be difficult at first, since you have no experience of the other realms. In this case, it may be more effective to sit by a sick person and imagine taking on his suffering.

When practising the second part of this meditation, imagine sending your body, wealth and virtuous actions to others. Transform your body into rain or cool air for those in the hot hells, and into a warm breeze for those in the cold hells. Imagine giving your body so that others may attain a human body, giving it as food to the pretas, and giving it to animals in the form of wisdom. Because humans are greedy, transform your body into all things that fulfil people's desires. For the anti-gods (who are always at war) transform your body into armour, and for the devas into objects of the five sense desires. And finally to the Buddhas and your gurus, you may transform your body into offerings. For all of these, imagine giving your body and wealth of the present and future but not of the past, and give your virtue of all the three times.

Important scriptures on this 'tong-len' practice are *spyod-'jug* by Shantideva: and the two sutras, *sdong-po bkod-pa'i mdo*, and *rdo-rje rgyal mtsan-gyi-mdo*.

After attaining confidence in the 'tong-len' practice using just your imagination, do it with your breathing as well. You then will not waste your breathing throughout the day. Tsong Khapa's disciple, Khaydrub, commented that if even your breathing is used to develop bodhichitta, all your actions will naturally follow suit. This is the theory—now it needs to be put into practice in your daily life. You cannot expect to attain the goal in a few weeks or a month. Shakyamuni attained enlightenment through perseverance—he did not start out perfect.

It will be helpful to read verses on bodhichitta, either your own or those of others, before meditating. The following lines were widely used by meditators in Tibet:

"Therefore (having recognized the fruitlessness of self cherishing and the great benefits of cherishing others) I request the adhisthana (the blessing and power) of my compassionate guru, enabling me to bring all living beings to permanent joy by means of my practice of sending all my virtues and happiness to others. May all sufferings, obstacles and defilements of all the motherly beings fall upon me this very moment."

Most verses in Tibetan have only four lines, but this has five, giving added emphasis to the importance of 'tong-len'. Reciting this verse is like a preliminary practice to developing bodhichitta, and some meditators have recited it one hundred thousand times.

The practice which follows 'tong-len' is the changing of all unfavourable circumstances to favourable ones and using them to develop bodhichitta. Understanding and spiritual growth are like precious jewels, and we follow the practice in order to protect them from obstacles and hindrances. This training of the mind is called 'the accomplishment of happiness'. Through meditation, even physical suffering ceases to be a hindrance.

There are many obstacles to the development of bodhichitta, including having a high, profitable position or wealth, as well as sickness or physical handicaps. Especially during this degenerate age, or 'Age of the Five Dregs', these must be carefully guarded against. The 'five dregs', (*snyigs-ma lnga*, or that which remains after all the good has been taken out) refer to: the characteristics of humans, kleshas, ideas, lifespan, and time. The body, speech and mind of humans are very resistant and not easily subdued. Ordinary peoples' kleshas are in their roughest form and are very difficult to abandon. The prevailing, or generally accepted, ideas and philosophies are full of delusions and because people's minds are set on them, they are difficult to correct. The average lifespan is decreasing, and the time is now one of war and new kinds of disease.

This kalpa, or world age, began with the Age of Completion, a time when everyone practised the ten virtuous acts. There was little sickness or war, and people did not need the light of the sun or the moon, for they radiated their own light. At that time, the earth's surface was smooth, but as virtue decreased, it became rough.

Now the practice of the Dharma is vanishing, and at such a time, the merit of practising just one of the ten virtuous acts is almost equal to that of practising all ten during a more favourable era. The maximum lifespan will continue to decrease until it reaches the limit of ten years. At that time, people will have large heads and small bodies like children and will be filled with much anger. Maitreya will then appear, having a very small, pleasing body, and people will admire him and seek to know how he became that way. He will then teach them virtue. He will be one of the manifestations of Maitreya, but not the final one, in which he will take on the nirmanakaya form and become a Universal Teacher.

Because of the five degenerated conditions, many distractions and obstacles to spiritual practice arise. This makes it all the more important to make use of all circumstances, making them causes for one's further growth. Whenever any misfortune such as sickness or harm from enemies arises, one always tends to blame it on others, but one should rather blame it one one's own self-cherishing. One must train oneself to blame all misfortune on self-cherishing, for misfortune would not arise without it. If one is travelling and someone steals all one's wealth, one blames it on the thief, but one's sorrow is actually due to self-cherishing.

Whenever any misfortune arises, try not to let it affect your practice, but rather be glad that this evil karma has ripened. Atisha once said that sickness and misfortune are brooms that sweep away kleshas and obstacles. Bodhisattvas prefer being sick to being well, for even a slight headache may be an effective means for removing obstacles. When they experience suffering, they wish for yet more in order to relieve others of their misery. Such people never have mental suffering, and they use their physical sufferings to remove their kleshas. They are grateful to experience such suffering, but otherwise they remain unaffected by it.

One follower of the Dharma had leprosy and was therefore cast out from human society. He used this rejection and by intensive practice gained high spiritual attainment. In ancient India there was a bhikshuni who had leprosy, but instead of succumbing to depression, she intensively followed the Dharma. By doing so, she became able to converse directly with Manjushri and Avalokiteshvara, developed bodhichitta and regained her health.

Misfortunes are actually teachings that remind us to collect merit in order to avoid suffering. They are also of great benefit because without them we would not seek a way out of delusion. There are many examples of this. When people are poor and helpless, they seek the Dharma, but as they grow wealthy and self-assured, they easily abandon it.

With inner peace, one can be happy anywhere, but, as Milarepa said, without it all is misery even in the best of external circumstances. There are many ways of changing all circumstances to favourable ones, and the possibility of this depends solely on one's own attitude. Whenever harm is experienced, let this be an opportunity to practise the Dharma, and remember that one's true enemy is self-cherishing. One who is accustomed to exchanging one's self for others holds the key to all spiritual practice and attainment.

This concludes the discussion on changing one's mental attitude, and now we turn to ways of action conducive to the growth of bodhichitta. Once again it should be stressed that there is no higher practice than developing bodhichitta, which is the main structure of the Mahayana.

There are four types of action which should be followed in order to cultivate the growth of bodhichitta:

1. Collecting all different kinds of merit. Before doing any virtuous actions, one should correct one's motivation, that is, one should always work towards enlightenment for the benefit of all sentient beings.
2. Applying the four opponent powers. One should eliminate all obstacles and apply these powers to even the smallest unvirtuous deed.
3. Seeking the assistance of the dharmapalas (*chos-skyong*). Some people seek their aid for worldly gain, but the true function of the dharmapalas, or protectors of the Dharma, is to help people attain spirituality, and towards this end they use their abilities to remove obstacles. One may offer food to them, perhaps one's own meals.
4. Offering food to the pretas. One does this by setting aside food with the strong intention of giving it to them. When going through a hazardous area, one is very careful where one steps, and one should be all the more careful to protect one's growth of bodhichitta from obstacles. While developing bodhichitta, be neither very rich nor very poor, but be strong

enough to face either of those extremes if they arise, using them to intensify your practice.

Know that whatever occurs is a result of one's own black and white karma. While seeking happiness, one uses up one's past collection of good karma. There are only two kinds of merit that cannot be used up: that which is dedicated to attaining enlightenment and bodhichitta.

A Bodhisattva welcomes abuse and dislikes praise, for the latter increases pride and self-esteem. Abuse may help one discover one's kleshas and eliminate them. There was once a very virtuous man living near Lhasa. Everyone praised him highly, and he never had arguments or conflicts with anyone. The result was that although he did not become proud, he failed to do anything with his life. When he recognized this as an old man, he bemoaned the praise that had been heaped upon him.

Bodhisattvas always think of themselves as the lowest among living beings. Holding high position satisfies one's pride, but it confines one and takes away one's freedom. If one instead takes the lowest position, one lives in harmony with all beings.

Through understanding shunyata one comes to realize the non-self-existence of others whom one thinks of as being harmful, and one gains insight into one's own void nature. Again, make every effort to change all circumstances to favourable ones. If during this era of degeneration, one does not develop strong will-power and strength over depression, there is no way to attain higher states. Shantideva wrote: "Even suffering has its good qualities. Experiencing one's own suffering increases one's longing for freedom, and seeing the suffering of others aids the growth of mercy."

Teaching others about bodhichitta will lead to the source of the world's problems, such as pollution and war. There is little that can be done if one deals only with the outward manifestations of suffering. The best thing to do is first to tame our own minds, then guide others.

Je Tsong Khapa devised a method to aid the growth of bodhichitta which combines the two previous meth-ods, called the eleven-round contemplation (*dmigs-skor bcu-gcig*). The steps of this meditation are as follows:

1. Equanimity (*btang-snyoms*).
2. Holding all beings as one's mother (*mar-shes*).
3. Remembering the kindness of one's mothers, both one's present mother and all living beings (*drin-dran* and *drin-dran khyad-par-pa*).
4. Repaying the kindness of one's mother (*drin-gzo*).
5. Cherishing others above self by remembering that all beings, like oneself, seek happiness (*bdag-gzhan mnyam-pa*).
6. Contemplating the many disadvantages of cherish-ing oneself more than others (*bdag-gces 'dzin-gyi skyon-sgo du-ma-nas bsam-pa*).
7. Contemplating the advantages of cherishing others (*gzhan-gces 'dzin-gyi yon-tan sgo du-ma-nas bsam-pa*).
8. With forceful contemplation on mercy, accepting the suffering of others (*snying-rje'i dmigs-pa rtsal-du bton-te de-dang sbrags-nas len-pa*).
9. While meditating on love, sending forth one's virtue and joy (*byams-pa'i dmigs-pa rtsal-du bton-te de-dang sbrags-nas gtong-ba*).
10. Generating the pure wish to take on the burdens of others (*gzhan-don khur-du 'khyer-ba'i lhag-bsam*).
11. Developing bodhichitta, seeking enlightenment for the benefit of all sentient beings (*gzhan-don-du rdzogs byang thob-'dod-kyi sems-bskyed dngos*).

The teaching of the oral tradition on this contemplation is no more elaborate than this. How detailed one makes it and how effective it is depends on the individual. When practising, spend equal time on all eleven points and, at the end, imagine yourself to be a Buddha, sending a clear light of wisdom out from your heart, enlightening all beings. The meditation should end in great joy. This teaching is found only in the oral tradition and was not previously found in books.

Nagarjuna wrote that one short meditation period on bodhichitta has more merit than even the Buddhas can estimate. We are like the only son of a loving mother (the Buddha), and as we grow and ripen, she is very pleased and relieved. Simply forming the intention to help others has great merit, but actually doing so, even in minor ways, has very much more.

Previously, this meditation was taught only to disciples prepared to practise it three times daily, and the lama would first test each disciple to see if he was fit to benefit from it. Now, because of the disappearance of the Dharma, it is openly taught here.

When meditating, do not look at bodhichitta, rather transform your mind into bodhichitta—let there be no gap between the two. If after performing this meditation for a few days, you do not feel any difference, do not be discouraged, but simply continue. Tame the mind especially with regard to bodhichitta, for this is the direct remedy for self-cherishing. To one who gains a deep realization of one point of the Dharma such as bodhichitta, understanding of all the other subjects will come easily. But if one flits from one subject to another, it will lead only to discouragement, not insight. After having developed bodhichitta, one will be able to use all of Buddha's teachings towards higher attainment. It is like a mirror, reflecting all images and leading to an understanding of any apparent contradictions in the Dharma.

It is primary in tantric practice that one visualizes oneself as a Buddha before the actual attainment, as is practised during the eleventh round of this meditation. This method is called 'sem-kye dra-bui lam-khyer' (written *sems-bskyed 'bras-bu'i lam-khyer*), or 'bringing the goal into the practice'. Thus, the Paramitayana is called the Vehicle of the Cause, and the Tantrayana, the Vehicle of the Effect. It is in the latter that both cause and effect develop simultaneously.

If by performing this meditation, shunyata is even slightly developed, one is fit to receive tantric teachings. It is bodhichitta which makes tantra so high and exclusive.

When practising the main points of the Dharma, such as Guruyoga, do not continually rely on notes or texts. Internalize the teachings and make them your own. Especially when practising this eleven-round contemplation, do not simply follow the notes, counting each point off one by one.

One needs bodhichitta from the beginning of one's practice until its fulfilment, and it must accompany one throughout like one's shadow.

The following are five methods of practising the Dharma in its most condensed form in one lifetime (*tshe-gcig-gi nyams-len bsgril-nas ston-pa-la stobs-lnga*).

1. The power of the beneficial intention (*'phan-pa'i stobs*). Remembering the value of the fully endowed human body, decide to make full use of it this year, this month, and especially today. Wishing to take the fullest advantage of this opportunity for the benefit of all sentient beings is the proper motivation, and it should be present from morning till night. All acts, whether killing an insect or deciding what to have for lunch, are determined by one's motivation. All actions of those who do not follow the Dharma are directed towards ego-gratification. The beneficial motivation is as rare as a star seen in the daytime. A string tied to a finger or belt may help to remind one of the proper motivation. In

many caves in Tibet such phrases as "Don't let your mind wander!" are written all over the walls. Form a strong determination never to abandon bodhichitta or the path to enlightenment.

2. The power of the white seed (*dkar-po sa-bon-gyi stobs*). Direct whatever is done through body, speech or mind towards the development of bodhichitta, rather than to benefits in this present life. Even if one is a great solitary meditator, one's practice is not so intense without this power.

3. Complete disgust with one's self-cherishing attitude (*rnam-par bsun-'byin-pa'i stobs*). This is the same as the second of the four opponent powers and includes disgust with all unvirtuous actions along with an intention to refrain from them in the future. If a snake enters the room, one immediately jumps up and drives it away. One's reaction to self-cherishing as soon as it arises should be the same, even to the extent of actually jumping up or waving one's arms if this helps.

4. The power of acquaintance (*goms-pa'i stobs*). To become acquainted with bodhichitta, strong and continuous effort, even during sleep, needs to be given for its development. One should not be discouraged if now one is unable to follow the practices of the great Bodhisattvas. Do what is possible and pray for greater ability in the near future. There is both relative and ultimate development of bodhichitta. The relative is compassion, and the ultimate is based on the understanding of shunyata.

5. The power of prayer (*smon-lam-gyi stobs*). At the end of each day, one should look back on one's actions, recognizing faults, applying the four opponent powers, and rejoicing in one's virtue. Then just before sleep, dedicate the merit gained that day to

one's enlightenment for the sake of delivering the world from suffering. As with giving, it is not the outward prayer that is authentic, but rather one's state of mind. All actions should be devoted to the growth of bodhichitta.

These five methods are the way to attain bodhichitta in one lifetime. Most people would not even like to hear these teachings on bodhichitta, so recognize your present great opportunity and make full use of it. Shunyata may be attained in months or years, depending on one's effort. But even if it is not fully attained in this life, the practice will lay a foundation for the next life, and it will easily be attained then. One needs to maintain a strong intention to use one's entire life towards developing bodhichitta and to do so even during the *bar-do*, for this is the best means for transferring one's consciousness.

Death and the uncertainty of one's lifespan is something one cannot doubt, and only one's practice of the Dharma can be of help at the time of death. There are five corresponding practices to be performed at the time of death, and in order to perform them successfully, one needs control and intimate acquaintance with them. So begin now. If one wishes to die without regret, one needs to practise during this life. It is by following these simple methods that the great sages of the past, such as Naropa and Marpa, attained their wisdom.

1. One needs to come to the firm decision to benefit others and increase bodhichitta even during the *bar-do* and in the next life.
2. It is extremely important not be attached to one's possessions, relatives, or even to one's guru or to a statue of the Buddha at the time of death, for this would lead to rebirth in one of the lower states. It is a custom in Tibet to make offerings to the poor

after a person has died, but it would be better for that person if they had practised giving during their lifetime.

3. It is good to try to receive initiation just before death, for one has probably not kept the vows of previous initiations as closely as one should. If this is not possible, then apply the four opponent powers, for it is important to purify oneself from non-virtuous actions before death.

4. The force of acquaintance should already have been gained through one's life practice.

5. At death do not make ordinary wishes for high rebirth but wish only for the growth of bodhichitta and enlightenment. One geshe died on his throne while giving teaching on bodhichitta, and in his next life, even as a child, he thought only of the welfare of others. When a person is about to die, it is best that they be alone so that they may keep their mind on virtue. It is best then not to give them medicine, but rather to read the scriptures and let them die in peace. Bodily position is also important, the best being the horizontal posture of the Buddha when he entered parinirvana.

Only by putting the five forces into daily practice will they be effective at the time of death. If one wishes to make the Dharma a living tradition, one must develop strong will power and perseverance. Look at the examples of the great Bodhisattvas of the past, but rather than simply admiring their attainments, carefully examine the paths they followed. The essential practice is to control and cultivate the mind and develop bodhichitta. Between the age of thirty-six and forty-eight, Je Tsong Khapa lived with twelve of his disciples in caves, meditating and eating only meditation pills. At the end of this time, they sold all their belongings in order to build a temple for Maitreya, but their possessions were so few that they only received three *sho* (a few cents) for them. All those who are highly attained have totally abandoned worldly desires for this life, having their minds focused on the goal beyond. If one feels that one's bodhichitta meditation is lessening one's self-cherishing attitude, the practice is successful. For Dharma practice one must have both the internal witness, one's own mind, and the external witness, other people. If others say that one's conduct is good, look inwards and see if one's thoughts, too, are virtuous. Of the body and mind, the mind is the chief, and must be constantly watched and guarded.

Whatever spiritual progress is attained should be kept private—don't tell others of it. Because these are degenerate times, to do so would only create hate and jealousy. Shanti-deva, who had fully developed bodhichitta, was known to others as one who did nothing but eat and sleep. Through our Dharma practice there should be a noticeable change in one day, or if not, in one month, or at least in one year. If within one year there has been no definite change, our practice has not been effective.

12
The Six Perfections

Having developed bodhichitta, one should not be satisfied with this alone, but rather should begin following the conduct of the Bodhisattvas. Bodhicitta is like the decision to go to Delhi. If one stops with the decision, one will never get there, but if one starts walking towards the goal, it is soon reached. The goal of our Dharma practice is the achievement of the rupakaya and dharmakaya, which are the Buddha's form and truth bodies. Those two bodies have two separate corresponding causes—method and wisdom. The Bodhisattva's conduct is the practice of the paramitas (*phar-phyin*) or perfections, of which the first five constitute method and the sixth, wisdom. The first four perfections are known as the common Bodhisattva practice, the last two, concentration and wisdom, constitute the extraordinary Bodhisattva conduct, the most exclusive practice being that of tantra. Practice of the perfections is necessary for both followers of the sutras and of the tantras, and it is essential for the attainment of Buddhahood as well as of the fully-endowed body. At the beginning, they involve simply the practice of virtue, but they are actually methods towards attaining the perfection of each of the six kinds of conduct.

I. GIVING (*SBYIN-PA*)

True selfless giving is a state of mind: the wish to give, rather than the act of giving. One may give material goods, teachings, and protection, but giving any of these without the proper motivation does not lead to the perfection of giving. For example, giving a piece of bread to a dog with proper motivation is a step towards the perfection of giving, whereas giving even a house of gold without that motivation is not. Do not give so that others will like you or think highly of you, but do it only for the welfare of others.

Whenever reluctance to give arises, immediately contemplate the effects of selfishness and attachment. But be careful when giving—make sure not to give more than you can afford and do not give to the wrong person, for you might later feel regret and this would erase the merit of giving. In such a case, it would be better not to give at all. A Bodhisattva tries to foresee the effects of his actions before he carries them out. When giving to someone of lower status than oneself, give with respect and concern for satisfying the other's needs or desires. People to whom one can give should be thought of as spiritual friends, for without them there would be no way to practise giving and thus attain this perfection.

Giving anything from a spoonful of rice to the sacrificing of one's own body is the giving of material goods. Before any act of giving, form the correct motivation and afterwards dedicate the merit of the act.

Teaching is the greatest gift, if one gives true teaching with no wish for payment or reward. Make the Dharma teaching interesting and pleasing, but never go to extremes so that the main points are obscured. Causing another person to act virtuously is teaching the Dharma and this may easily be accomplished in everyday conversation. Teaching others a craft or skill is also a practice of giving. One may give others protection from agents of destruction and harm, both human and non-human, and thus relieve others of fears. This includes helping people and even insects out of trouble or danger, such as removing an insect from a road. Be careful of what is given, for some things, such as weapons or liquor to a monk, are not fit to give.

Give what is possible now and pray to be able to give more later. Those lacking bodhichitta cannot, and should not, give their own bodies, but after one has developed great mercy, this would be possible. One can attain the perfection of giving and enlightenment with this body, so one should not sacrifice it, but rather use it towards attaining these goals. Even later, if sacrificing the body is only of slight benefit to others, do not do so. Demons may come wishing to interrupt one's practice and beg the sacrifice of one's body. A demon, in the form of a human, once asked Aryadeva for one of his eyes. He plucked it out and gave it, and the man promptly smashed it on a rock. Only the Aryabodhisattvas are able to give their bodies, for they alone know who is a demon and who is not. This knowledge comes with the attainment of the first Bodhisattva ground.

All of the six perfections may be practised in the act of giving. When giving, do not think of getting something in return. Guard your mind and concern yourself only with the welfare of others. Patience should be applied if someone continually asks for more. When meditating on mercy and patience, one should concern oneself especially with people one dislikes. Always give with respect, and the fruit will be happiness and an increased desire to give. Whenever beggars approach a Bodhisattva, he becomes very happy. Practice giving with diligence and apply samadhi on rejoicing over the act of giving. In oneself, in the gift, and in the recipient there is no self-existence, and contemplating this leads to prajna. By doing so, one comes to understand shunyata while giving. Samsaric giving, on the other hand, is giving with the belief that the giver, the gift and the recipient are independent entities.

Giving to an Arya, to a sick person, to one on the verge of attaining enlightenment, or to a person teaching the Dharma results in especially great merit. The karmic result of giving is the attainment of wealth.

II. MORALITY (*TSHUL-KHRIMS*)

One who practises giving but fails to practise morality takes rebirth in one of the lower realms or as a naga. Morality is refraining from harming others and the development of the corresponding change in attitude. Recognize the importantance of others, for without them there would be no way to practise giving or morality. There are three types of morality:

A. Avoiding breaking one's vows such as any of the Pratimoksha vows (vows of individual liberation).
B. Being of benefit to others, that is, giving medicine to the sick or helping the blind.
C. Having the bodhichitta motivation in all activities.

Even great practice of morality without bodhichitta leads only to nirvana, the attainment of the Hinayana Arya, but with bodhichitta, the practice leads to enlightenment.

A. Of the three kinds of vows, (Pratimoksha, Bodhisattva and tantra), most important are the Bodhisattva vows. Even if all the ten virtuous actions are carefully heeded, but bodhichitta is lacking, one is not a Mahayanist. If the ten virtuous actions are not always followed but bodhichitta has been developed, one is a Mahayanist.

B. There are eleven ways of helping sentient beings:

1. Helping suffering sentient beings such as the blind or sick.
2. Helping sentient beings who are ignorant of the Dharma or of the difference between virtuous and unvirtuous actions.
3. Helping sentient beings while remembering their kindness. One may give them food, clothes and the

greatest gift, teachings to help them towards enlightenment. Contemplate the kindness of all sentient beings as though they were one's parents.

4. Protecting sentient beings who are in danger, as
from a wild animal or a powerful person. This
includes helping those who are fearful even though
they are not actually in danger, their fear being a
result of having caused fear in a former life. Helping such beings leads to great peace of mind in the
future.

5. Helping sentient beings who are in misery, such as
someone who has lost their parents or wealth. One
should explain to such people the nature of samsara, the truth of impermanence, the inevitability of
death and so on. Through practising this, one experiences less misery in the future.

6. Helping sentient beings who are poor, lacking food
or clothing. This means giving not only to beggars,
but to whomever is in need, including those in need
of the Dharma.

7. Helping those who are without a home, country, or
a teacher, by giving them whatever they lack.

8. Raising the attitude of sentient beings. This includes
consoling and encouraging those who are depressed
or in misery, thus making it possible for them to
resume their Dharma practice. As for those who are
in misery due to the evil they have committed,
encourage them to combat their kleshas.

9. Helping those who are on the true path (that of
hearing, contemplation and meditation). Encourage
them in order to keep them from straying. If one
discourages a small child by telling her that she is
incapable, she will not study. If one encourages
others when they practise virtue such as giving, it
will increase both one's own and the others' happiness.

10. Helping those who are on a wrong path. To those who follow non-virtue, point out its results and advise them to apply the four opponent powers and perform such practices as prostration to the Three Gems.

11. Helping sentient beings by means of super-normal powers. For example, if one meets someone who disbelieves in the hells, create for them, if possible, a vision of hell. Most people do not have such powers, but are able to practise the previous ten methods. In order to practise the last method, one must develop calm abiding medita-tion (*shamatha, zhi-gnas*).

C. Protect these three types of morality just as you guard your own eyes, and pray that you will be able to follow the Bodhisattva conduct.

All the perfections may be applied while practising moral-ity. One may practise giving while keeping pure morality unsullied by the Hinayana attitude of thinking of oneself only, and showing others how to follow this way of life. Patience and diligence may also enter the practice of morality by rejoicing in one's own and others' practice. Practise concentration by keeping your mind firmly set in the Mahayana attitude and in maintaining pure morality. Wisdom is developed through recognizing that morality, the one who practises it, and the object of morality are all without independent self-existence.

All Mahayana teachings are based on bodhichitta and shunyata, and one who has gained insight into both has grasped the entire teaching. If you practise the ten virtues without bodhichitta you are not a Bodhisattva, and if you lack understanding of voidness, you have not destroyed the illusion. Insight will come through practising the Dharma.

III. PATIENCE (*BZOD-PA*)

The fruit of patience is having a sound, healthy body in the future, whereas lacking it may result in the destruction of the merit gained through the first two perfections. It is the armour against such evils as abuse and protects one from anger, the root cause of rebirth in the lowest realms. With patience one will retain equanimity even if harmed by another or while experiencing a misfortune. This is essential because there are many different kinds of people, many of them evil. Rather than trying to cover the earth with leather in order to protect one's feet from thorns, it is far easier to cover one's own feet—and the effect is the same. Likewise, it is impossible to destroy all bad people, for the attempt makes yet more enemies; but by destroying one's own anger, one brings an end to enemies. One needs only to destroy anger, not change the external world.

Contemplate the negative aspects of anger in terms of both the visible and invisible effects. The obvious effect of anger is that any angry person makes himself and others unhappy and may even end his own life or take the life of one of his friends. If an angry person is given good food, he cannot even taste it. Anger destroys the wisdom of discriminating between right and wrong. The unseen effect of anger is rebirth in the hells in the next life and unfavourable birth thereafter. During the *bar-do* one is able to see one's future rebirth and through clairvoyance know its causes. Be heedful now. When you look back on your past acts during the *bar-do*, it will be too late to change. When an angry person again attains a human rebirth, he experiences much sorrow, has an unhealthy body and receives much abuse. Patience also has two effects, the seen and the unseen. One with patience experiences happiness and this spreads to others. All people like such a person and try to help him. When such a person dies, this virtue leads to a high rebirth.

Meditate upon these qualities of anger and patience (in Tibetan the word for meditation means 'acquaintance with virtues'). Before getting angry, practise patience, for anger destroys virtue.

In Tibet there was once a meditator who lived on a mountain with his cook. A thief came to steal from them, but the cook caught him and began beating him. The meditator told him to stop, but the cook continued with the beating until finally the meditator called out "Patience!" and he ceased.

Shantideva wrote that there is no better virtue than patience, and that anger is the worst non-virtuous action because it destroys the merit of past virtuous acts. If a person on the path of insight becomes angry, he destroys his virtue of one hundred aeons, and if he is a Bodhisattva, the merit of one thousand aeons is destroyed.

One cannot tell who is and who is not a Bodhisattva, for when a person attains this state, their outward form does not change. For example, Tilopa, who had such great insights but a very unpleasing form. Marpa appeared to be an old farmer who had thirteen wives and nine sons and who always fought with his neighbours. He once told Milarepa that if he killed some people for him by means of black magic he would teach him the Dharma. When Milarepa came to him for teaching, Marpa would beat him with a stick, and he also beat his wife for helping his pupil. When treated poorly or with anger, do not think of others as having an evil nature, for one simply does not know. There are many incarnations of Buddhas and Bodhisattvas in the world, and it is not possible to recognize them by their outward appearance.

Patience may be categorized into three types: (1) not taking revenge if someone harms you; (2) willingly taking on hardships while practising the Dharma; and (3) distinguishing right from wrong understanding.

1. If a sick or insane person were to fight with his doctor, the latter would not fight back, for he would know the person was demented by his illness. It would be the same if a son were to fight with his father.

Thieves once came into the cave of a disciple of one of the Panchen Lamas, and after he had given them a rope to tie him up, they beat him and took all his possessions. Afterwards he went to his lama to report all that happened, and his lama was very glad upon hearing that he had not become angry.

Pymee Dorje, one of my lamas, was in retreat on a mountain when soldiers came and demanded his possessions. He willingly gave them all he had, except his robes and begging bowl, articles which every monk should have with him. Then when more people came and demanded these as well, he chased them away with a knife. His guru later admonished him saying that if he had killed someone, the karma would have remained with him, whereas he could always get more robes. Thereafter, he was always willing to give up anything he had in his possession.

One should realize that angry people are mad with delusion and should therefore try to relieve their sufferings. Destroy anger, not the person who is moved by it. If an angry person comes and hits you with a stick, it is the stick which causes you pain. Just as the stick is wielded by that person, so is he moved by anger. So hate anger, not the person.

If you try to catch fire in your hand it will burn, yet the fault is not with your hand but in your trying to catch it. Likewise, if a person causes you pain, know that you have given her pain in the past and thus rejoice that this karma has ripened.

Anger towards any object, even a table or the weather, is very harmful, especially if one is practising tantra.

2. Voluntarily enduring suffering and harm is the second kind of patience, and its object is the person or thing that inflicts the pain upon us. Bodhisattvas look for unfavourable circumstances and upon finding them, feel that they have found a treasure. An object of patience is much more rare than an object of giving, and we need them in order to develop patience. Even Hinayana practitioners try to eliminate anger, so all the more should Mahayanists strive for this.

In order to develop this kind of patience, one needs to develop an indifferent attitude towards external pains or troubles and the ability to endure suffering willingly, accepting it as an ornament. The Buddha declared that if one is unable to accept sufferings, then there is no way to overcome them. When sick, one may have to take very unpleasant medicine, but it is taken willingly in order to recover. When suffering, be grateful that this karma has ripened and make good use of this opportunity to develop renunciation and mercy. Accept suffering like a person who, though condemned to death, has only her arm cut off. Sick people are willing to take injections and have operations; likewise, be willing to accept hardships and suffering in order to relieve yourself of mental illness or delusion.

Dharma practice will be neither stable nor lasting without patience. You must be willing to be the loser. Suffering lessens one's pride and makes one aware of the way of samsara. Further, it is a reminder that one is still producing unvirtuous karma, and it may help one to be more aware of the feelings of others. When sick, adopt this attitude: "In my countless lives, I have experienced all levels of joy and pain, but to no purpose. Now I will make use of this suffering." There are many people who work all day, enduring many hardships just for the pleasures of this life. In working towards liberation, one should be willing to take on at east as much hardship. All suffering can be eliminated totally.

This type of patience is divided into the following categories:

(a) Accepting physical sufferings, such as the pain of sitting in the lotus position while meditating, or the hardship of doing 100,000 prostrations as a preliminary practice to tantra.

(b) Observing the voluntary acceptance of pain. Train the mind constantly to observe the Dharma, not letting it slip into idle matters. This is especially difficult.

(c) Disregarding all luxuries and comforts, while accepting whatever is available. If the firm decision is made to devote oneself to intensive Dharma practice, one's environment will be of little importance. After attaining enlightenment, Milarepa observed his skeleton-like body and reflected that even his enemies would pity him, yet his mind was the pure truth body.

(d) Combining endurance of physical and mental harships.

(e) Taking on the sufferings that come in the course of saving the lives of others.

(f) Trying to abstain from all the trival actions in which people involve themselves. Make life intensive by practising only the Dharma.

3. This type of patience involves the acceptance of any hardships that arise due to one's practice of the Dharma. When going to a discourse, try to distinguish between the meaning of the words and the intuitive understanding they represent, and at the same time recognize the relationship between the two. This requires special effort.

This patience is practised in relation to the following eight objects:

(a) The object of faith, the Triple Gem.
(b) The object of intutive understanding, shunyata.
(c) Meditation on enlightenment and those who have attained it.
(d) The object of spiritual practice, meaning virtue and its fruit.
(e) Enduring the strain of the effort given to examining one object.
(f) The complete attainment of enlightenment.
(g) All the Bodhisattva practices.
(h) All the scriptural teachings.

In the process of attaining these eight objects, one must be able to endure all hardships. This type of patience may always be practised with one's body, speech and mind. Hold the Three Gems as the ultimate refuge, trusting totally to their power which is authenticated by means of one's own reasoning combined with sciptural knowledge. The effort of trying to understand the teachings as deeply as possible is this third type of patience.

This armour of patience is especially necessary during this present age of degeneration. One should apply patience to the present situation and pray that one will attain the patience of the Aryas. It is most important to practise patience in all circumstances. While developing patience, one may give teaching on it to others. Likewise, the other perfections should be followed while practising patience.

The *Avatamsaka Sutra* (*mdo phal-cher*), the *Bodhisattva-bhumi* (*byang-sa*), and Shantideva's *Bodhicaryavatara* (*spyod-'jug*), are the scriptural references for this practice. All spiritual practice should be soundly based on either the sutras and tantras. In scientific exploration new methods may always be found, but the methods taught by the

Enlightened Ones cannot be improved upon. There is nothing the Buddha does not know, and his Teaching does not grow old. Through following the Dharma, we attain the fully-endowed body, happiness even while remaining in samsara, and ultimately enlightenment.

IV. ENTHUSIASTIC PERSEVERANCE
(*BRTSON-'GRUS*)

This virtue is the root of all the perfections and it means virtuous conduct motivated by one's own enthusiasm rather than by some outside force. With it one's goal is ever-present and one has the means to attain it. All actions of the three doors then become meaningful, and full advantage is taken of the fully-endowed body. Without it, one would always be looking for a more effective method, switching from one to another always with new hope, but never attaining the goal. It is not beneficial to spend one's life sampling the tastes of different spiritual paths—it is better to keep to one and follow it assiduously. Diligence is practised if one makes the effort to endure the pains of sitting in meditation, but with enthusiastic perseverance one is so totally absorbed in the object of meditation that the pains are not even noticed. Applying oneself to meditation without this perseverance is as difficult as driving a donkey up a hill. Skill in meditation is not inherent, but once can train oneself to accomplish it by making the meditation periods short at first and by making the practice as interesting as possible. Practise accepting some pain in order to develop diligence, but not in excess, or all enthusiasm will be destroyed. Some children do seem to have this trait innately, but it is due to familiarity with it in a past life. If such traits did not carry on from one life to the next, eveyone would be the same at birth. To understand enthusiastic perseverance, one must understand its opposite, laziness, or the reluctance to take an interest in anything one wishes to do. There are three kinds of laziness (*le-lo*), listed as follows:

1. Laziness due to discouragement or an inferiority complex.

2. Procrastination: perhaps one wishes to meditate, but puts it off because today one's knees ache, or one has not learned the position well yet, and so forth. Whenever this occurs one should contemplate impermanence and the fully-endowed body, keeping in mind that there are thousands of forms other than human that one might have taken. Like changes in the weather, the duration of one's life cannot be guaranteed. Even when there is no external interference with the practice of the Dharma, there may be internal conflicts—as though there were two people in the mind, the first luring one away from the Dharma. People often do not realize that death may come at any time, and this ignorance is the factor that causes them to stray from the Dharma.

3. Being totally absorbed in something that yields no fruit or spiritual attainment. There are many different occupations, and if people take them to be ultimate, they fall into this form of laziness. For example, most farmers are wholly concerned with farming matters throughout the entire day, even in their dreams, and this is a total obstacle to Dharma practice. Recognizing this kind of laziness, observe the fruits of such action and realize that they will be left behind at death. The sole attainment that carries on after death is that resulting from Dharma practice. Cultivate the ability to follow both worldly activities and the Dharma, bringing the two together in harmony.

Try intellectually to grasp all the teachings that have been given up to this point, but develop intuitive understanding of one point at a time by means of examination meditation. Meditate until intuitive understanding is attained, then move on to the next point, concluding each meditation period with a brief meditation on the rest of the main points of the teaching. Now develop an intuitive understanding of impermanence until you have a natural drive to practise the Dharma, no longer needing to force yourself. Just as progress is made in science, there will be progress in your own mind by means of hearing, contemplation and intuitive understanding.

In reference to the first type of laziness, many people speak of the difficulty of attaining enlightenment, but by making false excuses they create their own obstacle to the practice. Arya Bodhisattvas are willing to sacrifice their own lives for the benefit of others and sometimes actually do so. Do not think of this as being an unattainable ideal. Having been imprisoned in samsara so long, one should be willing to make such a sacrifice in order to attain liberation. It is necessary to develop will power so strong that one would be willing to spend one's entire life on developing insight into just one point of the Dharma. Whenever laziness arises, call to mind such people as farmers and factory workers who exert themselves greatly in work concerned only with this life. Yet the Dharma gives fruit that accompanies one like one's shadow from one life to the next.

Because of the Buddha Nature in all sentient beings, all may attain full enlightenment. Even with proper guidance, one's level of attainment depends wholly on one's individual practice. No one was enlightened from the beginning. Shantideva wrote, "Why always live with these forms of laziness? Shakyamuni said that even a fly may attain enlightenment. Since we humans are endowed with the power of discrimination, we should always be optimistic in our practice."

While cultivating the mind, great changes can be seen from one year to another, making one ashamed of past actions. As in the practice of liberality, give now as much you are able, even if it is only a few pennies. Then as you develop, you will be able to give away something to which you are attached, and eventually giving up your own body will be easy. My Lamas told me that if one wishes to become a Bodhisattva, one should study and practise the teachings of Shantideva's *Bodhicaryavatara*.

The human attitude towards the practice of Dharma is wrong in that people always try to compromise in order to make it easier for themselves, thus ignoring vices and postponing true practice. Some people gladly sacrifice their lives for political reasons. In striving for enlightenment, should one not be willing to do as much? Non-virtue arises as easily as water flowing down a hill, and practising virtue is as difficult as rolling a rock up a hill. Now is the time to turn towards virtue. The nature of laziness is conscious or unconscious reluctance. While meditating on the fruits of spiritual practice, realize that the effort required is an ornament rather than a burden.

There are three types of perseverance:

1. The strong armour-like perseverance. Equipped with this, one is willing to remain for cosmic ages in the three lower states of existence if doing so would help other sentient beings. If one practises only the perfections, the full attainment of Buddhahood requires aeons. If one recognizes this and follows tantra simply because it is a quick method, one is totally unfit for tantric practice. The only worthy motivation for tantric practice is that, seeing the great suffering that now exists in the world, one is moved by great compassion to the desire to attain the goal for the sake of relieving others of their pain. A Bodhisattva may also remain in samsara,

not due to the force of delusion, but solely out of compassion. The sphere of samsara is not harmful to a Bodhisattva—in fact it is actually more beneficial for her to live in a city than in seclusion.

Enthusiastic perseverance should be like a stream: study and practise without break. Some people begin with great enthusiasm and energy, but after a few years abandon their practice. To guard against this, do not have expectations of immediate intuitive understanding from meditation. Intuitive insight arises only after the object has been understood intellectually, and it becomes a part of the mind. As with bodhichitta, whenever the object arises naturally and without effort, intuitive understanding has been attained. This is the full experience, and it is attained by means of contemplation and formal meditation. Further, intuitive understanding is reached when the mind and its object become one. Before then, the mind intellectually understands its object as something separate. To think of relative bodhichitta as a moon disc and understanding of shunyata as a vajra is, at the beginning, only a method of visualization, but it is the seed of intuitive understanding.

2. Perseverance applied to virtuous conduct. This should be applied after the armour-like perseverance has been developed, thus conjoining all the actions of the three doors of body, speech and mind with the six perfections.
3. Perseverance in benefiting sentient beings by means of the eleven practices of morality. Rejoice in helping others both in ordinary and extra-ordinary ways.

Take every opportunity to develop and practise enthusiastic perseverance and pray to be able to follow the conduct of the Aryas in the future.

V. SAMADHI (*BSAM-GTAN*)

Samadhi is defined as a powerful state of mind that can control mental activity and the arising of kleshas like a powerful ruler. After attaining samadhi, any object of meditation remains in the mind as firmly as Mount Meru. This ability can be used for many types of meditation and can be directed towards both virtuous and nonvirtuous actions. It is easy to apply the mind to nonvirtue, but difficult to keep it fixed on virtue. One guru described samadhi as the guideline to mental and physical ecstasy and ultimately to the great bliss of enlightenment. If one wishes to practise the Dharma intensively, samadhi must be developed. This and prajna are the extraordinary practices of the Bodhisattvas. When the mind can be made to stay on virtuous thoughts with no mental scattering or dullness, samadhi has been attained.

There are two kinds of samadhi in terms of its nature. The first is the samadhi developed by beings still in samsara. The second is the samadhi of the Aryas who have transcended samsara through insight into shunyata.

Categorically there are three types of samadhi: (1) samadhi of shamatha (*zhi-gnas*) or calm abiding meditation, (2) samadhi of vipasyana (*lhag-mthong*) or specuial insight meditation, and (3) samadhi of the combination of shamatha and vipasyana.

Functionally there are also three types of samadhi: (1) mental and physical bliss, (2) intuitive understanding, and (3) helping other sentient beings. There are many ways of using the power of samadhi, such as for attaining psychic powers, happiness, calmness, intuitive understanding, and as a means for helping others. The method of developing it will be explained separately.

VI. PRAJNA (*SHES-RAB*)

The perfection of prajna, or discriminating wisdom, is the fully-developed insight into shunyata, and it is the means by which one cuts out the root of samsara: ego-grasping (*bdag-'dzin*). It is the torch which dispells all the ignorance caused by ego-grasping and is the treasure of knowledge dealt with in all the sutras and their commentaries. After recognizing all the qualifications and advantages of attaining the perfection of prajna, one should generate great energy in developing it.

Without prajna one would not know if one were truly following the Dharma. One would likely mix many different spiritual paths and traditions, not knowing which to follow, thus being led into confusion. Spiritual paths differ in order to serve people with different mental capacities and inclinations. Further, without prajna, one would have no insight into the other five perfections and never be able to perceive the harmony of the sutras and tantras. One who has faith but lacks wisdom remains in doubt with respect to one's practice and never attains stability.

One who has developed a high degree of prajna recognizes that all objects and living beings are spiritual friends and thereby learns from them all. There is no way to know the value of the Dharma without prajna. It is defined as 'the secondary mind which examines and discriminates between right and wrong.'

There are three kinds of prajna as follows:

1. Understanding phenomena in terms of their conventional levels of existence.
2. Understanding of the ultimate truth, or non-self-existence and shunyata.
3. Knowing how to benefit sentient beings with the most appropriate means.

This concludes the teaching on the six perfections. Having understood the teachings given thus far, you now have a general understanding of the steps to enlighten-ment and the order in which they are to be practised. You know what needs to be done. It is now up to you to apply your energy to these practices and begin to advance spiritually.

SHAMATHA (*ZHI-GNAS*)

The last two perfections, which include shamatha (calm abiding) meditation and vipasyana (special insight) medita-tion, are the most difficult to practise and understand. Shamatha is a form of meditation practised not only by Buddhists but also by followers of other spiritual traditions.

The following is an outline of the teaching which must be received in order to fully develop shamatha:

A. The conditions necessary for attaining shamatha.
B. Obstacles to the development of shamatha.
C. How to attain the nine mental stages of shamatha.
D. How the nine stages are attained by means of the six forces.
E. The four types of attention developed through the nine stages.
F. The full attainment of shamatha.

These instructions were not given in the teachings which apply to the persons of middle scope, as the teachings for those of the two lower scopes are meant to be stepping stones to the teaching for those of great scope. If shamatha is developed along with compassion, it leads to Buddha-hood; but if it is developed solely with renunciation, it leads to nirvana.

Shamatha is like a container to hold together all the teachings we receive. Its development is essential because in order to cut the root of samsara, the understanding of non-self-existence and shunyata is needed, and this can only be completely attained with single-pointed concentration. To observe the details of a painting in a dimly-lit room, one needs a steadily held light. Likewise, to realize shunyata, concentration and prajna are necessary. The difference in the practice of Dharma with and without shamatha is like the difference between the footprints of an elephant and those of a mouse. Enthusiasm alone is not enough, one must know the definite need for shamatha to cut out the root of samsara. Knowing this with surety, meditation will be intense and effective. This instruction on the development of shamatha has been carried down through oral transmission directly from Shakyamuni and Maitreya Buddha.

A. THE CONDITIONS NECESSARY FOR ATTAINING SHAMATHA

There are eight conditions which are essential for attaining shamatha:

1. A quiet place for meditation, free of the sounds of water or birds, and having an expansive view. If possible, it is good to stay in a place where a great meditator has previously practiced.
2. Food should be easily attainable so that one does not need to go to town with its crowds of people.
3. A meditation teacher who is available if problems arise in meditation.
4. A dry place with good water and healthy conditions.
5. Full instructions on shamatha before going into retreat. (This is the most important of the eight.)
6. Limiting one's desires and avoiding those which

cannot be satisfied while in retreat, such as desiring a better place to meditate.

7. Avoidance of activities other than meditation, such as seeing other people or reading books.
8. Lack of attachment to the five sense objects.

These conditions are of great importance, for after they have been acquired, shamatha will develop naturally. Many people have recently attained shamatha in three, six or twelve months. The reason others take so long is that they do not have these conditions. It is helpful to keep a vow during the period of retreat, for by keeping it purely the rough sort of mental wanderings are eliminated. At least keep the purity of the ten virtues if no vows are taken. Just as the earth is the foundation of all life, so moral discipline is the foundation of all spiritual attainment.

Review these preparations and instructions again and again until you know them by heart before beginning your meditation. It is the tradition for the guru to give meditation instructions four times, each time in a more condensed form so that the disciple is completely familiar with them. Make sure that your place of retreat is in a suitable environment, and one in which you will not be hindered by spirits. If you have a companion, they must be one with the same attitude and interests as you, firm in their own practice and able to aid your meditation. During the day there should not be such distractions as people, running water, or wild animals. You must be content with what you have and hold only the least desire for these. On the Hinayana path to becoming an Arya, contentment is of primary importance.

After you have begun meditating, avoid going to public gatherings which will draw your mind outward, making it very difficult to bring it back again. Contemplate again and again the disadvantages of desire and clinging to sensual objects. Each morning when you rise, wash your body,

make offerings, meditate briefly on the succession of subjects from the teachings for one of small scope right up to
bodhichitta, then practise shamatha meditation for as many
short periods as possible.

It is important to sit in the lotus position for this meditation (it is also essential in tantric practice). Place your
right hand upon the left, with the thumbs touching (this
aids the generation of bodhichitta) at the level of the navel
(in tantric practice this helps to generate heat). Your arms
should be bent in bowshape, your back straight, and your
head slightly inclined forward. Do not lean against a
pillow, but keep your back and the channels (nadis, psychic
'wind' passageways) which run through it straight, for this
helps to keep your mind clear. Otherwise you will quickly
become sleepy. The tip of the tongue should touch the roof
of the mouth to prevent the saliva from forming and your
becoming thirsty. Your eyes should gaze down at your lap.
This is the position of Vairochana, and sitting thus leads
one to the attainment of his qualities.

Since it is not possible to do two things at once, bring
your mind to neutrality at the beginning of each meditation
period. You can do this by closely watching twenty-one
breath cycles and by counteracting any tendencies towards
ignorance, hate, or desire that may arise.

B. OBSTACLES TO THE DEVELOPMENT
   OF SHAMATHA

Before beginning shamatha meditation, it is essential to
know the five interruptions and their eight remedies. This
method is common to both Mahayana and Hinayana, and
it can be found in the teaching of Maitreya as given to
Asanga and in texts written by the Pandit Kamalashila. The
instruction given here has been synthesized from a number
of oral traditions. In tantric practice there is no separate

shamatha meditation, for during the developing stage of the Highest Yoga Tantra, shamatha is an integral part of one's meditation. An oral tradition contains the key points of great scriptures, and some are more effective than others. They are formed by means of scriptural research, organization, and synthesis and are needed because an individual's lifespan is too short to study all the scriptures. The sutras and their commentaries are like a vast ocean, the tantras like the treasures found within, the oral tradition like the boat, and the guru who passes on the tradition like the oarsman. Full confidence will not be gained unless one relies completely on only one tradition.

The five interruptions are as follows:

1. Laziness (*le-lo*).

This is the feeling that the meditation is too difficult, coupled with reluctance to make effort towards its attainment, especially for a prolonged time. One must be convinced of the effectiveness and great value of shamatha, as this will lead to the intention to meditate with enthusiastic perseverance. Inspiration can be found through contemplating the physical and mental ecstasy experienced with the attainment of shamatha as well as the resulting supernormal powers and clairvoyance. By analogy, if a person wants to make some food and has an idea of how good it will taste, he or she will make it with continuous enthusiasm. Shamatha lessens the force of delusion and can be applied even in one's sleep. One needs conviction and faith in this meditation, arrived at through knowing what can be done with its full attainment. Faith (*dad-pa*): this causes enthusiastic perseverance (*brtson-'grus*); and this leads to contemplation on the qualities of the meditation (*shin-sbyangs*).

2. Forgetting the instruction received and the details of the object of meditation (*gdams-ngag brjed-pa*).

A strong, pillar-like object of meditation is needed to which to tie the wild-elephant-like mind. In addition, one needs the strong rope of mindfulness and the iron hook of alertness, used to tame the elephant while it is tied to the pillar.

An ordinary object with which one is familiar may be used, but if a Buddhist develops shamatha, it is important to practise it with an image of the Buddha as the meditation object (this is stated in the *Samadhirajasutra*). This causes one to continually remember the aspects of the Buddha and thereby accumulate merit. Further, whenever one makes an offering, it is easy to visualize Buddha, and one has no problems in remembering his qualities at the time of death (this eliminates the possibility of birth in the three lower realms). It is also a great aid to tantric meditation in which the practitioner visualizes oneself as a deity.

According to the oral tradition, it is better to have a physical object for meditation, but for some an abstract concept like 'non-self-existence' is better. Look at the object, either a statue or a picture, and try to remember its details. Then when meditating, visualize it as life-like as possible, being first concerned with its general form only, not the details. Be satisfied at the beginning if you can keep your mind firmly on the general form of the object. After this, begin developing the details, going carefully from head to foot. The problem at first is one's inability to hold the mind even on the general form, so this must be dealt with first. Since the mind continually wanders off to other things, not being able to stay on one object for even a minute, one needs to apply the remedy, mindfulness. In the beginning, set your attention for five minutes, meditating for this time with the greatest possible intensity. Keep the object before your attention as if you were holding a rosary tightly in hand.

3. Mental agitation and dullness (*bying-rgo*).

At first one need not be concerned with agitation and dullness, for these do not arise until the duration of holding the object increases. Later on, if meditation is filled with agitation and dullness, energy is wasted and it becomes torture both to mind and body. The ability to sit in the meditation position does not necessarily imply that one has developed inward concentration— elimination of these two obstacles is essential.

There is coarse mental dullness and subtle mental dullness: the coarse form is the cause of the subtle, and it occurs when the mind is obsessed with a klesha or is simply unable to do anything. Whenever one is greatly worried, shocked or has other mental problems, this results in coarse dullness or sluggishness. The coarse form of dullness exists when most of one's attention is placed on an object, but there is no clarity or distinctness. It is easily recognized when it occurs.

The subtle form is very difficult to understand and recognize, so much so that some people think it is true meditation, thus blocking any further progress. With this form of dullness, one has both mindfulness and clarity of the object, but the full force of the attention is lacking. Each meditator must recognize this for herself. After attaining a firm hold on the object and seeing it with clarity, the mind relaxes and there is no longer forceful attention. This is like reading a book and seeing it clearly but, after closing it, not remembering what you read. In order to recognize mental dullness, develop sharp attention and mindfulness. Some people become very proud of themselves when, with mindfulness and clarity, they become absorbed in the object and even cease breathing. Yet there is still subtle dullness, and their satisfaction blocks further progress. If one remains at this level, neither liberation nor higher rebirth is attained. Instead, both wisdom and one's power of mindfulness become diffused in this life, and in the next life one takes birth as an animal.

Mental agitation arises due to desire and as a result of mental wanderings. For example, if one goes to a play and enjoys it very much, then later remembers it during meditation and cannot take the mind off it, agitation has set in. Mental wandering, such as thinking about other Dharma practices, virtue, and so forth, arises abruptly and is of very short duration. Agitation is always due to desire, and is both subtle and of long duration. Thus, the great meditators of the past point to this, not to mental wandering, as a major obstacle.

There are two forms of agitation, coarse and subtle. The former is easily recognized. The mind holds the object for a moment, then wanders off, gradually becoming more and more occupied with some distraction, until finally the object of meditation is completely forgotten. The subtle form, like a stream flowing beneath a layer of ice, is difficult to identify. This occurs when one slight part of the mind is directed elsewhere than on the object. Whenever happiness suddenly arises during meditation, it is a result of subtle agitation.

The remedy for both agitation and dullness is mental alertness. This is like a watchman who reminds one to be careful. When dullness occurs, contemplate the happy aspects of the Dharma, and when agitation arises, contemplate the impermanence of life and of phenomena in general. Alertness is like a spy who does not do anything himself, but reports what he sees to headquarters (the mind), which then takes action. Do not try to use this special alertness all the time; it may itself become agitation, but use it only once in a while as a remedy. Were one never to apply alertness, the result would be like a thief coming into the room and stealing everything unnoticed. One would also be unable to mark any progress in one's meditation.

At first, simply develop acquaintance with the object and do not be concerned about applying special alertness. This will come later when your attention span is longer. However, alertness is important at all times whether or not you are meditating, for it helps you to understand what you are doing. Meditation is like holding a cup of tea: one holds it firmly (mindfulness) with the eyes, watching the tea to see that it does not spill (clarity). The intensity of concentration should be like the strings on a lute—neither too loose nor too tight. If it is too tight, agitation arises, and if it is too loose, dullness sets in.

4. Neglecting to apply the remedies (*'du mi-byed*).

The way to deal with this obstacle is to exert effort towards the elimination of dullness and agitation. Succumbing to it is like standing in one's field and seeing animals eating all one's crops, but not doing anything about it.

5. Unnecessary application of the remedies when interruptions are no longer a problem (*'du-byed*).

To this obstacle apply equanimity. This obstacle is analogous to parents continuing to correct a child even when he is behaving. It simply disturbs the child.

Meditation is an effective means of counteracting the three poisons. When meditating, sit up very straight with your hands resting comfortably in your lap, otherwise you will become tired. If you are bothered by pains from sitting in this position, contemplate the qualities of the Buddha and this will give relief. Your meditation periods should be great moments of peace in this disturbed world.

The tradition is to visualize the object one foot away at eye-level, but many meditators find it easier to visualize it one foot from the navel. Find out which is better for you. In shamatha meditation one is trying to collect the whole world in one object, and if this is done too intensely, it may be dangerous. You must trust yourself completely to the Triple Gem and pray for the success of your meditation. If you are sometimes unable to bring your mind back to the object while meditating, you may become frustrated and angry at other people and objects without reason. Whenever this anger arises, take walks through the woods, look out upon distant views, and meditate on compassion. If shamatha is not practised skilfully, it may cause insanity. You must judge for yourself if your concentration is too loose or too tight, and to recognize this, you need very sharp alertness. It is both very difficult and important to develop the correct tone in your meditation.

Since dullness and agitation are such major obstacles to meditation, they shall be discussed further. The coarse form of each, like enemies who are unkind to one, are easily recognized, but the subtle forms, like enemies who pretend to be friends, are far more difficult. When the object is there but there is no clarity, coarse dullness arises and the mind becomes completely relaxed. This is like trying to do something without having the strength to carry it out. Both forms of dullness are due to the mind's being withdrawn into itself. When this occurs, relax your concentration somewhat and if necessary, completely let go of the object for a short time (while remaining in the meditation posture). If this fails, contemplate the fully-endowed body, the circumstances of your meeting with the Dharma, and the qualities of the Triple Gem. If you are well practised in the small-scope contemplations, this will be refreshing like cold water splashed on your face. Another method is to visualize a clear light filling your room. (If you wish to sleep lightly and be aware of your dreams, practise this before sleeping.) If these remedies are successful, immediately return to your meditation. However, some sorts of dullness may still remain and in such case, visualize several times a clear light in your heart rising up to your head, then beyond to the sky and finally disappearing. If all of these methods fail, take a walk, look at distant views, and wash your face with cold water. As soon as this has its remedial effect, return to your meditation. Coarse dullness is easily recognized but difficult to overcome, while subtle dullness is difficult to recognize but easy to overcome.

Coarse agitation occurs when there is concentration on the object but part of the mind wanders off. Counteract this by contemplating the impermanence of life and suffering, then return to your meditation. Being continually happy is a great obstacle to meditation and to any spiritual attainment. If this is not effective, use the forceful method of carefully observing twenty-one cycles of breath. Each meditation period should begin with this breathing exercise. Carefully count the breaths as they go by, and if you lose count, start again. At other times when one is very unhappy, this exercise helps. When you can hold the mind to your breathing for twenty-one cycles without a break, you have attained the first stage of the meditation. At first this concentration can be held for only three or four breaths. If this method also fails, break your meditation.

Before starting, decide how long you will meditate. If you make the duration too long, you will get discouraged and lose the will to meditate. If two people part on good terms, they will be glad to see each other again. So you should look forward to your meditation periods. Some days your meditation will be very poor. This may be due to the psychic wind not flowing properly and is not something to worry about. At the end of your predetermined meditation period, stop, whether or not your meditation has been good. If it was clear, this will make you want to return to it. While developing the first mental stage of placing the mind on the object, keep your meditation periods short, perhaps even less than five minutes, and eliminate all dullness and wandering. Each day meditate for eighteen such periods. After doing this for some time, you will get a natural fixing of the mind on the object. Then you will be ready to proceed to the next mental stage. When you can concentrate well for five minutes eighteen times each day, you can gradually lengthen the periods to one hour.

For your meditation use a square cushion and lay two straws of kusha grass on it with their points touching at the centre (signifying single-pointedness and purification). Another kind of grass having many joints (it is used for attaining a long life) should be laid beneath the cushion. The kusha grass also helps to bring the psychic 'wind' into the central channel. For firmness, scatter a clockwise swastika of grain on the cushion.

C. How to Attain the Nine Mental Stages of Shamatha

The nine mental stages (*sems-gnas dgu*) in the development of shamatha are as follows:

1. Placing the mind (*sems 'jog-pa*).

This first stage is attained by means of the force of hearing, and it entails withdrawing one's attention and focusing it on one object.

If the disciple is practising intense meditation, the teacher explains only this first stage, no further explanation being given until the disciple has attained it. There are three teaching methods: (1) the teacher gives the entire instruction all at once (*bshad-'khrid*); (2) the teaching is given in stages at a pace corresponding to the disciple's progress (*nyams-'khrid*); and (3) the teacher gives instruction by drawing from his own experience, then waits until his disciple has attained the same experience before giving further teaching (*myong-'khrid*). All teaching of the Dharma should be of the third type, and this was the method most prevalent during the time of Atisha. At the beginning it is not bad if one thinks there are more uncontrolled thoughts than usual while meditating. One is simply perceiving for the first time thoughts that have been there all along. For example, a person standing by a highway but not really looking, would not see very much traffic, but if he began paying attention, he would think there was more traffic than usual.

When concentration lasts for the duration of twenty-one breaths, the first mental stage has been attained. At first, concentration will not be pure for more than the duration of about three breaths.

2. Placement with continuity (*rgyun-du 'jug-pa*).

This stage is attained through the force of contemplation and awareness of the meditational object. Concentration is like the flow of a river in a gorge, constantly interrupted by wanderings, then returning to the object, then again wandering. During these first two stages, wanderings are so frequent that dullness and agitation cannot be recognized. To counteract these, apply intensive 'squeezing' attention, attaining a very strong grasp on the object of meditation. This stage is achieved when concentration continues for the time it takes to recite "Om mani padme hum" twice around the rosary.

3. Patch-like concentration (*glan-te 'jog-pa*).

During the first two stages, wanderings are not immediately recognized, but at this stage one becomes aware of them as soon as they arise. Thus, the duration of the wanderings is much shorter. Now all the force of mindfulness must be used in order to shorten their duration.

4. Close placement of the mind on the object (*nye-ba 'jog-pa*).

At this stage, the mind and the object become almost inseparable. In contrast to the first three stages, the attention is now well-fixed on the object, but one should not be satisfied with this achievement alone. Coarse mental dullness is the main obstacle encountered during this stage. With the full development of the power of mindfulness, the third and fourth stages are attained. During the latter, the mind becomes completely absorbed into the object, which leads to coarse and subtle dullness.

5. The controlled mind (*dul-ba byed-ba*).

Because the mind is too absorbed innto its object at this stage, subtle dullness is the main problem. To counteract this, relax attention from the object and with part of the mind contemplate such things as the Triple Gem and the fully-endowed body. This is to be done while still holding the object of meditation. Both can be done at the same time, like walking along a path and talking to friends on the way. During the fourth stage, the coarse forms of both dullness and agitation occur, but in this stage only the subtle form of each remains.

6. The pacified mind (*zhi-ba byed-pa*).

During this stage, the mind is very happy, and this leads to the subtle form of agitation. The full force of alertness is needed, and this remedy needs to be applied as soon as agitation arises. The fifth and sixth stages are attained by means of the force of alertness and during the latter this force is fully developed.

7. Complete pacification of dullness and agitation (*rnam-par zhi-ba byed-pa*).

Subtle dullness and agitation still occur during this stage, but because of the developed forces of alertness and mindfulness are combined with enthusiastic perseverance, they are eliminated as soon as they arise and therefore do not affect the meditation. The difference between the power of concentration of this stage and that of the fifth stage is enormous. Even concentration for a short time eliminates many kleshas during meditation. As progress is made through these stages, one learns to make use of one's present potentials of alertness and mindfulness. Since dullness and agitation have not been totally discarded during this stage, one must always be ready to apply effort towards eliminating them. During each of the stages, dullness and agitation must be dealt with differently. During the sixth stage, one needs to be intensely on the alert for them, but during the seventh, such intensity is not necessary.

8. Single-pointed concentration (*rtse gcig-tu byed-pa*).

At this stage, dullness and agitation are completely abandoned, and one no longer needs to be concerned with them. With little effort one can immediately perceive the object, and it remains for as long as desired. Only a little effort is needed at first in finding the details.

The first four stages are like approaching a very powerful enemy. During the fifth and sixth, the enemy is overpowered and the during the seventh, it is almost vanquished. Finally during the eighth stage, one attains victory over the enemy, dullness and agitation, and the force of uninterrupted attention is gained. The seventh and eighth stages are attained by developing the force of enthusiastic perseverance. Even these higher stages are a continuation of the same stream of consciousness that has carried on from the beginning. Moving from one stage to the next is like climbing a staircase. One ascends higher and higher, with each new step resting on the foundation of the steps already traversed. Only upon attaining Buddhahood is the entire path transcended, as when one's ship is abandoned after having crossed the ocean.

9. Placing the mind on the subject with equanimity (*mnyam-par 'jog-pa*).

At this stage only a minute amount of effort is needed to enter the meditative state. It is like knowing a prayer very well—after having begun it—even if the mind wanders elsewhere, the recitation is completed naturally. This minute effort is required until the attainment of Buddhahood. This stage is the highest single-pointed concentration attainable by beings in the realm of desire, but it is not the highest single-pointed concentration, the full accomplishment of which is far beyond the understanding of beings of this realm. The ninth stage is attained with the force of complete acquaintance. The full attainment of shamatha goes beyond the realms of desire and form to the formless realms.

In brief, the differences in the stages are as follows: between the first and second stages, it is the duration of placement of attention; between the second and the third stages, it is the duration of wanderings; between the third and fourth stages it is forgetting the object; between the fourth and fifth stages, it is coarse dullness and agitation; between the fifth and sixth stages, it is minute dullness; between the sixth and seventh stages, it is less need for intense alertness for obstacles; between the seventh and eighth stages, it is having no dullness or agitation; between the eighth and ninth stages, it is the difference in the degree of effort required. The feeling at the seventh stage is almost like that of the ninth. It is as if one has conquered the enemy, but it still tries occasionally to make trouble.

D. HOW THE NINE STAGES ARE ATTAINED BY
   MEANS OF THE SIX FORCES

This has been covered in the previous section, so only an outline need be given here:

    1st stage—the force of hearing (*thos-pa'i stobs*).
    2nd stage—the force of the contemplation (*bsam-pa'i stobs*).
    3rd & 4th stages—the force of mindfulness (*dran-pa'i stobs*).
    5th & 6th stages—the force of alertness (*shes-bzhin-gyi stobs*).
    7th & 8th stages—the force of enthusiastic perseverance (*brtson-'grus-kyi stobs*).
    9th stage—the force of complete acquaintance (*yong-su 'dris-pa'i stobs*).

E. THE FOUR TYPES OF ATTENTION DEVELOPED
   THROUGH THE NINE STAGES

During the first two stages, 'squeezing attention' (*bsgrims-te 'jug-pa yid-byed*) is required since one's concentration is so weak. From the third to the sixth stage, one develops interrupted attention (*chad-cing 'jug-pa'i yid-byed*), which is disturbed by dullness and agitation. During the seventh and eighth stages, uninterrupted attention (*chad-pa med-pa 'jug-pa'i yid-byed*) is gained, during which interruptions no longer occur once the subject has been found. Finally during the ninth stage, the natural achievement (*lhun-gyi grub-pa 'jug-pa'i yid-byed*) is gained. At this point, it is almost as if the object tries to find the meditator, rather than his seeking it.

F. THE FULL ATTAINMENT OF SHAMATHA

Even the attainment of the ninth stage is not full shamatha for the completion comes only after the experience of mental and physical ecstasy. Mental ecstasy (*shin-sbyangs*), which is a lightness and clarity of the mind coupled with the ability to use it in any way desired, precedes physical ecstasy and is like a piece of gold that has been completely freed from dirt. During physical ecstasy, the psychic 'wind' that powers the instinctive kleshas subsides, and one is able to use the body in any way desired. Until shamatha is developed, the mind cannot be used effectively, but after its attainment, the mind can be used to attain any intuitive understanding. Mental ecstasy leads to physical ecstasy, which is a result of having controlled the movement of the psychic 'wind'. The body then feels light and flexible, as if one could ride on one's own shoulders.

Physical bliss precedes mental bliss, and with the latter there is the feeling that one can concentrate on each atom while gazing at a wall. When there is the feeling that the self has been completely absorbed into object, shamatha has been attained. This is the first immutable state of the realm of form and is totally beyond the realm of desire. Having attained shamatha, one can attain all states in the form realm, and during the period of meditation, one passes beyond the reach of kleshas, but only temporarily, for one must still take rebirth. For this reason, one needs insight meditation, or vipashyana. Meditators following some non-Buddhist traditions attain all states of the realm of form and take this to be the ultimate. But later, when their power of concentration fades, they conclude that there is no nirvana. Pandit Ashvaghosha stated, "Those who are attached to an incorrect concept of freedom remain in samsara, no matter how high their attainment." He was first a great non-Buddhist teacher, then later became a Buddhist.

A Buddhist's sole reason for developing shamatha is to understand shunyata, for the joining of shamatha and vipashyana is the one method of severing the root of samsara. Mistaking something else for liberation is like confusing copper with gold. Neither shamatha nor vipashyana alone leads beyond samsara. Vipashyana should ride upon shamatha, for it is only these two together that can completely destroy all kleshas.

13
Vipashyana

Since intellectual studies are first needed in order to realize shunyata, the six scriptures of Nagarjuna should be relied upon. In several sutras, the Buddha gave exact prophecies about his coming, and all great pandits who have realized shunyata have relied upon Nagarjuna's teachings. The fundamental texts on shunyata are the *Madhyamakavatara* by Candrakirti, the *Buddhapalita* by Pandit Buddhapalita, and the *Six Collections of Logic* by Nagarjuna. There are many texts on shunyata, but it is upon these six by Nagarjuna that one should rely most strongly.

Intuitive understanding of shunyata may take a very long time, depending entirely on each individual's practice, but even intellectual understading alone softens the coarseness of samsara. Maitreya said that it is only a very fortunate person with good karma who develops even this relative understanding of shunyata.

Great care must be taken in teaching shunyata, for incorrect understanding of it may ruin a person's life. Understanding of shunyata is described as the Mother of all the Buddhas of the past, present, and future. Teaching it to followers of the three lower philosophical schools (Madhyamika being the fourth and highest school) is of no benefit to them whatsoever. One must learn and understand shunyata, but at the same time accept phenomena as they exist on an operational level. Before learning it, one must have a great collection of merit such as that attained by doing prostrations and so on. When the word 'shunyata' or 'voidness' is mentioned, if one feels naturally drawn to it, it is an indication that one is ready for the teaching. Trying to understand shunyata is like holding a poisonous snake, for there is the danger that one might simply negate everything. The object is to separate the self from self-grasping. There is a self to be refuted and a self to be accepted. Self-grasping is to be refuted.

The teaching on vipashyana *(lhag-mthong)* is divided into three sections:

I.   Establishment of the concept of non-self-existence of the person *(gang-zag-gi bdag-med gtan-la 'bebs-pa)*.
II. Establishment of the concept of the non-self-existence of phenomena *(chos-kyi bdag-med gtan-la 'bebs-pa)*.
III. The method of developing vipashyana *(de-las lhag-mthong skye-tshul)*.

Self-grasping is the clinging to the belief in independent self-existence, and this is to be refuted. Mistaking the five skandhas, or aggregates of the person, as having independent self-existence is like mistaking a striped rope for a snake, and this error leads to fear and kleshas. By realizing the voidness of an independent self among the five skandhas, one is freed from fear and ceases to produce kleshas.

I. THE NON-SELF-EXISTENCE OF THE PERSON

Since it is easier to understand the non-self-existence of the person *(gang-zag)* than that of phenomena *(chos)* in general, the former is explored first. Two methods that are used to develop this understanding are: (1) space-like contemplation on non-self-existence *(mnyam-bzhag nam-mkha' lta-bu'i skyong-tshul)* and (2) post-meditational contemplation on the illusory nature of phenomena *(rjes-thob sgyu-ma ta-bu'i skyong-tshul)*. The former is meditation on shunyata, similar to gazing into empty space, and involves no intellectual understanding. The latter entails seeing all things as being void of self-existence and having the nature of a mirage or magically created appearance. There are three levels of understanding these mirage-like creations; (1) a person having relative understanding of shunyata sees them but does not believe that they are truly existent and thus has no attachment to them; (2) a person having no understanding of shunyata thinks that these creations are true and is attached to them; (3) an Arya, or one having full understanding of shunyata, is like a illusion-creator who has destroyed all his creations and no longer sees or believes in them.

In addition to these two methods, the four points of analysis (*gnad-bzhi*) are of great importance in gaining realization of shunyata. These entail the following:

A. The point of being certain as to what is to be refuted (*dgag-bya nges-pa'i gnad*).
B. The point of absolute certainty (*khyab-pa nges-pa'i gnad*).
C. The point of separating the illusion of an independent self from the five skandhas (*bden-pa'i gcig-du bral nges-pa'i gnad*).
D. The point of searching for an independent self within the collection of the five skandhas (*bden-pa'i du-bral-du nges-pa'i gnad*).

If one meditates on shunyata using these four points, the danger of wrong understanding is avoided.

A. THE POINT OF BEING CERTAIN
   AS TO WHAT IS TO BE REFUTED

The relative self is mixed with the concept of a false or non-existent self, and it is on this error that light must be shed. For example, if there is an enemy, one must first recognize him and know where he is. To successfully do this requires intelligence, a strong collection of merit, faith in understanding shunyata, and visualizing the guru as being one with one's tutelary or meditational deity.

In this point of analysis, one contemplates how the self could exist independently of the five skandhas, by trying to determine what characteristics it would have. The more one meditates on this illusory self, the more clearly one understands the relative self which depends upon the five skandhas. The ultimate philosophy of the Madhyamika-Prasangika school (*dbu-ma thal-'gyur-pa*) is that ultimate truth, or shunyata, is understood by means of understanding the relative, and relative truth, principally the law of cause and effect, is fully grasped through understanding shunyata. If this point is carefully analyzed after acquiring the necessary prerequisites of merit and so forth, realization of shunyata is not difficult. Shortly before the invasion of Tibet, there was a young monk (not a very learned one) who did intensive analysis on this first point and realized shunyata while chopping wood.

Do not be satisfied with shamatha alone. The goal is Buddhahood, so why settle for anything less? From the beginning of one's development of shamatha, have the motivation of using it with vipashyana as soon as it is attained. Pandit Ashvaghosha stated that with the combination of shamatha and vipashyana, one can go beyond all the great obstacles of demons. Without them, even if one is a Bodhisattva, one's actions are samsaric, that is, stained with self-grasping. One needs to understand shunyata in order to follow all the great practices, including those of the Bodhisattvas.

In order to understand shunyata intuitively, one needs to understand the philosophy of the Prasangikas, in which the minute form of non-self-existence is defined as the voidness of independent self-existence. The other three philosophical schools define it as the non-existence of a self that exists by itself, separate from its parts, or attributes.

Human lifespan is too short to understand shunyata solely through reading the sutras, since they are so great in bulk. Thus, one needs to rely on the two traditions of the vast and the profound teachings. Nagarjuna was the founder of the latter of these traditions, and by following it, all mistakes are avoided. There is no doubt about the validity of his teachings, as he was prophesied by the Buddha. While trying to develop understanding of shunyata, one must rely on the scriptures, for to rely solely on one's own experience may lead to dangerous self-delusion. Chandrakirti stated that following any method other than that taught by Nagarjuna will not lead to full understanding of shunyata. If there were a second door to liberation, one might enter there, but if not, one should follow Nagarjuna. His teachings are accepted by both Madhyamika schools.

Of Marpa's thirteen gurus, the one who taught him about shunyata, Pandit Maitripa, told him, "Tell the people of Tibet that it is impossible to understand shunyata without following the teachings of Chandrakirti and Nagarjuna." Atisha also said this when he came to Tibet. Chandrakirti is relied upon because he simplified the vast teachings of Nagarjuna. At the beginning, the mind is like a white cloth in that one has no fixed ideas about shunyata. It can be dyed any colour, so one needs to depend on a sound reference for developing correct understanding. When Je Tsong Khapa asked Manjushri if he could rely on Chandrakirti, the reply was, "You may rely on him for understanding both the sutras and tantras. He came to earth solely for the purpose of clarifying the teachings of Nagarjuna."

Understanding of the relative level of truth is developed by practising the small and medium scope contemplations, especially on the law of cause and effect and the qualities of the Buddha. When these are well understood, the teachings on non-self-existence should be studied. There is no difference between the non-self-existence of the person and that of the five skandhas, but the former is easier to understand.

In the first of his six main works (*rtsa-ba shes-rab*), Nagarjuna shows the logical reasonings, or methods, used to gain understanding of shunyata. The three types of reasoning he sets forth are as follows:

1. The king of logical reasonings concerning interdependence (*rigs-pa'i rgyal-po'i rten-'brel-gyi gtan tshig*).
2. The seven-aspect reasoning (*rnam-bdun gyi rigs-pa*). An example of this would be looking at a carriage and trying to find which part of it is the carriage itself. This attempt results in finding only a collection of parts, never the entity which intrinsically bears the name 'carriage'. This reasoning is dealt with at length in the *Supplement to the Middle Way*.
3. The logical reasoning which shows that things do not exist independently either as a whole or as many (*gcig-du bral-gyi rigs-pa*). One thesis using this reasoning is as follows: "Take the person as an example. Why has it no independent self-existence? Because it does not exist independently as a whole or as many." This relates directly to the first point of analysis dealing with what is to be refuted.

This logical reasoning should be used with all four points. In order to understand non-self-existence, one must try to imagine how independent self-existence could be true. Apply much effort to this point, for one's own personal experience is essential. To shoot an arrow, one needs a target, and likewise, the target of this point of analysis is that which is to be refuted. If merit is first collected by such means as the preliminary practices, when this firt point is analyzed, understanding will come easily. Contemplate your own self and alternate periods of analysis with shunyata meditation.

If the self exists independently, it must exist either as one or as many. Since it has many parts (the five skandhas) it does not exist as one, and since the many parts do not exist independently, the self does not exist independently as one or as many. One must be careful not to negate the relatively existing self while analyzing this point. By following this reasoning many times, using oneself and all phenomena as its object, one gains confidence in the truth of non-self-existence.

According to the Madhyamika-Svatantrika school (*dbu-ma-rang-rgyud-pa*) the relative, or conventional, self is mental consciousness, one aspect of the consciousness skandha, and it is this which carries karmic seeds and continues from one life to another. When studying this more extensively, first explore the teachings of the lower three philosophical schools (Vaibhashika, Sautrantika and Chittamatra) and gradually work up to the Prasangika school. Prasangikas teach that it is most important in the beginning to have a deep understanding of what is to be refuted: otherwise, all further understanding of shunyata is blocked, and one is likely to fall to the view of nihilism. An example of such fallacious reasoning would be to examine a vase and after recognizing that no part of it is the vase, concluding that it does not exist. Using correct reasoning, true, independent self-existence of the vase is refuted, but not the vase itself.

There are two kinds of self-grasping, inherent and intellectually-formed. Inherent self-grasping is the feeling in all sentient beings, including insects, that the self exists separately from the five skandhas: and the latter kind is the result of philosophical beliefs in independent self-existence.

There are three ways of apprehending the distinction between the self and the person. A person with understanding of shunyata holds the view that the self does not have independent existence. Others believe the contrary. The view that the self exists independently of mental imputation is fallacious, for it accepts that which is to be refuted. Thirdly, there are those who have never studied philosophy and have no view on the nature of the self, yet they see and understand the conventional existence of phenomena and apply this likewise to themselves. This is the proper understanding of the relative self and things or phenomena in general.

When meditating on non-self-existence, examine the five skandhas as if you were separate from them, and by this means the truth will become clear. It is essential to understand the difference between the second and third views mentioned above. When someone praises or abuses you, you catch a glimpse of what is to be refuted, but it lasts only meomentarily—when you try to examine it, it vanishes into the five skandhas. When you are happy, suffering, or angry, you have the best opportunity to recognize this false self. Also, if someone unjustly accuses you of stealing, you experience a cold, uncomfortable feeling in the chest and your whole mind strongly reacts with self-grasping. Then as soon as part of the mind tries to examine this, it disappears like a rainbow. The practice called 'chöd' (written *gcod*) involves going to cemeteries and other fearful places in order to have the opportunity to examine self-grasping.

The self which is grasped at is sometimes identified with the body and at other times with the mind. For example, when walking along a cliff, it is identified with the body, and, when viewing one's non-virtue and fearing birth in a low realm, with the mind. The urge for self-preservation which strongly arises while walking along a cliff is not self-grasping, but is accompanied by it. Even the Buddha has the instinct of self-preservation, for it is this which preserves the well-being of the relative self.

The feeling that the self exists independently of mental imputation is based upon an illusion, and it is because of this, the root of samsara, that all kleshas arise. Sentient being have remained in samsara for countless aeons due to confusing the relative self with this illusion. When a finger is pressed to the eye, two moons are seen, but one is perfectly sure that only one exists. In the same way an Arya understands shunyata.

At first, when analyzing this first point, one needs to rely on the scriptures and the Lama's teaching; but later, as one's own experience arises, the teachings may be left behind. This point is like a great hammer which crushes self-grasping, and it deserves much time and effort. Having analyzed this well, the later steps will come easily.

B. THE POINT OF ABSOLUTE CERTAINITY

When dealing with this point, examine more carefully whether the illusory self exists with, or separate from, the five skandhas. Further test whether it can exist independently as a whole or as many. By first examining one's own self, then using many other examples, one attains absolute certainty that this self is an illusion.

C. THE POINT OF SEPARATING THE ILLUSION OF AN INDEPENDENT SELF FROM THE FIVE SKANDHAS

In this analysis, one determines whether the illusory self exists as the unity of the five skandhas. If this were the case, it would be a mistake to think that there is one self, for since there are five individual skandhas, there would likewise have to be one self per skandha. Further, one would be forced to conclude that either the self dies with the body or that all five skandhas would take birth again having the same form. For example, an animal would always take birth as an animal since this is the nature of its form skandha. Also, if the self exists as the compound of the five skandhas, there could be no birth in the formless realms, since these lack the form skandha. On the other hand, if the illusory self exists independently of the five skandhas, it would not have to experience any of the results of the actions of those skandhas. And such is obviously not the case.

The person is the relative self, and it is this which is mistakenly believed to have independent existence. Having clearly explored this point of analysis using logic, one gains complete confidence that the independent self is an illusion. This is a difficult point, but it is one that needs to be dealt with.

D. THE POINT OF SEARCHING FOR AN INDEPENDENT SELF WITHIN THE COLLECTION OF THE FIVE SKANDHAS

Now each of the five skandhas are examined separately to determine if an independent self exists. By grasping at the view that the self exists separately from all the skandhas, one ignores the relative self, and such phrases as "I am sick" or "I am old" would bear no relation to reality. When one has seen the impossibility of such independent existence, the proof is complete, and relative understanding of shunyata has been attained for oneself from one's own experience. When this happens, one may feel either great joy or a sense of loss, depending upon one's accumulation of merit. To the latter kind of person, this realization comes as a great shock, and he feels as if he has lost his most prized possession. Collecting merit and faith are prerequisites to entering this study. Do not approach it as one would any other subject.

Padmasambhava and the founders of the other three spiritual traditions in Tibet followed Nagarjuna's teachings,

and all agreed that the use of logic is a necessary preliminary to shunyata meditation. Je Tsong Khapa wrote,
"Understanding Nagarjuna's teachings is as difficult as the
opening of the utpala flower, which opens only under the
light of the moon. Chandrakirti's teachings are like moon-
light." Je Tsong Khapa respected all the great pandits, but
most of all Nagarjuna and his disciples, who opened his
mind to shunyata. A person having understanding of
shunyata sees no fundamental difference among the four
religious traditions in Tibet.

To aid development of bodhichitta, make prayers and
offerings to Avalokiteshvara, and for understanding of
shunyata, perform devotions to Manjushri. Je Tsong Khapa
thought of going to India to learn of shunyata but he first
asked his teacher for advice. His teacher consulted Vajrapani, who replied, "If you go to India, it will be good for
you and you will soon realize shunyata. But you can most
benefit others by remaining in Tibet and establishing direct
contact with Manjushri." Strong faith in understanding
shunyata is of great importance, for the mind must not be
divided in this pursuit.

Relative understanding of shunyata is a key to understanding all the scriptures, including both sutras and tantras. In preparation for intense study of shunyata, it is
important to begin doing daily prostrations to the Triple
Gem. Also practise this analysis as well as calm abiding
meditation for a short time each day in order to keep them
fresh in mind. Shunyata may be contemplated at any time,
even during sleep. One can always practise Dharma in the
mind, even if the body and speech are involved in worldly
activities. Again and again Atisha said, "Develop bodhichitta. Give up attachment to this life!" A person's past
experience determines how he reacts when he has proved
to himself that the illusory self is non-existent. While
experiencing shunyata, there is nothing one can point to

and say, "I have experienced that." It is really a feeling of emptiness.

In developing understanding of shunyata, two types of reasoning are used, both of them arriving at the negation (*dgag-pa*) of the illusory self. The first is deductive reasoning (*ma-yin dgag*). For example, if one mentions a "mountainless plain", one first knows to refute the existence of a mountain, then by deduction to conclude that there is a plain. First there is the negation, then the logical inference. The second type of reasoning is direct negation (*med-dgag*). Using this one-step reasoning, the non-existence of an independent self is immediately apprehended, then words are left behind. Beyond this point they are no longer applicable.

In contrast to these two ways of reasoning, there is a third which is used to understand things in terms of their relative existence. In this case, instead of negating, one affirms (*sgrub-pa*) information about an object. This reasoning is like letting everyone enter a building, whereas deductive reasoning is like allowing some people to enter, and direct negation is like admitting no one. The first reasoning is totally inapplicable to understanding shunyata, and the latter two are necessary preliminaries to actual shunyata, or space-like meditation. There is a difference between reaching certainty of non-self-existence and totally cutting out the concept of such existence. On fully realizing this negation, appearances (*snang-go*) are no longer seen as having independent existence; rather, one directly understands the true state (*nges-ngo*) of phenomena.

Shunyata is the essence of all the Teachings, and since it is also the most difficult subject in the scriptures, its understanding requires much effort and a large accumulation of merit and faith. Even the Pandit Vasubandhu did not understand shunyata during the earlier part of his life when he followed a Hinayana philosophical school. Only later in his life did he change to the philosophy of the

Prasangikas. In developing understanding of shunyata, one must constantly forge ahead until full realization is attained. Even if a glimpse of shunyata is gained, this may be lost if further effort is not made.

When practising the space-like meditation on the voidness of independent self-existence of the person, one needs to become wholly absorbed in shunyata, leaving behind all that exists on the conventional level. Only after meditation does the relative self reappear. Then during the postmeditional periods, one contemplates the illusory nature of all phenomana and by this means comes to a clear realization of the non-existence of an independent self and of the relative existence of the true self, which is obvious when, for example, one is stuck with a pin. The relative self is then seen to have the nature of a mirage which one has created. Space-like meditation is incomplete, for it ignores relative existence; but, when the fruits of both types of meditation have been attained, both levels of truth are clearly seen and this is the full understanding of shunyata. One having this understanding is like a person who has magically created visions of animals, and since he knows them for what they are, is able to destroy them at any time. Other people, however, are deceived by his creations.

At the start, these contemplations are very difficult because sentient beings have been ignorant for so long. Then, after glimpsing shunyata, it is difficult to retain understanding of relative truth. Gradually the middle way is found and one's understanding of each level of truth supports the other. There are both subtle and gross forms of relative truth, but at the beginning, one understands only the latter. After becoming experienced in both types of shunyata meditation, insight into the subtle form is gained as well.

The two levels of truth are dependent upon one another; thus even shunyata has no independent existence since it depends on relative truth. In order to understand this, contemplate the nature of interdependent existence. The logical argument used here (*rten-'brel-gyi rigs-pa*) runs as follows. "Take a sprout as an example. Why has it no independent self-existence? Because its existence is dependent upon other circumstances, such as seeds, moisture, heat and fertilization." Usually when one first sees a sprout, one ignores even the earth. This ignorance must be abandoned by clearly recognizing the cause of phenomena.

The Tibetan word 'ten-drel' (*rten-'brel*) is a synonym for shunyata and shows why both absolute negation and positivism are to be rejected. The root 'ten' means 'to depend', thus refuting absolute existence, and 'drel' means 'connection' or 'link', which refutes negation since the links between phenomena do exist. Through understanding shunyata, one avoids the extreme of positivism and by understanding relative truth, nihilism is rejected.

If there were true self-existence, a child would always remain as such. Thus old age and all momentary changes help one to realize the illusion of self-existence.

All these teachings on shunyata have sound references in the words of the Buddha as recorded in the *Kangyur* (*bka'-gyur*). Anyone studying the Dharma should be able to point out his references in the sutras. Pandit Chandrakirti wrote, "Once interdependent arising is understood, shunyata is comprehended, and all actions of body, speech, and mind become meaningful." With understanding of shunyata, the other teachings are more fully appreciated and one gains deeper insight into them. Immeasurable merit is gained from even a moment of contemplation on shunyata. Nevertheless, the idea that only understanding of shunyata is important, thus ignoring taking refuge, bodhichitta, and the rest of the method aspect of the Teachings is like cutting off one leg.

II. THE NON-SELF-EXISTENCE OF ALL PHENOMENA

This aspect of non-self-existence refers specifically to the five skandhas and is also known as the non-self-existence of phenomena (dharma), which means in this case, 'that which holds its own individual identity'. For example, a pillar is a phenomenon because it has its own identity. The Buddha has stated in many sutras that if one understands the non-self-existence of the person, understanding of the non-self-existence of all phenomena comes easily. The Mahayanist's purpose in developing understanding of non-self-existence is to liberate all living beings from suffering.

There are two main categories into which all phenomena fall: collected and uncollected.

A. COLLECTED PHENOMENA (*'DUS-BYAS*)

Collected phenomena are divided into three categories:

1. Form (*gzugs*)
2. Consciousness (*shes-pa*)
3. That which is neither form nor consciousness (*ldan-min 'du-byed*)

This third type includes terms such as 'human beings', 'impermanence' and 'time', which do not refer to a specific object.

All sentient beings who have an ordinary consciousness (that is, not having attained the wisdom of the Aryas) are deluded by gross (kleshavarana) and subtle, or instinctive (jneyavarana), ignorance. These may be likened to a moth-ball and its odor. Just as the odor remains even after the mothball has been removed, so does instinctive ignorance remain after gross ignorance has been dispelled.

Shunyata contemplation involves creating a concept of what is to be refuted, then refuting it. This method should be used when examining the three types of collected phenomena.

1. Form.

All objects are dependent upon mental imputation. Ordinary individuals see objects and their mental imputation as being inseparable, but in truth they exist separately. Knowing this, one can cognize the voidness of independent self-existence of the object. Since the object is dependent upon its mental imputation, which is interdependent with the imputation of other objects and is therefore a compound, the object is likewise a compound. For example, the term 'north' only has meaning in relation to the other three directions, all of them being interdependent. Nothing can exist independently either as a whole or as a compound. To understand this, consider carefully that all labels are mentally created and do not stand for independent things.

2. Consciousness.

Consciousness is defined as a clarity of the mind which can be focused upon an object, thereby enabling one to understand its nature or aspects. The primary mind understands only the rough nature of an object, and the secondary mind makes the fine distinctions. Consciousness is a stream of momentary changes and does not exist independently either as a whole or as a compound. When, for example, the faculty of vision is focused on an object, and there is consciousness of a visual object, it is wrong to believe that this consciousness is independent.

If consciousness did exist independently as a compound, then after taking away this morning's and this evening's consciousness, one should be able to point to today's consciousness as the independent compound of those two. But such an entity is not to be found. On the other hand, if consciousness existed independently as a whole, it could not have any parts, and one would have to conclude that all moments of consciouness exist in one moment. For example, today's consciousness could not be different from that of this evening's con-sciousness. But since this morning's consciousness cannot exist in the evening, if consciousness exists as a single unit, one must conclude that today's consciousness is non-existent.

Consciousness, the subject (*yul-can*) referring to the person, and its object (*yul*) are interdependent and each exists because of the other. The fact that all the people in a room perceive one object, such as a table, shows the dependence of consciousness on the object. The table is seen and recognized by the secondary mind. It is formed by the collective karma of all sentient beings and by the work, or karma, of actually building it. In the *Abhidharmakosha*, the matter of the universe is compared to a pot and all sentient beings to the food (*bcud*) in the pot. All things are created by collective karma and individual karma. In any part of the universe where sentient beings collectively follow virtue there is no war, famine, disease, and so forth.

Once you have analysed these points carefully and come to a strong conviction about the truth of non-self-existence, begin alternating periods of analysis with formal meditation.

3. Neither form nor consciousness.

Taking 'time' as an example, the concepts of 'year', 'month', 'day', etc., seem to be something substantial, but in fact they are all composites. Thus, this concept of an independent 'year' which is devoid of months, and days is refuted. Since one year equals twelve months, if the year exists as a unity, there must be one year per month. On the other hand, if twelve months and one year exist separately, having taken away twelve months, there should still be one year remaining.

This is the same argument as that used when dealing with the self: if the self exists as an independent unit of the five skandhas, there must be five selves since each of the skandhas is separate. The only other possibility is that the five skandhas do not exist as such. Having clearly understood this arguments, it can be applied to all concepts. By proving the impossibility of one year existing independently either as a whole or a composite, it is seen that 'year' and, more generally, the word 'time' refers to a composite of dependent parts.

B. UNCOLLECTED PHENOMENA ('*DU MA-BYAS*)

Examples of uncollected dharmas, or phenomena, are the truth of the cessation of suffering, shunyata and space. By examining the concept 'space', we see that it is a direct negation involving nothing tangible. Thus, nothing needs to be affirmed before comprehending space. Although it has no cause or conditions, it does not exist independently since it is composed of parts, such as the four directions. If space were independent of its parts, one would conclude that eastern space and western space were the same. But this cannot be, since it may be raining in the west, but sunny in the east. Following the same argument as before, if space is an entity separate from its parts, one should be able to point to this independent self after taking away the ten directions of space.

At this point, a brief discussion of the five skandhas might facilitate understanding of the non-self-existence of the personality and all phenomena. The five skandhas, or aggregates, are the group of parts, like five piles of grass, which make up the person. They include form, feeling, recognition, volition and consciousness.

The definition of form is 'anything that is fit to be la-belled as form' (*gzugs rtags-su rung-ba*). The human body is included here as it is made up of atoms which give it form.

Feeling is the secondary consciousness which experi-ences happiness, suffering and indifference. This skandha includes all types of feeling, including fear. At the time of death it is left behind.

Recognition is the secondary consciousness which dis-tinguishes the fine differences between objects. We have many recognitions, one for each labelled object. First we have direct observation, then recognition and labelling of the object. This skandha also fades away at death, as when a person is no longer able to recognize her relatives.

The skandha of volition includes every aspect of the person which does not fall within any of the other four categories. For instance, prajna and samadhi are included here. This skandha is made up solely of secondary con-sciousness (*sems-byung*). The only way to understand it is to examine oneself, categorize all that is observed into the skandhas, and see what does not fit into any of the others. Anything that fits into one skandha cannot be included among any of the rest.

The consciouness skandha includes the six primary consciousnesses (*rnam-shes*) of the eye, ear, nose, tongue, body and mind. These perceive the rough qualities of things, while secondary consciousness motivates the mind. The Buddha's mind is comprised of both primary and secondary consciousness, but bodhichitta is only primary consciousness. No living being has any skandha other than these five, and not all beings have them all.

When learning of shunyata, there is the danger of casting aside one's understanding of relative truth, and it is for this reason that disciples are always taught relative truth before shunyata. In Tibet, disciples were first taught logic, then the *Abhisamayalamkara* and all the other works of

Maitreya. Using this as a foundation, they then learned the Madhyamika philosophy by study-ing the works of Nagarjuna, the *Madhyamakavatara* and the commentaries in that order. The teaching given here will form a framework for later intense study of shunyata.

All things existing relatively have two aspects—how they actually exist (*gnas-tshul*) and how they appear to exist (*snang-tshul*). It is easier to deal with the latter and by doing so recognize the illusion of an independent self-existence. For example, if one looks in a mirror, only the mirror can be seen, but one thinks that one is looking at one's own image.

Anything that is not Sunyata is a relative truth, or 'truth for an obscured one' (*kun-rdzob bden pa*) meaning 'false'. Shunyata has only the one characteristic of voidness, but it is not independent. Relative truth can be likened to a person who feels one way but acts in another, whereas shunyata is like one whose feelings and appearance are the same. It is very difficult to correct the view that shunyata has independent self-existence, so avoid this view from the start. The belief that relative truth has independent self-existence can easily be corrected, like using water to quench a fire; but when trying to correct the view that shunyata is independent, it is as if the water itself has caught fire. Shunyata depends both on its mental imputation, which is the direct negation of true independent self-existence, and upon objects in general. If there were no object, there could be no void nature of the object.

There are twenty million types of shunyata, but in their most condensed form they fall into four categories.

1. External shunyata, the voidness of all objects that do not have consciousness.
2. Internal shunyata, the voidness of bodies that are conscious. A person's head and limbs are included here, whereas the tips of hairs and fingernails have

external shunyata.

3. External and internal shunyata, which includes the voidness of all the sense organs. For example, the eyeball has an outward appearance, but the actual sense organ of the eye inside the head is grasped by consciousness and thus has both inner and outer voidness.

4. Shunyata of shunyata. This term refers to the fact that shunyata also lacks independent self-existence.

III. THE METHOD OF DEVELOPING VIPASHYANA

The attainment of the nine mental states and the completion of shamatha do not by themselves give insight into shunyata, but this ability is used to examine the four objects of analysis. Firstly, one gains confidence with respect to the non-self-existence of the person, then one concentrates single-pointedly on this voidness of independent existence. Because the object of meditation is now so different from that of shamatha, the force of meditation may at times decrease and, whenever this occurs, one needs to return to analyzing the four points.

Using the attainment of shamatha in vipashyana meditation is the ultimate means of realizing shunyata. During formal meditation, most of the mind is concentrated on shunyata, but a small part of the mind deals with the four points. Mental ecstasy grows from this meditation and this is followed by the full accomplishment of vipashyana.

The full combination of shamatha and vipashyana (*zhi-lhag gzung-'brel*) is the framework of the attainment of Arhatship and enlightenment. Shunyata is the mother of the attainment of the Prayekabuddha and Shravaka, and when it is joined with bodhichitta, the father, enlightenment, is born. Shunyata is like a mother who can produce any kind of child depending on her mate.

Nagarjuna wrote, "After attaining shunyata realization, one can take the means to enlightenment into one's own hands and thus shape one's future."

I urge you to arouse great enthusiasm in yourselves by meditating constantly on the value of shunyata meditation and on the disadvantages of ignoring it. One can practise the virtue of giving by bestowing upon others one's understanding of shunyata.

This concludes the teaching on vipasyana.

THE FOUR MEANS OF CULTIVATING
THE MINDS OF OTHERS
(*GZHAN-RGYUD SMIN-PAR BYED-PA'I BSDU-BA'I DNGOS-PO BZHI*)

By applying these four means, one helps others to conquer their kleshas. They are explained in the *Mahayanasutralamkara* (*The Ornament of Sutras*).

A. Giving material aid

Since all beings appreciate worldly things, these are given first. One should give not with the intention of making others serve one, but in order to afford them the opportunity to attain a higher level of existence in the next life, nirvana, or enlightenment.

B. Giving encouragement

One should speak with others at their own intellectual level, giving them teachings that can be best used by them. If one has high attainment or strong renunciation and speaks with a person who is just starting out, the other will feel a great gap unless one speaks to him as a comrade, stressing the similarity between one another. Show the other person the reasons for practising the Dharma, speaking of a way of life rather than just theory. There are times when it is not fitting to speak of the Dharma; instead speak of worldly matters gradually leading the conversation to more meaningful things.

First one should try to help one's enemies, or those who have tried to harm one. It is the natural tendency to return abuse for abuse, and that attitude must be reversed. This is difficult for anyone. The second difficulty is trying to teach those of very low intelligence. One should be willing to spend even a lifetime to help just one such person, never allowing oneself to be discouraged. The third difficulty is trying to subdue very irreligious people.

These three difficulties must be dealt with only by those who wish to learn. If someone is following another path, do not try to change them, but rather help those who are without a path and do not know how to help themselves. By trying to effectively teach those who have a hard time learning, one will easily be able to teach others.

With those whose minds are not cultivated in the practice of the Dharma, start with worldly conversation and cleverly lead to the Dharma. To those whose minds are cultivated, speak immediately of specific teachings, such as bodhichitta and shunyata.

C. Teaching specific practices on the path to enlightenment

This practice includes giving vows and ordinations to disciples, leading them to higher and higher spiritual attainments. If another person has his mind set on other views but has the potential to follow the Dharma, make effort to guide him. In short, try to help others regardless of their mental capacity, skillfully teaching them practices which will bring them to fulfillment.

D. Being a perfect example of one who follows the teachings

Others do not listen to someone whose own conduct does not reflect what they teach. If one seeks to lead others to enlightenment, one must either attain it oneself, reach a level of attainment close to it, or at least gain a greater realization than those whom one wishes to teach.

These four methods and the path of the six perfections constitute the path of all Bodhisattvas of the three times. These practices are the only path to enlightenment.

The following scriptures contain the complete teachings on the Bodhisattva practices, and are the source references for the teaching given here. Like a stream and its source, all sutra practices must have their source in the teachings of Buddha Shakyamuni, and all tantric practice must be based on the teachings of the Buddha as he manifested himself in the form of Vajradhara.

1. *mdo-sde, The Collection of Sutras.*
2. *byams-chos, The Five Works of Maitreya.*
3. *rigs-tsogs, The Six Works of Nagarjuna.*
4. *sa-sde, The Five Works on the Spiritual Stages* by Asanga.
5. *skye-rabs, The Garland of Births* by Ashvagosha.
6. *spyod-'jug (Bodhicaryavatara)* by Shantideva.
7. *bslab-btus (Shikshasamuccaya)*, Shantideva's commentary to the former work.
8. *lam-sgron (Bodhipathapradipa), Lamp to the Path of Enlightenment* by Atisha.

14
The Five Paths of the Hinayana

One having the potential to follow Mahayana practice should do so, but if not, turn to Hinayana. There is an axiom in Tibet, "Why cross a river twice if you can cross it just once?", and this applies here, for one who follows the Hinayana must later follow the Mahayana before reaching fulfilment. Follow your inclination towards one or the other, and this will indicate your potential.

Although one may claim to be a Mahayanist, one should never look down upon a Hinayanist, for by truly following Mahayana practices, one sees the great value of the Hinayana path (*theg-dman gyi sa-lam*). The term 'Mahayana' (*theg-chen*) refers to taking on the burden for oneself and all sentient beings, whereas 'Hinayana' (*theg-dman*) refers to taking on the burden only for oneself. The latter term has never referred to a specific tradition such as Theravada. The paths of the Shravakas and the Pratyeka-buddhas are the two Hinayana paths. Both of these and the Mahayana path each involve five paths, or stages of spiritual growth.

I. THE FIVE PATHS OF THE SHRAVAKAS
(*NYAN-THOS-KYI SA-LAM*)

A. THE PATH OF ACCUMULATION (*TSHOGS-LAM*)

In order to attain this first path, intensive renunciation and complete non-attachment to samsara must be developed. If one wishes to abandon samsara, look within, where it truly exists, and not to the outside world. samsara is defined as the state of 'a being that takes rebirth in the various states of existence, from the hells to the deva realms, due to its being uncontrollably propelled there by karma.' A being in samsara is like a naked person carrying a bundles of thorns tied to their back. There can be no freedom until the rope binding one to samsara is cut and this is done by freeing oneself from the forces of klesha and karma. By gaining a clearer understanding of samsara in general, one's own samsaric existence, and the sufferings of samsara, one develops a strong desire to escape from one's body and all suffering. When this state of mind has been attained, the path of accumulation is reached.

In order to develop this renunciation, one must be free of attachment to the pleasures of this life and of future lives. By meditating on the law of cause and effect and on the sufferings of all samsaric states of existence, one is freed from attachment to the pleasures of future lives. The sole way of attaining freedom is by taking advantage of the fully-endowed human body. Samsara is like a sick person who never dies, a guest who never arrives, and a prisoner who is never freed. It never ends until effort is made in applying skillful means towards this goal.

After developing renunciation, one realizes that wherever one goes there is suffering, because we carry it along with us. All Dharma teachings should be used to aid one in this development and to clearly recognize that samsaric pleasure is never satisfactory. People delude themselves by thinking that those at other social levels are happier. Kings think that the simple peasants are the happiest of beings and vice versa. Senseless envy is the result.

The path of accumulation has three stages. As one progresses through them, attachment to one's own body, then to all of samsara is completely abandoned, and finally all mental prejudices are eliminated. During the initial stage, one gains insight into the four objects of close contemplation (*dran-pa'i nye-bar bzhag-pa bzhi*). During the intermediate stage, the four states of complete abandonment (*yang-dag spong-ba bzhi*) are attained. And during the final stage, the four states of samadhi (*rdzu-'phrul-gyi rkang-*

pa bzhi) are achieved. These three attainments are the source of:

1. All paths to the wisdom of the Buddha,
2. All paths of perseverance, and
3. All paths to single-pointed concentration.

One who attains the initial stage regards the human body as a magnet for suffering and is thus able to abandon most kleshas. One's only concern becomes the attainment of freedom. Miraculous powers and clairvoyance are another result of the attainment of this path. After becoming aware of these attainments of the Shravakas, there is no excuse for ever looking down on the Hinayana path.

B. PATH OF PREPARATION (*SBYOR-LAM*)

On this path one develops a clearer understanding of shunyata, for one's former understanding was stained with preconceptions. The path is divided into four stages: heat (*drod*), peak (*rtse-mo*), patience (*bzod*), and supreme worldly Dharma (*chos-mchog*), beginning with the practice of meditation at the heat stage. Through these stages, the five powers (*dbang-po lnga*) and the five forces (*stobs lnga*) are attained. These will all be explained at a later point.

C. THE PATH OF INSIGHT (*MTHONG-LAM*)

With the attainment of this path one gains pure understanding of shunyata, devoid of any false concepts. One then becomes an Arya and is able to abandon all coarse mental obstacles, but not inherent kleshas. To abandon these one needs even deeper understanding of shunyata.

D. THE PATH OF MEDITATION (*SGOM-LAM*)

It is while following this path that the inherent kleshas are abandoned. At the beginning of one's practice, the grossest kleshas are combatted by the weakest mental power, then as one progresses on this path, the more subtle kleshas are dispelled by an ever stronger force of the mind. Whenever one experiences suffering or feels disturbed, klesha has arisen. Asanga wrote, "When klesha arises, there comes a change from the normal condition of mind, which is apparent even on one's face." Step by step one abandons the kleshas of the realm of desire (*'dod-pa'i nyon-mongs skor-dgu*) of the realm of form (*gzugs-med-kyi nyon-mongs skor-dgu*) and of the formless realm (*gzugs-med-kyi nyon-mongs skor-dgu*). There are nine types of obstacles in each realm, which are divided into the levels of great, medium and small, then again sub-divided into a total of nine levels. When all of these have been abandoned, one attains the final path of no more learning (*mi-slob lam*) and becomes an Arhat.

II. THE FIVE PATHS OF THE PRATYEKABUDDHAS
(*RANG-RGYAL-GYI SA-LAM*)

The only difference between the paths of the Pratyeka-buddhas and those of the Shravakas is that the former collect merit for many ages, whereas the latter do not. The Pratyekabuddhas are known for their ability to impart teachings without using words, and they remain alone in the forest like the rhinoceros.

15
The Five Paths of the Mahayana

The Mahayana called 'great' for the following reasons:

1. The aim is great, because it is for the benefit of all sentient beings.
2. The purpose is great, for it leads to the omniscient state.
3. The effort is great.
4. The ultimate goal is great, because it is Buddhahood rather than mere freedom from samsara.
5. The concern is great, as it is for all sentient beings.
6. The enthusiasm is great, as the practice is not regarded as a hardship.

Bodhisattvas look for opportunities to help others, and take joy in doing so, whereas Hinayanists are concerned primarily with their own attainment.

There are two ways of spiritual development within the Mahayana, called the Paramitayana and Mantrayana (tantra). Both of them follow the five paths of the Mahayana (*theg-chen gyi sa-lam*). The former is like taking a roundabout route to one's destination, and the latter is like taking all the short-cuts. Before practising tantra, one must have a clear general understanding of the Paramitayana, the five paths and the ten Bodhisattva grounds.

The Tibetan word for these paths is 'sa-lam' meaning 'grounds and paths'. They are called 'grounds' because each stage is a foundation of wisdom which supports all further growth of insight. 'Path' here means the development of a state of consciousness which has been grasped by the force of renunciation. 'Path', 'ground' and 'wisdom' all have the same meaning in this case. It is absolutely necessary to follow a path in one's Dharma practice.

A. THE PATH OF ACCUMULATION (*TSHOGS-LAM*)

During this initial path, one develops love and mercy by meditating on the suffering of all beings. Not being able to bear this suffering, one generates a strong wish to liberate all sentient beings and, by the time this path has been attained, one has a firm development of bodhichitta. Bodhichitta is then not a contrived motivation, but a natural one which accompanies one always. From this point until enlightenment, bodhichitta continues to grow in intensity and is the impetus for attaining ever greater wisdom by means of hearing, contemplation and meditation. The practice of collecting merit with this motivation is a true basis for all further development.

The path of accumulation is divided into three stages of development. Bodhichitta and the four objects of close contemplation are attained during the initial stage (*tshogs-lam chung-ngu*). The four objects of contemplation are the body (*lus*), feelings (*tshor-ba*) the mind (*sems*), and all phenomena (*chos*). One meditates on the body in order to realize its impurity, on feelings to realize that they are all unsatisfactory, on the mind to realize that it is a stream of momentary changes (thus changing the belief that it is permanent), and on all phenomena to realize their non-self-existence. The characteristics of impermanence, suffering, voidness, and non-self-existence are found to be true for each of these objects.

By meditating closely on the body, one gains a clear understanding of the first noble truth, the truth of suffering. Most people are attached to their present bodies and wish for permanent life, but with this meditation one develops a strong wish for liberation.

This leads one to seek out the cause of suffering, and by meditating on the different feelings, one sees that suffering is caused by the desires which arise from them. The actual feeling itself is not the cause (Buddha, too, has feelings), but one needs to abandon any feeling of joy or sorrow which causes desire.

After recognizing this second noble truth, one meditates on the mind, and thus gains insight into the third noble truth of the cessation of suffering. One comes to realize that there is no permanent independent self to be grasped, but that there does exist a momentary, relative self.

The fourth object of contemplation includes all secondary consciousnesses except feeling. By meditating on the virtuous and non-virtuous states of secondary consciousness and weighing them in the mind, one sees the reasons for following virtue, and thus arrives at an understanding of the truth of the path to the cessation of suffering.

There are many reasons for meditating on the body. When it is recognized as the source of suffering, the urge to sever the rope of karma and be rid of the delusions which bind one grows. One may feel proud of one's pure physical form, but if each part of the body is examined, one realizes that beauty pertains only to the skin that covers it. If all bodily matter were taken out of its bag of skin, one would be revolted by it. Only the skin, form and life are attractive; if one sees a corpse or skeleton, one feels disgusted. One should constantly be mindful of the points developed during these meditations.

The study of the Buddha nature (*sangs-rgyas-kyi rigs*) complements that of the five paths. The mind is temporarily clouded by a veil of delusion which can be removed. To do so, one needs to know what paths to follow. If it is not known that one possesses this essence, one's Dharma practice is based on blind faith. There is always room for mental progress. At birth people cannot think or talk, but later they are almost like different beings—and the growth goes on. At death, one should at least be on this first path, enabling one to proceed in the next life.

All teachings deal with the three principles of the path, the essence of the Dharma, and in order to attain the first path one needs relative understanding of these. Only when one has developed pure renunciation and seeks either liberation or enlightenment, has one entered the path. There are many methods of attaining prosperity, but only one's internal practice gives true happiness. For this one needs to rely on external teachings (oral and scriptural), the concepts of which must be embodied in one's own practice. One must develop understanding of the three principles of the path and attain perfect renunciation for the sake of all sentient beings. When this is accomplished, the path of accumulation is attained.

Contemplation of the five paths also · helps one to understand the Three Refuges. While meditating on the qualities of the Aryas, one realises that they first attained the path of accumulation, and in order to have deep faith in them, one needs to know what they attained and how they attained it. With understanding of the five paths and ten Bodhisattva stages one has a clear outline of what one will be doing in the future and what obstacles lie ahead. All the paths and stages are experienced by one stream of consciousness; that is, there are no breaks from one level to the next.

When the intermediate stage of the path of accumulation has been completed, one no longer has selfishly-motivated thoughts (such as of seeking one's own liberation) and the four states of complete abandonment have been attained. These four include:

1. Abandoning non-virtuous actions before they occur.
2. Abandoning non-virtuous actions which occur to the mind.
3. Developing virtuous actions which have not yet occurred to the mind.
4. Cultivating virtuous actions that have already been developed.

Before attaining any of the paths, one needs to be able to discriminate between virtuous and non-virtuous thoughts and actions. A simple guide-line is 'whatever non-virtues are committed result in unhappiness, and any action that causes happiness is virtue.' By meditating on the effects of different actions, both virtuous and non-virtuous, one gains a clear understanding of virtue and non-virtue. By knowing its effects, one will avoid non-virtue just as one would avoid entering the car of a drunken driver.

The understanding of the four noble truths gained during the initial stage induces enthusiastic perseverance to attain the four states of abandonment. The bodhichitta developed during the first stage is like the earth, the foundation of all further attainment, and that of the intermediate stage is likened to pure gold. During the initial stage, if one meets with a very evil person and feels that one cannot in any way help him, one's bodhichitta has been destroyed and one may fall back to the Hinayana path. During the second stage, there is no longer any danger of this happening.

Someone once approached Shariputra, one of the chief disciples of Buddha Shakyamuni, and asked him for his right hand. Shariputra immediately cut it off and held it out to him with his other hand. The person, actually a manifestation of mara, then refused to accept it since Shariputra had been so discourteous as to give it to him with his left hand. Shariputra then became very discouraged and wondered, "How can I ever develop bodhichitta when there are such evil people in the world?" As soon as this attitude arose, his bodhichitta faded and he took to the Hinayana path. If it faded even for him, we must be all the more careful to guard our bodhichitta at a time when the world is so full of evil people.

When the pandit Dignaga was beginning to write his great text on logic, he first wrote the salutation to the objects of refuge, then went away for a short time. In the meantime a non-Buddhist erased what he had written, so when he returned, he wrote it again. And again the non-Buddhist erased it. Dignaga then challenged him to come out in the open and debate with him. The challenge was accepted, but when he was defeated by Dignaga, the non-Buddhist took revenge by producing fire from his mouth and burning his robe. In despair, Dignaga threw his slate up in the air, saying that if it fell to the earth, he would follow the Hinayana path. Manjushri then appeared, and held it aloft, while giving him words of guidance. One must especially follow Bodhisattva conduct when confronted with those who are rough and delight in evil.

During the final stage of the path of accumulation, the four states of samadhi, literally 'the four legs of miraculous action' are attained. These are the four main methods, or legs, which support the full attainment of single-pointed concentration, although there are many other factors involved besides. One may then go to the celestial spheres to make offerings and acquire merit, and all one's spiritual friends and statues of the Buddha are seen as actual Buddhas (not in their ordinary form, but in the nirmanakaya). One's bodhichitta at this stage is like a new moon, which increases steadily until full enlightenment.

While traversing all of the five paths, one needs the use of the power of samadhi, and this is attained during this stage. The four kinds of samadhi are defined as 'meditational knowledge having the eight powers of single-pointed concentration, being devoid of the five interferences.' They include the following:

1. The samadhi of intention. Like the wood needed for building a fire, this is strong intention to attain samadhi.
2. The samadhi of enthusiastic perseverance.
3. The samadhi of the mind. This is the realization of the inherent potential of the mind. Sakya Pandita

wrote, "Even if you are going to die tomorrow, never stop meditating or acquiring new knowledge." Do not demand results in this life, but know that by meditating one will gain familiarity with the practice which will ensure fast progress in the next life.

4. The samadhi of examination. With this ability one examines and tests the teachings on samadhi given by the guru. One also tests one's own level of attainment of samadhi, watching for interferences and applying skilful antidotes to aid progress.

Just as love and mercy are called conquerors since those who attain them become conquerors, so do many terms, including the above four, refer both to the means and their fruits.

The reason for learning of these stages of the path of accumulation is to become acquainted with the progress of one's future development. During the initial stage, one has the seeds for the attainments of all three stages, but lacks the power needed to realize them. By developing close contemplation on the four objects, one gains understanding of the four noble truths, and this leads to the attainment of the power of abandonment. The first two noble truths are to be abandoned and the latter two are to be adopted. The purpose of the four states of samadhi is to attain the power to abandon gross kleshas and all attachment to samsaric pleasures.

Signs of the various stages are experienced as progress is made through them. With the attainment of the initial stage one has complete, almost instinctive, understanding of which acts are unskilful, and one firmly establishes oneself in those that are skilful. During the intermediate stage, one minutely follows the course of cause and effect and by being constantly aware of this, all one's actions become skilful. In the final stage, one attains the ability to remain in samadhi at all times. Whenever one wishes to examine anything, the full power of concentration is there for use. One also has 'the ability to remember all streams of knowledge' (*chos-rgyun-gyi ting-nye-'dzin*), never forgetting any of the teachings one has received. Finally, one is able to listen to spiritual teachers and Buddhas while seeing them in their enlightened forms. Two people who have both attained the path of accumulation can feel each other's physical vibrations and instinctively recognize each other's attainment, whereas one at a lower spiritual level cannot.

When this path has been fully attained, one should break meditation and acquire much merit by doing preliminary practices (such as prostrations, offering the mandala, and taking refuge). After this, one should begin meditating on shunyata and thus enter the next path.

B. THE PATH OF PREPARATION (*SBYOR-LAM*)

The first two of the five paths are called the paths of ordinary individuals. The difference between the first and the second is like that between the earth and space. Although the practice remains the same, during the second path one develops much greater insight into shunyata. The path of preparation includes all the levels of development from the attainment of the wisdom that is gained by means of meditation at the heat stage to that gained at the stage called the supreme worldly Dharma. The full development of samsaric meditational wisdom is completed during this path. As progress is made along the path of preparation, one's mental forces grow and the mind becomes purified. When this path is completed, the samsaric path comes to an end and that of the Aryas begins.

The path of preparation is made up of four stages, graded according to one's degree of insight into shunyata.

1. The wisdom of the heat stage (*drod*). This wisdom aids in abandoning kleshas, but during this stage one may still hold wrong views. In the same way that a boxer takes on certain opponents that he can overcome but leaves others to fight with a stronger adversary, so are different kleshas combatted at different stages along the paths, depending on the strength of one's opponent forces.
2. The wisdom of the peak (*rtze-mo*). Having attained single-pointed wisdom, one totally abandons the extremes of nihilism and positivism and thus discards the seeds of wrong views.
3. The stage of patience (*bzod-pa*). At this stage one is assured of never again taking rebirth in any of the three lower states. All fears of losing one's self-identity are abandoned, and one has a great capacity to take on suffering.
4. The wisdom of the supreme worldly Dharma (*chos-mchog*). The great value of having a human body is illustrated by the fact that this wisdom is attained solely by humans in the realm of desire. Other beings, such as devas and those in the formless realms, cannot attain this fourth stage because they have little knowledge of suffering and thus a low potential for renunciation. Beings in the form and formless realms experience no suffering, but when their lives come to an end, they may take rebirth in any realm. The human form is the best for attaining liberation.

During the first two stages, one attains the five powers needed for the development of the understanding of the Aryas. All people have these powers now, but their full potential does not become manifest until the attainment of this path. They include the following:

1. Faith (*dad-pa'i dbang-po*). This is strong conviction in the truth of the law of cause and effect and the four noble truths.
2. Armour-like perseverance (*brtzon-'grus-kyi dbang-po*). This is the perseverance of well-trained Bodhisattvas, who have the wish to remain for aeons in the three lower stages of rebirth if this would benefit even one sentient being.
3. Keeping in mind the characteristic of the four noble truths (*dran-pa'i dbang-po*).
4. The combination of shamatha and vipashyana (*ting-nye-'dzin-gyi dbang-po*).
5. The ability to examine the void nature of the four noble truths (*shes-rab-kyi dbang-po*).

These five powers are developed during the path of preparation and are retained thereafter until the attainment of enlightenment.

The five forces, which correspond directly with the five powers, are gained during the second two stages of this path. Once the five powers are developed, their opposites (faithlessness, laziness and so forth) may only arise during post-meditation periods. With the attainment of the five forces, they no longer arise at any time. The five forces include the five powers (but not vice versa) and are defined as kinds of wisdom which cannot be overcome by any of their opponents. They bring one to a quick attainment of the next path, which occurs during meditation at the end of the path of preparation, when one feels competent to attain full realization of shunyata.

C. THE PATH OF INSIGHT (*MTHONG-LAM*)

The definition of this path is the actual understanding of truth, or shunyata. Before its attainment, shunyata is confused with one's impression or image (*don-spyi*) of it. The difference is like that between recalling the visage of a friend and actually seeing him. From the guru's teaching on shunyata, one forms an impression of it which is mistaken for shunyata itself. This is abandoned when shunyata is experienced directly. According to the Prasangikas, all states of consciousness of ordinary beings, including their sensory consciousness, are deceptive, and this is due to their confusing truth with their conception of it. The Aryas, or those who have attained the path of insight, have two states of consciousness. They have non-deceptive understanding of shunyata, but deceptive consciousness of the five senses as well as instinctive kleshas.

Attaining the path of insight involves seeing the bare truth for the first time, and it is on this path that all intellectually-formed kleshas (*kun-btags*), which arise from invalid reasoning, are eliminated. For example, when one sees a table, one automatically thinks that it exists independently; this tendency is an inborn klesha. Believing by relying on reasons that it exists as such is an intellectually-formed klesha.

Upon attainment of the path of insight, one is freed forever from throwing karma, which is caused by self-grasping. After this, there is no chance of rebirth in any of the three lower realms. Since the force of throwing karma has been destroyed, one has control over one's future rebirth.

During this path the seven causes of enlightenment (*byang-chub yan-lag bdun*) are attained. The Tibetan term for 'enlightenment' (*byang-chub*) is a composite of two terms meaning 'freedom from both kinds of kleshas' and 'the ability to encompass all that is to be known within one's wisdom.' These seven characteristics that are the exclusive attainments of Aryas are as follows:

1. Memory as a pure cause of enlightenment (*dran-pa yang-dag*). This is the non-samsaric form of pure memory. One who attains it never forgets further goals or virtuous conduct.
2. Discriminating wisdom and direct, fresh understanding of non-self-existence (*chos rab-tu rnam-'byed*).
3. Pure enthusiastic perseverance (*brtson-'grus yang-dag*). This perseverance is more intense than that of earlier paths.
4. A pure state of gladness (*dga'-ba yang-dag*). This is both a mental and physical happiness which one never experiences until the attainment of this path. The word 'pure' when applied to these terms means 'non-samsaric'. That which is samsaric is stained by self-grasping, or the instincts of ignorance. For example, if one goes to a magic show and is taken in by the illusions, one's reaction is samsaric.
5. Pure ecstasy (*shin-tu sbyangs-pa yang-dag*). This is more intense than the ecstasy that results from the attainment of Shamatha.
6. Samadhi (*ting-nge-'dzin*).
7. A pure state of equanimity (*btang-snyoms*). During this state one has relative freedom from obstacles. One of the signs of having attained this path is that one no longer experiences physical suffering. There is then no difficulty in giving away one's body or cutting off one's limbs if this would benefit other sentient beings. Freedom from the following five states of fear is also attained:

    (a) Fear of not obtaining food and clothing. These come naturally without effort.
    (b) Fear of expressing thoughts to large groups of people. One receives direct teachings from the

Buddhas and is able to establish close communication with other people.

(c) Fear of death. One is able to choose one's own time of death, for this is no longer governed by the force of karma or klesha.

(d) Fear of birth in the three lower states. One has great confidence in the fact that all one's seeds for low birth have been destroyed.

(e) Fear of teaching to the very learned. One does so with complete relaxation, confidence and assurance of one's understanding of shunyata.

On the path of insight, one hundred and ten qualities are attained. They include the ability to pass through concrete objects, to see one hundred Buddhas at one time and receive teachings from them, non-samsaric clairvoyance, and the ability to manifest oneself in a hundred forms at once in order to help others.

D. THE PATH OF MEDITATION (*SGOM-LAM*)

During this path, one develops greater acquaintance (*sgom*) with shunyata. The initial realization of it is like meeting a person for whom one has been waiting for a long time. Thereafter, one needs to live with him and come to know him well in order to be fully benefitted by him. There is much to be attained on this path, including almost all the Bodhisattva stages. Only the first Arya Bodhisattva stage, or bhumi (literally meaning 'earth' or 'ground') is attained during the path of insight.

The following are the essential definitions of the five Mahayana paths, listed in order:

1. Direct understanding of the Dharma (*chos mngon-rtogs*).

2. Direct understanding of the profound meaning of the Dharma, as opposed to the mere literal meaning (*don mngon-rtogs*).
3. Direct understanding of truth (*bden-pa mngon-rtogs*).
4. Post-meditational direct understanding of truth (*rjes-la mngon-rtogs*).
5. The wisdom of the abandonment of both types of mental obstacles (*sgrib-gnyis spong-ba'i mkhyen-pa*). This is not a characteristic of the Hinayana fifth path.

By following the path of meditation, fulfilment of the eight-fold path (*'phags-lam yan-lag brgyad*) is attained. This includes the following branches:

1. Perfect view (*yang-dag-pa'i lta-ba*) or the wisdom arising from the realization of shunyata.
2. The intention of Bodhisattvas to express their understanding (specifically of shunyata) to others (*yang-dag-pa'i rtog-pa*).
3. Giving precise teachings on shunyata, presented in an orderly manner, free of contradictions (*yang-dag-pa'i ngag*).
4. Perfect physical action, including complete restraint from the ten non-virtues (*yang-dag-pa'i las-kyi-mtha'*).
5. Perfect livelihood (*yang-dag-pa'i 'tshor-ba*). This is completely free of the following five wrong ways of acquiring things:

   (a) Putting on an act in order to impress others and thereby gain something.
   (b) Giving something in the hope of receiving more in return.
   (c) Flattering in order to gain some desired object.
   (d) Implying or hinting at a desire in the hope of its thereby being fulfilled.

(e) Using an invalid excuse in order to exploit others.

6. The effort to abandon all inborn kleshas (*yang-dag-pa'i) rtsol-ba*).
7. Memory more highly developed than during the lower stages (*yang-dag-pa'i dran-pa*).
8. The use of samadhi for the attainment of the full clairvoyance of the Buddhas (*yang-dag-pa'i ting-nge-'dzin*). With this attainment, one knows the thoughts of others as easily as seeing the reflection of a light shining on a mirror. The Buddhas never neglect to help these who are ripe, and their ability to know which beings can be helped is developed on this path.

Once the two types of mental obscuration have been eliminated, they never return. Intellectually-formed kleshas and inborn kleshas are called kleshavarana (*nyon-sgrib*). Instinctive mental obscuration, which is abandoned only by the Fully Enlightened Ones, is called jneyavarana (*shes-sgrib*). This may be likened to the odour of a mothball which lingers on after the mothball (the kleshavarana) has been removed. Only during the eighth Bodhisattvabhumi does one begin to eliminate the instinctive mental obscurations.

There are two kinds of Bodhisattvas. The first completes all the Hinayana stages of development, then goes on to start from the beginning of the Mahayana practices. The second engages from the outset of their spiritual practice in the Mahayana paths, seeking the liberation of all. When the former attains just the first stage of the Mahayana path of accumulation, he is free of all coarse delusions, whereas the latter is not.

The branches of the noble eight-fold path fall into the following four categories:

1. The method of cutting the root of ignorance (*gcad-pa byed-pa'i yan-lag*). The first of the eight branches is included here.
2. The method of imparting understanding to others (*go-bar byed-pa'i yan-lag*). The second branch falls into this category.
3. The method of bringing others to a strong conviction about the truth of the Dharma, thereby causing them to mould their lives into perfect examples of the Teachings (*yid-ches-pa'i yan-lag*). The third, fourth and fifth branches are included here.
4. The method of applying opponent powers to kleshas (*gnyen-po'i yan-lag*). The remaining branches fall into this category.

The eight branches may also be divided into the three trainings of the Buddha's teachings (*bsal-pa gsum*). There is no understanding of either the literal truth of the teachings (*lung-gi bden-pa*), or the truth apprehended through direct insight (*rtogs-pa'i bden-pa*), that is not included in these three trainings. The relationship between the three trainings is shown in the Wheel of the Chakra kings, a common symbol for the Buddha's Dharma. The fourth and fifth branches are aspects of the training in moral discipline (*bslab-pa tshul-khrim-kyi bslab-pa*) symbolized by the hub of the wheel. The eighth branch is the fulfilment of the training in concentration (*bslab-pa ting-nge-'dzin-gyi gslab-pa*), represented by the rim of the wheel (meaning that it encloses all attention). The remaining branches are aspects of the training in wisdom (*bslab-pa shes-rab-kyi bslab-pa*), represented by the spikes protruding from the wheel (showing that it destroys all its opponents). The eight branches are symbolized by the eight spokes.

The first four of the five paths are Bodhisattva paths, and the last is the path of the Buddhas. The first two paths are those of ordinary Bodhisattvas, and the next two are those of the Arya Bodhisattva. One who follows these latter two paths has the understanding with which one attains enlightenment for the benefit of all sentient beings. One's sole motivation is love and mercy for all sentient beings, and this is reinforced by the power of one's true understanding of shunyata. All the types of wisdom of the Arya Bodhisattvas (such as love and mercy) are not necessarily combined with true understanding of shunyata, but they are grasped by the power of this understanding. At the beginning of the path of insight one becomes an Arya Bodhisattva, and the first of the ten Bodhisattvabhumis or stages is attained.

16
The Ten Bodhisattvabhumis

In order to understand these stages, one first needs understanding of the six perfections and the four additional Perfections of method, power, prayer and transcending awareness (*ye-shes*). These four are in fact aspects of the sixth perfection. The final one, which is awareness of all there is to be known, is the tenth Perfection and the direct cause of enlightenment. The following are brief explanations of the ten Bodhisattvabhumis (*byan-sa bcu*):

1. The Joyful One (*rab-tu dga-'ba*). With the attain-ment of this stage, one feels like a beggar who has found a treasure, for one realizes that one's wishes for oneself and for others can be fulfilled.
2. The Stainless One (*dri-ma med-pa*). At this stage, all non-virtuous acts are abandoned.
3. The Illuminating One (*'od-byed-pa*). During this stage, glimpses of enlightenment are gained, which, like the rising of the sun, burn away many kleshas.
4. The Radiant One (*'od-'phro-ba*). The light of one's understanding of shunyata now radiates in all directions and can be used in many ways.
5. The One Difficult to Conquer (*shin-tu sbyangs-dka'-ba*). During this stage, all the difficult obstacles to meditation are overcome.
6. The One Becoming Clearly Obvious (*mngon-du gyur-ba*). Understanding of samsara and nirvana now becomes ever more clear.
7. The One Which Goes Far (*ring-du song-ba*). During this stage, one moves far away from the Hinayana motivation. In a hundredth part of an instant (an instant being the duration of a snap of the fingers)

one is able to enter and rise from shunyata meditation.

8. The Unshakable One (*mi-g.yo-ba*). One's thoughts now become steady and unmoved by disturbing prejudices.

9. The One Having Good Discrimination (*legs-pa'i blo-gros*). Words, their meanings, and four other things are understood during this stage.

10. Cloud of Dharma (*chos-kyi sprin*). Just as rain falls from a cloud bringing crops to fruition, one with this attainment is motivated by a cloud of love and mercy to help and teach others by drawing from one's experience.

The first stage involves a development of wisdom coupled with the perfect practice of the first perfection and the following stages likewise correspond with the remaining nine perfections. Each stage comprises the following three phases:

(a) An uninterrupted phase free of all interferences.
(b) A phase of separation.
(c) A post-meditational phase.

During the first phase, one overcomes specific kleshas or obstacles; during the second, complete freedom from them is attained; and during the third, one rises from meditation on shunyata and acquires physical merit, such as by making pujas and doing prostrations in preparation for advancing to the next stage.

The definition of the uninterrupted phase of the first stage is 'the wisdom of perfect understanding of shunyata, which destroys the belief in independent self-existence'. This phase forms an unbroken link between the path of insight and the path of meditation. The last phase of the path of preparation and the initial and intermediate phases of the path of insight are all attained during one meditation period. During each of the stages, certain kinds of kleshas are abandoned, each stage having its own share of opponents (*rang-gi ngos-skal-gyi spong ba*). Each stage of the gradual process of eliminating ever finer subtleties of klesha is like casting water on a fire directly in front of one rather than trying to douse the fire in all directions at time (that is, tryingto eliminate all kinds of klesha at once). Intellectually-formed delusions (about the nature of shunyata) are the type which are eliminated during the initial stage of the first stage, and during the second stage, the abandonment of innate (inborn) delusions concerning independent self-existence is begun. The former type of delusion being of a grosser nature, it is more easily abandoned than the latter. At first one believes in the existence of a true, independent self, but upon recognizing impermanence, doubt arises. When first seeing a heap of stones upon a distant mountain, one may mistake it for a man. But having some doubt, one draws closer and closer until finally its true nature is discovered. In the same way these delusions are dispelled by applying the logic of the four-Point Analysis. However, these delusions are not totally abandoned during the initial stage. Like a thief put out of a door which is not locked behind him, they may return until complete freedom from them has been attained during the second stage.

During the path of insight, eight kinds of patience (*bzod-pa-brgyad*), are attained, which act as opponent forces against one's delusions concerning the four noble truths. Of these, the first four (*chos-bzod*) are the opponent forces for the delusions of the realm of desire, and the latter (*rjes-bzod*) four are the opponents of the delusions of the realms of form and formlessness. These latter are applied only after the delusions of the realm of desire have been conquered. In this way eight types of understanding (*shes-pa brgyad*) are attained. The first four (*chos-shes*) are the result of the abandonment of the delusions of the realms of desire, and the latter four (*rjes-shes*), of abandoning the delusions of the form and formless realms. During the path of meditation, there are one hundred and eight inborn delusions to be abandoned, and these are divided into nine categories, ranging from the coarsest to the subtlest of delusions. These categories are named as follows: (1) the coarse of the coarse, (2) the intermediate of the coarse, (3) the subtle of the coarse, (4) the coarse of the intermediate, (5) the intermediate of the intermediate, (6) the subtle of the intermediate, (7) the coarse of the subtle, (8) the intermediate of the subtle, and (9) the subtle of the subtle. All of the coarse of the coarse delusions are abandoned during the first stage, the intermediate of the coarse during the second, and so forth, with one category corresponding to each of the stages. By the end of the path of meditation, all kleshavarana are eliminated.

The uninterrupted stage of the tenth stage (*rgyun-mtha'i bar-chad med-lam*) is followed by complete separation from all jneyavarana, and enlightenment, which goes beyond this final stage, is attained.

17
The Four Buddhakayas

The four kayas, or bodies of a Buddha (*sangs-rgyas kyi sku-bzhi*), which are attained upon full enlightenment, are as follows:

A. The svabhavikakaya (*ngo-bo-nyid sku*) or nature body, is the void nature of the Buddha's omniscient mind (or wisdom).
B. The jnana-dharmakaya (*ye-shes chos-sku or rnam-mkhyen*) or wisdom truth body, is the conscious state of the Buddha's mind, which understands all there is to know. This is attained solely by the Buddhas.
C. The sambhogakaya (*longs-sku*), or body of bliss, is a psychic form, existing not as flesh and bones nor as a result of karma and klesha but rather due to the force of physical and mental merits. The following are five certain conditions that accompany the sambhogakaya:

1. Place. Those who attain this body always remain in the clear, non-samsaric Buddha fields.
2. Discourses. They teach only Mahayana since no one but Arya Bodhisattvas can hear them.
3. Physical form. The thirty-two major and eighty minor marks are always present.
4. Circle of disciples. This consists only of Arya Bodhisattvas.
5. Time. Their lifespan lasts until samsara's end. This duration cannot be reckoned by our standards, but since all sentient beings have Buddha nature, all can eventually attain enlightenment.

All statues and images of Buddhas belong to this kaya, but their real nature is not visible due to the impurities of our minds. The sambhogakaya is the physical form of the

Buddha's wisdom and, in tantric teachings, is known as the vajra of speech or as the voice of the Buddha.

D. The nirmanakaya (*sprul-sku*) or emanation body, is the transformation of the sambhogakaya into ordinary physical form. The five certain conditions do not apply to it, but it is, nevertheless a true manifestation of the Buddha, and its purpose is to enable a Buddha to communicate with those sentient beings having lesser attainment than that of the Arya Bodhisattvas. Those with pure karma are able to see the nirmanakaya form (the practice of guru devotion is very important in this respect), whereas others see only an ordinary sentient being. There are many examples of this. For instance, Asanga was able to see Maitreya only after making intensive efforts to purify his mind. The great disciple of Je Tsong Khapa, Khaydrub Je, who was himself a manifestation of Vajrapani, saw his master in his sambhogakaya form as Manjushri. Regardless of the level of attainment of the guru, as the disciple reaches greater and greater attainment, he sees his guru in the form of correspondingly higher kayas. When a preta comes upon the Ganges, he sees only sand, blood and pus, whereas humans see water, and devas see heavenly nectar. This depends solely on one's karma.

There are three kinds of nirmanakaya:

1. The first or supreme kind (*mchog-sku*) always appear as bhikkshus, complete with the thirty-two major and eighty minor marks. Such nirmanakayas, of which the Buddha Shakyamuni was one, always enact twelve major deeds for the sake of helping sentient beings. Whether or not his form appears on earth, the Enlightened Teacher's abode is the Akanishta heaven (*'og-min*).

2. The second way in which the nirmanakaya manifests is in the form of master craftsmen (*bzo-bo sku*). For example, Buddha Shakyamuni before his enlightenment once took form as a musician. At that time there was a certain deva who was very proud of his great skill at playing the lute. Buddha challenged him and they matched their abilities, playing first with all the strings, then with fewer and fewer. The deva was still able to play beautifully with only one string, but he became the loser and his pride was deflated when Shakyamuni continued to play after all the strings of his lute had been cut. The sculptor (*bzo rgyal-bu shva-karma*) of the famous Buddha figure in Lhasa was also such a nirmanakaya.

3. The third kind of nirmanakaya acts as a host in the deva realms (*skye-ba sprul-sku*). Any Universal Teacher must first be the host in Tushita heaven, acting as a religious guide for the devas. That is where Maitreya is now.

The nirmanakaya is the person, or personality, of the Buddha (*sangs-rgyas-kyi gang-zag*) but his actual body and voice do not belong to any of the four kayas.

18
Buddhahood

One who has attained full enlightenment, or Buddhahood (*sangs-rgyas kyi go-'pang*), is endowed with:

A. Ten powers of understanding.
B. Four kinds of fearlessness.
C. Four specific kinds of knowledge.
D. Eighteen kinds of knowledge that are exclusive to the Buddhas.

These are explained as follows:

A. THE TEN POWERS OF UNDERSTANDING

1. (*gnas-dang gnas ma-yin-pa mkhyen-pa'i stobs*). Understanding that virtuous actions must inevitably produce the fruit of happiness (for example, selfless giving leads to the attainment of wealth) and that they cannot possibly result in suffering (although this may superficially appear to occur at times).
2. (*las-kyi rnam-pa smin-pa mkhyen-pa'i stobs*). Understanding the ripening force of karma. The Buddhas are able to trace the causes in former lives of even such things as facial features, ailments, and so forth. All phenomena have their causes and no suffering occurs without its causes of non-virtuous action.
3. (*mos-pa sna-tshogs mkhyen-pa'i stobs*). Understanding the dispositions of individual sentient beings. Buddhas know the capacities and abilities of each being and can adapt their teaching accordingly.
4. (*khams sna-tshogs mkhyen-pa'i stobs*). Understanding the likings and potential for spiritual growth of each sentient being, thus knowing the most effective

methods for revealing each individual's Buddha nature.

5. (*dbang-po mchog-dang mchog ma-yin-pa mkhyen pa'i stobs*). Understanding the different levels of intelligence of sentient beings and teaching them accordingly.

6. (*thams-cad-du 'gro-ba'i lam-mkhyen-pa'i stobs*). Understanding the different spiritual paths and where they lead. The Mahayana path leads to enlightenment for the sake of all sentient beings, and the Shravaka and Pratyekabuddha paths lead to personal liberation.

7. (*kun-nas nyon-mongs-pa rnam-par sbyang-ba mkhyen-pa'i stobs*). Understanding that which is to be abandoned and that which is to be practised.

8. (*sngon-gyi gnas rjes-su dran-pa'i stobs*). The ability to remember the past lives of sentient beings. During the time of Buddha Shakyamuni, there was a bhikkshu who, no matter how hard he tried, could gain no attainment while sitting in meditation. The Buddha examined his past lives and, finding that he had been born a bull many times in succession, told him to meditate while lying down, as a bull usually rests. Arhats, too, can remember some past lives, but the Buddhas are able to look back much further into the past.

9. (*'chi 'pho-ba-dang skye-ba mkhyen-pa'i stobs*). The power to foretell all states of future existence and the place of death of all sentient beings. The Buddha sends forth rays that reach all sentient beings and are then reabsorbed into their source. If these rays strike one's knees, one's next rebirth will be in one of the three lower realms; if at the heart, the human realm; if at the throat, the deva realm, and if at the usnisa (crown of the head), in one of the higher deva realms. Much that came to pass in

Tibet, Buddha Shakyamuni prophesied and in his incarnation as Padmasambhava, made many prophesies about the future.

10. (*zag-pa zad-pa mkhyen-pa'i stobs*). The power to see which kleshas and obstacles each sentient being has overcome.

B. THE FOUR KINDS OF FEARLESSNESS

1. Fearlessness in expressing one's own intuitive understanding before all sentient beings, including Enlightened Ones.
2. Fearlessness in guaranteeing that one has abandoned all the obstacles to be abandoned.
3. Fearlessness in stating what sentient beings must abandon in order to progress spiritually.
4. Fearlessness in explaining which opponent powers are to be used against kleshas. For example, understanding of shunyata is the cure for instinctive kleshas and bodhichitta is the cure for ordinary kleshas.

C. THE FOUR SPECIFIC KINDS OF KNOWLEDGE

These four, relating to the spoken word and its meaning, are attained not only by Buddhas but also by Arhats and Arya Bodhisattvas who have abandoned kleshavarana.

1. Undeluded knowledge of the right means of communication.
2. Undeluded knowledge of the specific and general meanings of words.
3. Undeluded discriminating ability to understand all aspects of things.

4. Knowledge of the structure of words as opposed to random sounds.

D. THE EIGHTEEN KINDS OF KNOWLEDGE EXCLUSIVE TO THE BUDDHAS

The first six of these attainments are governed by the Buddha's action (that is, supreme Bodhisattva conduct).

1. The ability always to remain calm, free of any disturbed physical reactions.
2. Freedom from disturbed vocal responses in reaction to such things as danger.
3. Never-decreasing memory. The Buddha's total awareness is like the sun shining on all sentient beings. The more one removes the obstacles standing between one and his light, the more one shall be able to receive his blessings, for the Buddha never fails to help ripened beings.
4. Unbroken contemplation of shunyata. For the Buddhas there is no division between meditation and post-meditation periods, and they are able to do many things simultaneously.
5. Freedom from the concept of the independent self-existence of that which is to be abandoned and that which is to be practised, and of the attainment of enlightenment.
6. Never feeling indifferent towards any sentient beings, but always being ready to examine each individual's abilities, likings and disposition in order to give him all possible aid in advancing his spiritual growth.

It is helpful to meditate on the above six qualities when taking refuge. It is essential that an object of refuge be free of all internal and external fears. The following six traits are governed by the Buddha's insight and wisdom.

7. Never-decreasing intention to help sentient beings. Enemies and those who wish to harm one are the people whom one normally has the least willingness to help; but as they are the direct cause of the development of bodhichitta, one should truly make them the object of offerings and devotions.

8. Never-decreasing enthusiastic perseverance. Regardless of any difficulties involved, the Buddhas are always ready to act immediately for the sake of benefiting sentient beings. To illustrate this, there is the account of the Indian pandit Rahula's having gone to Tibet when, with his clairvoyance, he had seen a meditator there (who later became the founder of one of the two main Kargyu traditions) whose Buddha nature was ripening to the point at which he would need further initiations.

9. Never-decreasing awareness of the methods needed to help sentient beings. The Buddha, manifesting himself as the nirmanakaya, is able to assume forms such as trees, bridges and roads for the purpose of helping sentient beings. Both his wisdom and speech are able to take on physical form. After attaining enlightenment, it takes one at least seven weeks to realize the full extent of a Buddha's attainment. As opposed to this, most people's present awareness is as limited as that of nomads who came to Lhasa and were astounded at seeing bicycles, thinking the riders were people with wheels for legs. Similarly there was an old Tibetan woman who simply could not grasp the idea that there could be a lake bigger than her garden pond. It is valuable to become familiar with these at first

amazing and sometimes seemingly irrelevant qualities of the Buddhas.
10. Never-decreasing single-pointed concentration on shunyata.
11. Never-decreasing wisdom.
12. A never-decreasing omniscient state of mind invulnerable to kleshas.

The remaining six kinds of knowledge are the result of the union of Buddha's action and wisdom, but these shall not be explained here.

The difference between the Bodhisattvas' and Buddhas' intention to help sentient beings is that the former still need to make efforts towards this end, whereas the latter do not. Like a clear mirror, the Buddhas effortlessly bring images upon themselves, thus assuming many forms. Although his gross form has dissolved, Buddha Shakyamuni is still present in the world in his subtle form, which is visible to those with high spiritual attainment. Maitreya, though already enlightened, is now active in the world as a Bodhisattva.

This concludes the explanation of the stages in the Mahayana path.

May this offering of the Dharma be a blessing to all sentient beings, speeding them on their path to enlightenment.

Appendix 1
The Seven-Limb Puja

The Seven-Limb Puja (*yan-lag bdun-pa*) is an extremely valuable practice for purifying the mind in order to attain intuitive understanding, especially of shunyata. If an important guest were to visit, one would clean the house well beforehand, and in the same way one practises this puja to prepare the way for direct insight into shunyata. Like a seed and the conditions necessary for its growth, (such as moisture and heat), meditation is the direct cause of spiritual growth, while the Seven-Limb Puja provides the contributing conditions.

The practice of this puja may well precede any spiritual practice. Lack of true insight is due to poverty of acquired merit, and this puja, which yields physical merit, provides a perfect counterpart to mental merit gained through meditation. Tilopa instructed his disciple, Naropa, "Until enlightenment, collect mental and physical merit, which act as the two wheels of a carriage." Accordingly, this puja is practised even by those who have attained the tenth Bodhisattvabhumi.

A recent great lama in Tibet who attained enlightenment gave discourses on the stages of the path. Before a one-hour discourse, he would spend three hours in preliminary purificatory practices, and his disciples, thinking that much time was being wasted, asked him if more time could not be given to actual teaching. The lama replied, "If what you seek is dry, intellectual understanding, we should do as you suggest, but if you desire true insight, do as I say."

Before beginning this puja, or any other spiritual practice, it is of the greatest importance to correct one's motivation by developing bodhichitta. The following verse, which should be recited at this time, was composed by Vajradhara and contains both the verses of taking refuge and developing bodhichitta.

"I go for refuge to the Buddha, the Dharma, and the Supreme Community until the attainment of enlightenment. By the virtue of my giving and other wholesome deeds, may I attain enlightenment for the sake of all sentient beings."

Sang-gyae choe-d'ang tsog-kyi ch'og-nam-la
J'ang-chub b'ar-d'u dag-ni kyab-su-ch'i
Dag-g'i jin-sog gyi-paei soe-nam-ky'i
Dro-la p'en-ch'ir sang-gyae drub-par-shog

Following this, recite each of these Sanskrit verses of refuge, "Namo Gurubhya, Namo Buddhaya, Namo Dharmaya, Namo Sanghaya," twenty-one times as you go to them for refuge. As you do this, visualize the four objects of refuge before you, sending out rays of radiant light to you which fill and purify your body.

The first limb of the puja is prostration, the Tibetan term for which is the combination of two words meaning 'to sweep (defilements)' and 'to request (blessings)'. A correct full prostration as described in the sutras and tantras is as follows. First join your palms with your thumbs tucked inside, giving your hands the form of an oval-shaped jewel. Before you prostrate, first touch your hands to the top of your head (this is cause for the growth of the Buddha's ushnisha, or head protrusion), then to the point between your eyebrows (causing the growth of the urna, or wisdom hair), next to your throat (for obtaining the qualities of the Buddha's speech) and finally to your heart (for the growth of the complete wisdom of the Buddha). As you do so, repeat the verse:

I prostrate myself before the Gurus,
Who are the root of the Three Gems,
The Essence of Vajradhara,
And the collected body of all the Buddhas.

The verse for this first branch of the puja, which was composed by the Bodhisattva Shantideva, is as follows:

"As many atoms as there are in the thousand million worlds, so many times do I make reverent salutations to all the Buddhas of the three times, to the Dharma, to all the Excellent Community and to all the shrines and places where Bodhisattvas have been. I make profound obeisance to the teachers."

D'u-sum sheg-paei sang-gyae-kun
Ch'oe-d'ang tsog'-kyi ch'og-nam-la
Zhing-duel kuen-gy'i dr'ang-nye-kyi
Lue-tu peni dag-ch'ag-tsael

The second limb of the puja is making offerings. The Tibetan word for 'puja' means 'to please' (the objects of refuge) and this we are truly able to do not with external but rather with internal offerings, that is, our heart-felt devotion and practice of the Dharma. Milarepa once said, "Although I am poor, I repaid the kindness of my guru by putting all his teachings into practice." The true guru's attitude towards material offerings made to him is that of a wild carnivorous beast when presented with a pile of grass.

When making material offerings, at first offer only little things which you can give without attachment. Offering seven bowls of water upon your altar each morning is one form of devotion which everyone can afford. If you do not possess seven bowls, it is fine to use even your drinking cups—it is the devotion that is of importance, not the external paraphernalia. Cleanse the bowls each morning, then pour water into the first bowl and fill the others from this while reciting the mantra 'Om Ah Hum' three times. Candles, incense, flowers, food and any precious or beautiful things you have may be offered as well. If food is offered, you may leave it on the altar a short time, then eat it or give it to someone as you please. It is of equal value to make devotions totally in your imagination, such as offering the light of the sun and moon, or visualizing all your virtuous actions in the form of light and offering this to the Buddhas. But concentrate primarily on making the following peerless offerings of:

1. Practising the Dharma.
2. Making efforts to preserve the Dharma from defilement.
3. Developing bodhichitta (let your greatest effort be given towards this end).
4. Dedicating your merit towards the attainment of enlightenment for the sake of all sentient beings.

The verse for this second limb of the puja is as follows:

"Just as Manjushri and other Bodhisattvas make offerings to the Enlightened Beings, so do I make offerings to the Tathagatas and Bodhisattvas so that I may develop and expand bodhichitta."

> J'i-tar jam-yang la-sog-pa
> Gyael-wa nam-la ch'oe-dzae-pa
> D'e-zhin dag-g'i d'e-zhin-sheg
> Gen-po saoe-d'ang chae-name-ch'oe

For the third branch of the puja, confession, look back upon your recent nonvirtuous actions, then try to recall as many as possible since the time of your birth. By contemplating the effects of these actions, which you have committed both consciously and unconsciously, generate strong remorse and come to a firm intention to refrain from them in the future, even at the cost of your life. If three people went to a restaurant and due to accidentally eating poison, two of them died, the third would seek refuge in a doctor and follow her advice with utmost care. In the same way you should guard the actions of your three doors of body, speech and mind, having full consciousness that this is the sole means of safe-guarding your own well-being. After coming to this firm decision, take refuge and develop bodhichitta. The final step of confession is to practise virtue as a remedy for your non-virtuous acts. The six ways of doing this are as follows:

1. Repeating mantras of the names of the many Buddhas.
2. Repeating the Vajrasattva mantra.
3. Reading sutras on shunyata (especially the *Prajna-paramita Sutras*).
4. Contemplating shunyata (this is the best method).
5. Making offerings.
6. Making statues and paintings of Buddhas and building stupas.

The verse of confession is as follows:

"In this beginningless samsaric state, in this life and other lives, I have committed unfitting and non-virtuous actions or caused others to do so. Being confused by ignorance, I have taken pleasure and rejoiced in these non-virtuous actions. By confessing these to all the Buddhas and Bodhisattvas with a pure state of mind, I reveal them to the Protectors and apply the four op-ponent powers. The evil which I have heaped up through ignorance and fool-ishness, evil in the world of everyday experience and evil understanding and intelligence—all this I acknowledge to the Protectors. What is not wholesome, O Protectors, I will not do again."

T'og-ma me-daen k'or-wa-nae
Tse-rab di-am zhaen-d'ag-tu
Dag-g'i ma-tsael dig-gyi-pa-am
Gyi-d'u tzael-wa nyi-d'ang-ni

Ti-mug tr'uel-pae dag-noen-te
Je-su yi-rang g'ang-gyi-pa
Nong-pa d'e-ni t'ong-gyi-nae
Sam-pa t'ag-pae goen-la-shag

Rejoicing in your own virtue and that of others is the next limb of the puja, and it is a practice followed even by the Arya Bodhisattvas. Instead of being jealous and competitive with others, rejoice in their virtue and follow their example. The weight of the merit of this is tremendous. For example, a king once asked Buddha Shakyamuni how he, in his ruling position, could best practice the Dharma. The Buddha replied that he should develop bodhichitta, rejoice in virtue and dedicate his merit to the benefit of all sentient beings. By following this teaching the king attained Arhatship in that life.

Try to recall your virtuous acts since childhood and infer those of your former lives which have resulted in your present precious attainment of human life. By rejoicing in these you increase your own past merit and collect still more. By rejoicing as you go to sleep, you even collect merit during the night. There was once a king who was very proud of his lavish patronage of the Buddha and all his disciples, and in his kingdom there was a beggar who greatly rejoiced in the king's offerings. When he had finished teaching there, Buddha declared that it was the beggar who had gained the greatest merit, even greater than that of the generous but proud king. The Buddha dedicated all the merit gained thereby to the well-being of the beggar.

While rejoicing, repeat the following verse:

"I rejoice in the compassionate deed of giving happiness to sentient beings. I rejoice in the deeds of the Buddhas and Bodhisattvas in granting peace to sentient beings. I rejoice in their ocean-like wish to give permanent and ultimate happiness to all beings."

> Sem-chaen t'am-chae de-dzae-pae
> T'ug-kye ge-wa gya-tso-d'ang
> Sem-chen p'en-par dzae-pa-la
> Ga-wae je-su yi-rang-ngo

By following the next limb of the puja, requesting the gurus to turn the Wheel of the Dharma, you ensure that in all your future lives you will be born in a central place, that is, one in which the Dharma is taught and practised. As you request this, make a mandala offering to your guru. First make four piles at the points representing each of the four directions, placing the first pile closest to you and the others going around clockwise. Then four piles on each of the points representing the intermediate directions, and a final one in the centre. Visualize that you are making a thousand-spoked golden wheel and offer this to your guru. The disciple must request teachings many times to indicate his interest and sincerity and to exalt the glory of the Dharma. After his enlightenment, the Buddha spent forty-nine days testing the mental capacities of his future disciples before giving his first discourse. In ancient India, for example, during the time of Naropa, it used to be very difficult to receive teachings.

As you offer the mandala, repeat the following verse:

"Saluting them with folded hands, I entreat the Buddhas in all directions to shine the lamp of the Dharma for those wandering in the realm of suffering and delusion."

Ch'og-nam Kuen-gy'i san-gyae-la
T'ael-mo jar-te sol-wa-ni
Sem-chaen dug-ngael muen-t'om-la
Ch'oe-kyi droen-mae-bar-d'u-soel

Then imagine that your guru has agreed to fulfil your request.

The next limb of the puja is requesting the guru to live long. The Buddha and gurus, however, do not actually experience death: the nirmanakaya, which appears to die, only dissolves into the other three kayas. Of those other three, the svabhavikakaya and dharmakaya never die and the sambhogakaya remains until the end of samsara. Nevertheless, it is valuable to make this request in order to show your devotion to the Dharma and your guru, thereby increasing your own life-span. When doing so, build a five-mound mandala, one pile in each of the four directions and one in the centre, while visualizing a crossed vajra (the Tibetan word for 'vajra' is 'dor-je', meaning 'immutable'), symbolizing steadfastness and firmness. The verse to be recited is as follows:

"With hands folded in reverence I implore the Conquerors desiring to enter parinirvana to remain here for endless ages so that life in this world does not grow dark."

Gyael-wa nya-ngaen dae-zhe-la
T'ael-mo jar-to soel-wa-ni
Dor-di dong-war mi-goe-ching
Kael-wa dr'ang-me Zhug-su-soel

The final and most important of all the seven limbs of the puja is the selfless dedication of the merit of your acts of body, speech, and mind to the benefit of all sentient beings. With understanding of shunyata, give away your merit free of attachment, thereby protecting it from such non-virtues as anger, which could destroy it. The motivation at the beginning of your practice and the dedication of merit at the end are like the reins of a horse, because they control where your merit will take you to, and are thus considered to be of the greatest importance. Let your dedication be towards:

1. Your being cared for by a guru in all your future lifetimes.
2. The maintenance of the Buddhadharma, that it may long prevail and be a continual blessing to sentient beings.
3. Your own enlightenment for the sake of all sentient beings.

Conclude the puja by reciting the following verse:

"Having thus acquired all these merits and having performed all these virtuous actions in the past and present, empower me to lift the veil of suffering from all sentient beings. May the merit gained by these actions of mine relieve all beings of their suffering. My personalities throughout my existences, my possessions and my merit— all these I give up without regard to myself. Just as the earth and other elements are serviceable in many ways to the infinite number of beings inhabiting limitless space, so may I become that which maintains all beings, for as long as all have not attained peace."

> D'e-tar di-d'ag kuen-j'ae-te
> Ge-wa dag-gi sag-pa-g'ang
> D'e-ni sem-chaen t'am-chae-kyi
> Dug-ngael t'am-che sael-war-shog

The Seven-limb Puja is like a carriage, each of its parts being essential for it to be fully effective. When you practice the entire puja, you collect merit, purify your mind, and increase your virtue. Specifically, prostration, offering, rejoicing in the virtues of others, and requesting your guru to teach the Dharma and live long are all practices that result in the accumulation of merit. Confession serves to purify the mind, and rejoicing in your own virtue and dedicating your merit are practices which increase your virtue.

Each part of the puja also acts as an opponent of a specific klesha. Prostration acts as a force against pride; offering, against miserliness; confession, against the three poisons; and rejoicing in virtue is the opponent of jealousy. Requesting teachings on the Dharma opposes the inclination to discriminate between spiritual traditions, and requesting the long life of your guru counteracts any disrespect towards the Buddhas, Bodhisattvas and your gurus. The dedication of merit remedies the destructiveness of anger.

Finally, each of the limbs of the puja yields a specific result, or attainment. Prostration results in the formation of the ushnisha upon your attainment of enlightenment, and offerings lead to the acquirement of wealth. The Arya Bodhisattvas, for example, never lack anything that they want. Application of the four opponent powers leads to the elimination of both gross and instinctive kleshas. Once you have abandoned the ten non-virtues by this means, you develop understanding of shunyata, which pulls out all the kleshas by their roots. Rejoicing in virtue and trying to see the good in others causes you to have a pleasing form in future lives. Requesting the Dharma leads to your acquiring the qualities of Buddha's speech, and requesting the long life of your guru leads to the attainment of the undying state of Nirvana. Dedicating your merit results in your attainment of the general qualities of the Buddhas.

This concludes the explanation of the Seven-limb Puja.

Appendix 2
Guru Yoga

One renowned Kadampa geshe explained the need for a
spiritual friend by saying, "Since we need teachers for
learning ordinary crafts, how great then is our need for a
teacher to guide us to enlightenment!" Only such a friend
can show the way. There is sound scriptural reference for
guru yoga (*bla-ma'i rnal-'byor*), and in all traditions of Buddhism its practice is considered to be of prime importance.

Great care must be taken to choose a teacher having
complete knowledge. Maitreya set down the following ten
minimum qualifications of a Mahayana guru. The scriptural
references for these are the sutras: *sdong-po bkod-pa'i mdo*
(*Skt. Gandavyuha Sutra*) and *mdo-sde rgyan* (*Skt. Mahayanasutralamkara*).

The guru must have:

1. Calmness gained through the observance of a pure
   morality.
2. Inner peace due to mastery of single-pointed concentration.
3. Peace gained through having complete discriminating wisdom.
4. Knowledge greater than that of his disciples.
5. Ever-present enthusiastic effort and willingness to
   teach.
6. Full knowledge of the scriptures, oral traditions,
   and initiations.
7. Either complete intellectual knowledge or full intuitive understanding of shunyata.
8. Perfect means and intelligence in presenting the
   Dharma.
9. Sincerity and compassion in guiding his disciples.
10. Infinite patience, never succumbing to mental and
    physical fatigue.

For the relationship between the master and disciple to yield fruit, the disciple must have a balanced character, honesty and an attraction to the Middle Way. If a disciple realizes his own and other's mistakes but ignores them and refuses to apply opponent forces to them, he is not worth accepting. He must further have the ability to discriminate between right and wrong and have a strong interest in and enthusiasm for what he is doing.

A. THE ADVANTAGES OF PRACTISING GURU YOGA

The following eight advantages of making devotion to one's guru were taught by Buddha Shakyamuni and Vajradhara:

1. Every moment one draws closer to enlightenment.
2. It is the cause of intuitive knowledge and a source of joy for the Buddhas and Bodhisattvas.
3. One is protected against the influence of heretical gurus and maras.
4. The major and minor kleshas are automatically reduced.
5. One gains a constant growth of intuitive understanding and progress along the five paths and ten stages.
6. In all future lives until enlightenment, one will never lack a guru.
7. One is protected from rebirth in the three lower states in the next life.
8. All temporal wishes, such as for freedom from low rebirth, and the ultimate wish, that is, enlightenment for the sake of all sentient beings, will be accomplished easily.

These advantages will now be explained in more detail.

(1) There are two ways of approaching Buddhahood. The first is for a disciple to put all the teachings given by his guru into practice. If one practises tantra with intensive effort, one may attain enlightenment in this very lifetime. The second way is to make devotion to one's guru and please him. Attainment that would require aeons of practice on the Paramitayana can be gained in just one life-time by means of guru yoga. Nagarjuna wrote, "If a person steps off the porch of a house situated on the edge of a cliff, though he may not wish to fall, he must. In the same way, if one practises guru yoga, one will certainly gain spiritual insight." Another great Indian master said, "No matter where you are, by making guru devotions all your wishes will be fulfilled."

Bodhisattvas who live in total accordance with the Teachings come ever closer to enlightenment. The practice of guru yoga yields both mental and physical merits, which are necessary for the attainment of the wisdom and method aspects of the Dharma. Nagarjuna wrote that all offerings should be made to the guru, and Vajradhara stated, "It is more beneficial to make offerings to even one hair of the guru than to any of the other objects of devotion."

The guru shows enormous kindness by transmitting the knowledge of the Buddhas. One can only comprehend the true importance of guru yoga when one understands the advantages of putting it into practice and the disadvantages of acting in a contrary way towards one's guru.

(2) Just as the inhabitants of a country are pleased when their diplomats are treated well, so does one's relationship with the Buddhas and Bodhisattvas flourish when one shows devotion towards the guru. It is not offerings alone that please them, but rather the pure devotion with which even the smallest offering is given.

(3) The interferences that obstruct one's practice, which are caused by the influence of the maras, result from a decrease in one's collection of merit, and this is restored and increased by the practice of guru yoga. Every day the grip of one's delusions and internal interferences decreases and if one's has total faith in one's guru and his complete teaching, the ill intentions of others cannot affect one.

(4) Even if one lives far from the guru, one's kleshas will be lessened by the practice of guru yoga, and this is all the more true when one lives close to him, because one thereby becomes much more aware of one's actions.

(5) The practice of sincere guru devotion inevitably results in rapid spiritual growth. By following the Paramitayana, it is generally impossible to progress from the last stage of the path of accumulation to the eighth Bodhisattva ground. An exception to this, however, was the Bodhisattva Sadaprarudita, who for seven years made intense devotions to his guru, Dharmodgata. Without such devotions, even visions of Enlightened Beings are of little benefit.

When Atisha was in Tibet, among his disciples were Dromtonpa and two others from the region of Kham. Dromtonpa spent his time translating, while one of the latter two became a cook and the other meditated in a cave. Atisha gave much teaching to the meditator, so the cook, feeling that he was making no progress, became jealous. Realising this, Atisha sent Dromtonpa to him and he caused the cook to reveal all his grudges. He then explained the importance of guru yoga to him. Some time later when Atisha called the three together, it was found that it was the cook who had made the most progress.

(6) It is easy to make devotions to a high lama whom one rarely sees, but equal devotions must be given to one's

personal lama who is met regularly. One should test the guru carefully before accepting him as one's guide, and not go to just anyone for teachings.

(7) As a result of making guru devotions, causes of low rebirth in the future can instead manifest themselves as headaches or scoldings from one's guru. One great geshe said "If your guru scolds you, his words are mantras, and if he hits you, you are receiving a true initiation."

(8) As guru yoga is so effective in satisfying all wishes, both temporal and ultimate, one should never abandon one's guru even at the cost of life. Je Tsong Khapa, speaking from his own experience and attainment, advised this to anyone who has accepted a guru as their personal guide. The practice of guru yoga determines whether one is able to lead others to enlightenment and attain it oneself. Recall the great gurus of the past and their intense practice of guru devotion, and you will see that this is needed by even the highest Bodhisattvas. There are plenty of examples of Enlightened Beings, but none of beings who have attained lasting peace through material gain.

B. THE DISADVANTAGES OF IMPROPER BEHAVIOUR TOWARDS THE GURU

There was once a lion-headed dakini who prophesied that Milarepa would have one moon-like disciple (*Rechungpa*), and one sun-like disciple (*Gampopa*), twenty-five star-like disciples, and thousands of others on the path to enlightenment. Rechungpa disobeyed his master once by going to India to study Dharma when Milarepa had told him not to, and twice by going to central Tibet for the same reason. He thereby delayed his enlightenment for three lives, whereas he would otherwise have attained it in that life. One of the twenty-five disciples, on the other hand, followed all the instruction of his guru and attained fulfilment in that life.

The disadvantages of lacking a guru are simply the absence of the previous advantages, but there are eight other disadvantages of having a guru and behaving in an improper way towards him. Such conduct towards any kind of teacher, such as a master carpenter, is bad. The eight disadvantages include the following:

1. Despising one's guru is equal to despising the Buddhas of all three times.
2. For each moment of anger one has against the guru, a kalpa must be spent enduring the agonies of the deepest hell.
3. One gains no attainment or siddhis from tantric practice.
4. Tantric practice becomes a cause for rebirth in the three lower states.
5. New understanding is not gained and one's former insight decreases.
6. All kinds of miseries and unfavourable circumstances are met with in this life.
7. One will wander endlessly in the lowest realms.
8. In the future births, one will never meet a spiritual master.

The explanation of these eight is as follow:

(1) Like an ambassador of a country, the guru, as a manifestation of the Buddha, is the means by which the Buddha's speech is transmitted to disciples. The root text on guru yoga is *bla-ma lnga-bcu pa* by Ashvagosha, and it was the tradition in India to always give a complete explanation of this text before any major initiation. Although it has no Indian commentaries, there is an excellent one written by Je Tsong Khapa called *bla-ma lnga-bcu'u rnam-*

bshad. Among the tantras, the *Kalachakra-tantra* especially deals with guru yoga.

(2) If the guru is calm, it is easy to refrain from anger against him, but such is not always the case. For example, Marpa repeatedly designed houses and commanded Milarepa to build them, then upon their completion he would yell, "Who told you to build this house? Tear it down!" Gurus could not use such methods in guiding disciples in this present age of degeneration. On another occasion, one of Marpa's disciples came to him seeking an initiation and he brought with him all his possessions except a lame goat to present as offerings. But when he arrived, Marpa scolded him, saying, "Why didn't you bring the goat? Go back and get it and bring it to me as well." After the disciple had done as he was told, Marpa was well pleased and said that such determination was necessary in order to hear the Dharma.

(3) If for any reason a disciple despises his guru and wishes to have nothing to do with him, he thereby comes to the absolute end of his spiritual growth. In the *Guhyasamaja Tantra* it is written, "Even if one has committed all the ten non-virtuous acts and the five heinous crimes, it is still possible to attain enlightenment, but despising one's guru brings an absolute stop to all progress." Whether one has a spiritual or a worldly teacher, this teaching will be of great benefit.

(4) If the disciple is truly disgusted with her guru and she practices tantra, she gains no attainment, but rather casts seeds for her future low rebirth. The *Vajrahridaya* tantric text discusses this point.

(5) After a disciple breaks with his guru, not only does he gain no further wisdom, his former level of knowledge

decreases each day. If one is friendly with and drinks water from the same source as another who has broken with a guru, one's own attainment is harmed.

The three traditions of the Heruka tantric practice that came to Tibet had their sources in the great mahasiddhas Luipa, Drilbupa and Nagpopa. Nagpopa's guru, Zalendia, once told him to wait some time before entering meditation, but Nagpopa disregarded his counsel, and as a result, never saw the true form of Heruka or the dakinis. Nagpopa was remarkable for his ability to fly, always with seven banners fluttering overhead. On one occasion when he was flying with his disciples, who also benefited from his power, he saw a beautiful female leper standing on a river bank. She asked him to carry her across the river, but as a result of disobeying his guru, he ignored her. One of his disciples, feeling great compassion for her, then carried her across, whereupon she showed her true form as Vajradakini and, taking him in her arms, flew to the Buddhafields.

Tilopa once told his disciple, Naropa, not to debate with non-Buddhists, for he could be forced to relinquish his religion if he lost. Nevertheless, Naropa debated with them and when he found himself losing, prayed to his guru for assistance. Tilopa appeared to him in the form of a mahasiddha drinking blood and eating human organs, and Naropa was then able to turn about and win the debate.

For a long time Marpa refused to give Milarepa any teachings or initiation. Finally, Marpa's wife, Dagmema, who was known for her great compassion, forged a letter making it seem to have been written by her husband and told Milarepa to take it to Marpa's chief disciple and seek teachings from him. The plan was effective, and Milarepa received teachings, but from his meditation not only did he gain no insight, he did not even have an auspicious dream. Marpa's disciple then learned of the forged letter and told Milarepa that unless he received his guru's permission, he would gain no spiritual progress from teachings.

(6) Once a disciple comes to despise his guru, he encounters many problems in the same life and then experiences a violent death.

While one great teacher was giving a discourse to his disciples, his own guru, acting as a swineherd, approached while leading his pigs. His disciple, not wanting to look bad before his own disciples, ignored him. Only after he had finished his discourse did he come before his master and prostrate himself. His guru asked him, "Why didn't you honour me like this during your discourse?" He replied, "Because I didn't see you," and immediately both his eyes fell out. His guru later restored one of them but not the other.

(7) Breaking with one's guru results in the disciple's endless wandering in the lower realms. When Vajrapani asked Buddha Shakyamuni about the effects of scorning one's guru, he replied, "Please do not ask, for the answer would disturb the peace of the devas, and the Buddhas would vomit blood. Even you, Vajrapani, would faint." If one is unable to make proper devotions to one's guru, it is much better not to have one.

(8) After once breaking with his guru, a disciple never again meets with a spiritual master in all his future lives. If by some fluke he should happen to rise from the three lower realms and attain a human body, he would never have the opportunity of a fully endowed body.

Before accepting a guru, always test his and your own qualifications. If you think of your teacher as a lecturer, he is not your guru, but as soon as you feel he is your personal guru, one verse of Dharma spoken by him seals your relationship.

This concludes the teaching on guru yoga.

Glossary

Abhidharma The collection of Buddha's teachings dealing with knowledge and phenomenology.

Arhat One who has attained personal liberation.

Arya A Superior; one who has realized emptiness.

Aryabodhisattva A Bodhisattva who has realized emptiness.

Bar-do (Tib.) Intermediate state between death and rebirth.

Bhikkshu Fully ordained monk.

Bodhicitta Mind of enlightenment, altruistic aspiration for enlightenment for the sake of all beings.

Bodhisattva One who has generated the mind of enlightenment.

Bodhisattva-bhumis Stages of a Bodhisattva's development.

Buddha One who has overcome all obstacles and accomplished all qualities.

Deva A god.

Dharma Teachings of the Buddha; phenomena.

Dharmakaya Truth body of a Buddha.

Enlightenment The accomplishment of a Buddha, who has gained liberation and omniscience.

Hinayana The lesser vehicle.

Jambudvipa The southern continent; this world.

Jataka Stories of the Buddha's previous lives as a Bodhisattva.

Jneyavarana Obstructions to omniscience.

Kaya Body of the Buddha.

Karma Action.

Klesha/Kleshavarana Delusion; disturbing mental conception; obstruction to liberation.

Madhyamika Middle way; philosophy formulated by Nagarjuna.

Mahayana The greater vehicle.

Mara Hindrance; obstacle.

Moksha Liberation.

Nagas Subterranean beings similar to serpents.

Nirmanakaya Emanation body of the Buddha.

Nirvana Liberation from suffering.

Paramita Perfection; trancendent function.

Parinirvana Peace; state beyond suffering.

Prasangikas Consequentialist, proponents of Madhyamika tenets.

Pratimoksha Personal liberation.

Prateykabuddha Solitary Realizer.

Prajna Wisdom.

Preta Hungry ghost.

Rupakaya Form body of a Buddha.

Samadhi Meditative stabilization.

Shamatha Concentration.

Sambhogakaya Enjoyment body of a Buddha.

Sangha Spiritual community.

Samsara Cyclic existence.

Sautrantika One of the Hinayana schools of tenets.

Siddhis Attainments; feats.

Shiksha Training.

Skandha Mental/physical aggregate.

Shravaka Hearer; one who hears, practices and proclaims.

Buddha's teachings.

Stupa Buddhist reliquary object.

Shunyata Emptiness of true or inherent existence.

Sutra Speech of the Buddha; discourses, etc.

Svabhavikakaya Nature body of Buddha.

Tantrayana The vehicle of Secret Mantra.

Tathagata One Thus Gone; epithet for Buddha.

Theravada Vehicle of Elders; division of Hinayana Buddhism.

Tong len (Tib.) Giving and taking; practice of mind training to overcome selfishness and develop compassion for others.

Tushita Joyous Land; the pure land from which Buddha descended and where Maitreya now resides.

Ushnisha The fleshy protrusion on the crown of a Buddha's head.

Vaibhashika One of the Hinayana schools of tenets.

Vajra Diamond sceptre; symbol of the tantric vehicle, and practice of method.

Vinaya Discipline; rules governing the conduct of the Spiritual Community.

Vipashyana Special insight, particularly into emptiness.

Yogi A meditator.

Index